THE à BECKETTS OF "PUNCH"

Gilbert Abbott à Beckett.
Born 17th Feb. 1811.
Died 30th Aug. 1856.

THE à BECKETTS
OF "PUNCH"

Memories of Father
and Sons

BY

ARTHUR WILLIAM à BECKETT

WESTMINISTER,
A. CONSTABLE AND CO., LTD.,

1903

Detroit: Reissued by Singing Tree Press, Book Tower, 1969

Library of Congress Catalog Card Number 69—17341

THIS VOLUME

WHICH DEALS WITH THE

LIVES OF THREE WORKING JOURNALISTS

IS RESPECTFULLY DEDICATED TO THE

FELLOWS, MEMBERS AND ASSOCIATES OF THE

INSTITUTE OF JOURNALISTS AND THE

MEMBERS OF THE NEWSPAPER

SOCIETY BY ONE OF THEIR

PAST PRESIDENTS

THE AUTHOR

PREFACE

DURING the long career of *The London Chari-vari*, extending from 1841 till 1902, there have been three à Becketts closely associated with *Punch*. Gilbert Abbott à Beckett, the father of the others, was the chief à Beckett. The purpose of this work—which I venture to suggest is a good one—will disclose itself upon perusal. As the subject of my father's connexion with *Punch* has been recently discussed and may be discussed again, I have thought it advisable to say my say about the matter. I have an additional reason for the course I have adopted. My father was the firm and constant companion of Charles Dickens and Thackeray, and everything connected with the lives of the two great novelists of the nineteenth century has its value. I have certainly written nothing in malice, and hope and believe that these

PREFACE

pages are free from anything that can wound or give offence.

For the rest, I am told that reminiscences are very popular. I trust that my recollections of the life of a working journalist spent in the pleasantest toil amongst the most delightful of companions may consequently prove attractive and perchance even instructive. As the book has been written in some haste at a time when I have been exceptionally busy, there may be slips of the pen here and there discernible. If there be, these blemishes can be easily removed in the next edition. The date of that interesting issue will depend upon the will—the good will—of that best friend of the Author, the kind, the indulgent and the presently-appropriately-epitheted person,—the gentle reader.

ARTHUR WILLIAM à BECKETT.

GARRICK CLUB,
    September, 1903.

CONTENTS

5

CONTENTS

6

CONTENTS

CONTENTS

Chapter I

EARLY DAYS

I HAVE ventured to use the sub-title " Memories of Father and Sons," as it explains the source of half of my information. *Punch* was started in 1841, and my father, Gilbert Abbott à Beckett, was one of the little band of writers who contributed the copy to the initial number. He died in 1856 before I had entered my teens, but as a child I was a great friend of his. It may appear strange to make such an assertion, but it is a fact. My elder brothers and sister were at school, and although I had plenty of home lessons I was not sent to a boarding school—except once as an experiment for a few weeks—until after his death. I was an extremely delicate child, and I was carried by a nurse until I was six years old. It was in the days before the discovery of perambulators, and I imagine that our dear old family doctor must have ordered gentle exercise. Be this as it may, I used to walk across the park with my father from our house in Kensington to his court at Southwark very frequently. On certain special occasions I was allowed to accompany the magistrate on to the Bench itself, and these were my special delights.

THE à BECKETTS OF "PUNCH"

My father, who was in complete sympathy with his little son, used to make remarks for his delectation. In spite of his adventurous boyhood Gilbert Abbott à Beckett the moment he was appointed a magistrate—when he was in his thirties—became in manner the sedatest of the sedate. He frequently smiled but scarcely ever laughed, and used to say the most amusing things with a gravity that emphasized their incongruity. As I write I see before me the little court house with my father seated in front of his official desk on the raised platform of the Bench. On his right sits myself, a little boy with my legs dangling over the floor. My father has before him two females who have cross-summoned one another. It is the case of these ladies that each of them has tried to kill the other.

" She clutched hold of my hair and tore it out by handfulls, your Majesty," cried one of the litigants.

" I see," returned my father, " and I suppose that huge bundle under your arm contains your hair."

" It does, your Majesty."

" And who are you ? " asked my father, turning to the other party in the case.

" I am a poor lone widow, and she has treated me —— "

" What was the occupation of your husband ? " interrupted my father.

" He sold rags, your Lordship, and cherries strung on sticks."

" Ah, I see ; a rag and cherry merchant."

And then the case continued, and whenever my

father had occasion to refer to the widow she was always surnamed " the widow of the rag and cherry merchant." On one occasion I remember my father was cheered by the cabmen. This was due to a decision that the roadway of a railway station was a public place, and cabmen had a right to ply there for hire without paying toll for admission. But the " Railway Interest," always a strong body, were determined to have the ruling reversed, and they had their way. I do not know whether the matter was taken up to the Lords, but at any rate the famous decision which had provoked such enthusiasm among the cabmen was not upheld. It has been said that my father had a decided objection to cabmen, and that when my uncle Sir William à Beckett, first Chief Justice of Victoria, came over to England, the initial question my father asked him was, " How much has your cabman asked you ? " As a matter of fact there was no kindlier or more sympathetic man than my father, and he was charitable to a degree. It was his delight to help his poorer brethren, as he called them. I remember once that my father supported with his custom a bootmaker by paying him West End prices for very inferior boots. There were recriminations from the rest of the family.

" Very well," said Gilbert à Beckett, " I will at any rate wear the boots Johnston provides for myself." And he did.

So I cannot credit my father with harshness. In the forties and the fifties the cabmen were very mixed. Some of these fellows were good enough, but others were unmitigated brutes. It was their pleasure to take possession of some unfortunate old woman with luggage and then to fleece her to their hearts' content. With these bullies my father was very severe. So it came to pass that I had to take my morning walk with my sire, and during my peregrinations had to hear a good deal about the topics of the day. For my father was anxious to improve my mind ; he used to ask my opinion about everything, and correct it when in his judgment my view was at fault—so much for an explanation.

I shall have to say much about my father, for in my opinion he was the originator of *Punch*. Mr. Spielmann in his *History of Punch* has shown that he wrote in the first number and was by far away the most copious contributor, but he has said little about the papers which preceded the leading comic of the day. I shall briefly trace *Punch* to his predecessor *Figaro in London*, which my father founded and wrote. This will be the scheme of this work. If it proves to be a little egotistical I must ask pardon but plead *force majeure*. From the moment of joining the staff in 1874 to my last dinner in Bouverie Street on June 4, 1902, I abandoned every scheme of my life to *Punch*. I was called to the Bar and had a fair prospect of success, but *Punch* claimed my services and I retired from practice. I had a chance of success as a novelist, for my initial romance was extremely well received by such papers as the *Athenæum* and the *Spectator*, but *Punch* claimed my services and I practically abandoned this branch of literature. I wrote some half-dozen plays for the London theatres—none of them failed and they were all well received, but I abandoned writing for the stage for the simple reason *"Punch"* claimed my services and I had no time for attending rehearsals and the rest of it. Lastly my great delight was my connection with the Militia. For four weeks out of the fifty-two I was an officer on duty, a soldier, something more than in name, but *Punch* claimed my services, and after an attempt to dodge the training by exchanging from one battalion to another I had to give it up. But until June 4, 1902, I did not regret my life devotion to *Punch*. I was proud of the paper that my father had helped to found, and loyal to its interests to the backbone. For a moment there was a pang, because it looked to be a misspent life. But on reflection I do not regret a moment of my twenty-seven years' service —that twenty-seven years' service that during the last score of it yielded a holiday of not as many weeks. No, for I can look at that service as given to the paper founded by Mark Lemon and Gilbert à Beckett, and contributed to by my father's friends, Thackeray, Leech, Shirley Brooks, Dickey Doyle, Douglas Jerrold, Tom Taylor, Horace Mayhew and last, but not least, my dear old friend, John Tenniel. Of all those I have mentioned only one survives, John Tenniel. John Tenniel retired from *Punch* a couple of years before my place disappeared from the dear old table. At that table he and I had sat *tête à tête* concocting the cartoon of

13

the week when every other member of the staff
was away on a holiday. So I dedicate my life's
work, such as it has been, to the giants of the
Punch table—to the great dead. But mark me
well, I do not write as a man with a grievance—
let the past look after the past.

My father had three brothers and they were sons
of a solicitor. I remember my grandfather as a
very dignified old gentleman living at the Grange,
Haverstock Hill, devoted to genealogical studies ;
it was his pleasure to walk about the cricket field
in rear of the Grange and introduce me to every one
he met. I was toddling along carrying with both
my hands his walking stick.

" This young gentleman," he would explain, " is
Arthur William à Beckett, third son of my third
son, Gilbert Abbott à Beckett, Esquire, Metropolitan Police Magistrate, and nephew of my eldest
son, Sir William à Beckett, Chief Justice of Victoria." Then I used to take off my hat (or rather
his, for he used to lend me an old wide-awake which
came down over my eyes),return it,and go on riding
his walking stick as a horse in front of him. He
was always very kind to me, was this terrible old
gentleman. But he was perhaps feeling remorse,
for he quarrelled with all his boys. Three left England for Australia, and one, my father, remained at
home. But they were none of them on terms of genuine cordiality with him until they had all succeeded
in life. Then they approached the old gentleman
and the past was ruled out as forgotten. Of
course I knew nothing of these domestic jars at my

tender age, but I remember thinking it strange that my grandfather, who was as proud as Lucifer, but not in the least a snob, should be so anxious to emphasize the positions secured by his children. No doubt he was saying in his heart of hearts, " They have risen to this, thank God—in spite of me."

My father, who was born on February 17, 1811, was sent to Westminster School with his three brothers William, Thomas Turner and Arthur Martin. His elder brother and he were great friends and both had literary tastes. My uncles William and Thomas Turner soon left Westminster, one to read for the Bar and the other to prepare for the other branch of the legal profession with a view to his entering the firm created by his father. So Gilbert Abbott à Beckett was left behind for Arthur Martin was not yet old enough to join him. It was then that he made great friends with one of his school-fellows, Henry Mayhew, whose people knew his people " at home." At the time of which I am writing the bullying at Westminster was world-renowned. Forty years later, when my brother Gilbert Arthur à Beckett became a Queen's scholar, subsequently to proceed to Oxford as a student of Christ Church, the "ragging" was sufficiently severe, but in the twenties it was terrible. My father, who was not a strong child—he died before he had completed his forty-fifth year—complained to his parent in Golden Square. My grandfather treated the appeal with contempt. " It would do him good," said the old martinet, who prided himself upon the commission he held as Captain of the St. James' company of what now are the Queen's Westminster Volunteers. " It will do him good." Finding he could get no redress my father withdrew himself from Westminster, and never saw his father again on cordial terms until he had become a Metropolitan Police Magistrate.

Left to his resources he determined to make his way in the world, and this was to be done without any appeal to Golden Square. ' In spite of the bullying, Westminster had turned my father out a good scholar, and he was able to rely upon his knowledge. He applied for and obtained the post of usher, and I have always heard that much of the discipline described in Dotheboys Hall was founded on my father's description of his experiences. Charles Dickens and my father were fast friends, and in Nicholas Nickleby I can trace more than one family likeness. Nicholas himself was my father in his youth, and there is in Ralph Nickleby a suggestion of the stern old man in Golden Square. Not that Mr. William à Beckett was disliked by his neighbours—on the contrary, as my father told me with a smile, " he was greatly respected in the parish," so much so that the ratepayers presented him with a portrait which he subsequently engraved at his own expense. His father being so much respected, a serious thing for Gilbert Abbott à Beckett to do was to produce a paper that would outrage the feelings of Golden Square—so out came *Cerberus, or the Hades Gazette*, I am not sure that the second title was not more understandable by the people. The plan of the paper was that of the *Court Circular*. A list was given of arrivals and those shortly expected. But it never appeared—at the last moment the printer, alarmed at the character of some of the letterpress, went to Golden Square and sought an interview of the Captain. It was accorded, with the result that the type of *Cerberus* was turned into " pie " and the printers' bill was paid up-to-date. Unconscious of the fate of his paper my father and his eldest brother were watching the fortunes of an agent who, dressed as Mephistopheles, was distributing handbills. Unfortunately a boys' school broke up as he was passing the house dedicated to study, and the urchins surrounded him : the poor man had to fight for his life. My father came to the rescue with a constable ; what was left of Mephistopheles was conducted to the police office and there released at the instigation of his employers. I believe this was the first literary venture of my father's and was undertaken when he was still at Westminster. There were several others, amongst the rest *The Literary Beacon* and *The Censor*. In editing the latter he had the help of his brothers Thomas Turner and William. The latter was a poet in a small way. He wrote under the *nom de guerre* of Spforza, and sometimes turned out decent verses, and on his return from Australia shortly after my father's death he published *The Earl's Choice* and other poems. From the latter I quote one which referred to my father. It has the condescending tone of the elder brother to the younger, the Chief Justice to the magistrate, but it is neither displeasing nor inaccurate.

THE à BECKETTS OF "PUNCH"

IN MEMORIAM FRATRIS:

HE died in prime of manhood, not without
Repute beyond what he had hoped to gain,
Yet full of cares success could not shut out
From a too anxious heart and chafing brain,
The intellect, whose wit's too ready vein
Won Folly's laugh and Wisdom's kindly smile,
Fretted for loftier office, and the while
The world applauded, he with self disdain
Oft from his work recoiled, for in him lay
Capacity of nobler toil and thought
Than wake the utterance that suits the day;
And 'twas his hope, ere dying, to have wrought
A monument of more enduring fame
Than that which links the " Comic " with his name:

The Censor was published for the first time on
Saturday, September 6, 1828, when my father was
in his nineteenth year. In this initial number
appears a notice of Charles Kean. Speaking of
Mr. Price, lessee of Drury Lane Theatre, *The
Censor* (three gentlemen rolled into one, as the
writers explain in an introductory article) says :
" He commenced the season by introducing to the
stage Mr. Kean, junior, a young gentleman who
possesses no qualification whatever to fill the
station to which he aspired, a fact which Mr. Price
must or ought to have found out before he permitted the youth in question to appear upon the
boards ; but the wary manager relied on the name
of the performer to fill his house, and to effect that
object he did not care what disgrace he brought
upon the theatre. We shall however waste no
more of our valuable space upon this unimportant
subject." And here we have the tradition of the
paper. Years afterwards in 1841 (the date of the

appearance of *Punch*) it was the tradition to chaff Charles Kean. No doubt the buttons were taken off the foils when Douglas Jerrold quarrelled about " Dorothy's Fortune " at the Princess' Theatre. In later years I was introduced to both Charles Kean and his wife and found them both most kindly and delightful gentlefolk. But I never heard my father say a word in praise of the actor, and the last piece he wrote for the stage was a burlesque upon " The Corsican Brothers," which he called " Oh! Gemini, or the " Brothers of Corse." I remember that he, to quote my uncle's lines, "with self-disdain from his work recoiled." He said that burlesques and the Bench should be kept wide apart, and though he wrote to the very last for *Punch* and *The Illustrated London News* he had no more to do with the stage door of the theatre. For some time before coming to his decision he had collaborated with his friend Mark Lemon on the understanding that the rehearsals and production should be undertaken by his colleague. To return to the *Censor*—it cost three-pence—the price of *Punch*—and was very smartly written. Here is an extract : " If you would make others laugh, laugh yourself, there is much in sympathy, and besides, if you utter a good thing without appearing thoroughly to see the wit of it your auditors will very naturally suppose it to be the effect of chance ; and you will lose the credit of it accordingly." On one occasion a schoolfellow of the two brothers, a Mr. Whalley by name, wrote a paragraph called " Triple jeu de mots," which ran as follows : " At a great public dinner lately one of the party had agreeably entertained the company with some comic songs ; and on account of the heat of the apartment proceeded to open the window, when he was unanimously solicited to re-exert his lungs for his friends' amusement, but the singer thereupon expressed his determination " to give himself airs and them none." This feeble joke gave unlimited delight to the two editors. For ever afterwards Mr. Whalley was known as the author of the " Triple jeu de mots." On December 13, 1828, an editorial banquet was reported. It was described as being of " dazzling and dreamy magnificence," to which had been invited the friends and male contributors to their work. From the emphasis on the " male " it would appear that ladies were also on the staff. After announcing themselves, the editors call attention to the presence of a noble marquis, " whose name we could not learn," " the archbishop," and "the author of the ' Triple jeu de mots.'" The report continues, "The hall in which the dinner took place presented a perfect scene of enchantment, for as the editors had determined to devote the whole of the enormous profits of the publication to this one occasion several ruined noblemen had actually been brought over from the continent *incognito* for the sole purpose of devising extravagances." The description is very amusing. " From the ceiling depended three chandeliers of real emerald, each supported by a chain of golden circled hair culled from the brows of all the poetesses of England." After the chairman had proposed the toast of the sovereign,

" Crito " rose and " proposed success to *The Censor*
with 999 times 999, and after the arithmetician engaged for the occasion had calculated the required
number of hips the toast was drunk amid the most
hearty cheering and plaudits ever heard within the
island of Great Britain." Then the author of the
" Triple jeu de mots " proposed the Editor, and after
the response (fully reported) palanquins glided into
the banquet room ; " into these the Editors grace-
fully threw themselves, in which state they were
conveyed to their respective mansions, and in a few
minutes the once crowded and illumined hall was
dark and desolate." The account is delightful
reading and wonderfully clever considering that
it was the work of a boy in his teens.

My father was dramatic censor, and wrote on
April 4, 1829 : " We enter upon this portion of
our work not without regret, conscious that we
are addressing our readers (at least through the
columns of *The Censor*) for the last time." Gilbert
Abbott à Beckett had no intention of abandoning
the field of journalism. By this time his elder
brother was studying at Lincoln's Inn, on the
road to a call to the Bar, while Thomas Turner
(his immediate senior) had settled down to work
at Golden Square. *The Censor* stopped with the
sixteenth number, and William à Beckett, the
future Chief Justice, gathered together his verse
and published *A Volume of Poems, by Sforza,*
with the kind assistance of Messrs. Hurst and
Chance, of St. Paul's Churchyard. This was in
1828—sixty years afterwards Messrs. Hurst and

THE à BECKETTS OF "PUNCH"

Blackett were publishing for me in Great Marlborough Street. And by the way, I may note
that my father adopted in *The Censor* the *nom
de guerre* (I should like to write *nom de plume*,
as it seems more appropriate) of " Bertie Vyse,"
a signature I assumed when I wrote my earliest
comedy for the Royal Court Theatre, "About
Town" some thirty years ago. Moreover, I followed in my father's footsteps, succeeding him
in his creation of " Mr. Briefless " as his son,
" A. Briefless, Junior." The three young editors
of *The Censor* parted company, but William kept
long in touch with his younger brother. When
he was a dignified Chief Justice in Melbourne he
contributed to ι and, I believe, helped to found,
the *Melbourne Punch*. Through his recommendation my father wrote a London letter for one of
the Australian papers—I fancy the *Melbourne
Argus*—and now for nearly a century à Becketts
have been doing their best to keep up the prestige
of their name on both sides of the world. The
eldest son of " Sforza " died only the other day. He
inherited from his grandfather the love of genealogy,
and was said to be the best amateur herald at the
antipodes. When he left England—it turned out
to be for the last time—he spoke of a package
he proposed taking with him. " I am going to
have it stowed below, since I shan't want it
on the voyage." " What is it ? " I asked. " Something to surprise them with over yonder," said
he with a laugh : " a hatchment." He actually
was making arrangements for his own funeral !

EARLY DAYS

Poor fellow! W.A.C. he was called (William Arthur Callender) was a good sort. He was eccentric, but a very clever fellow. During the Gavan Duffy Ministry he represented the Government of Victoria in the Upper House.

My friend, Mr. M. H. Spielmann, in *The History of Punch*, has devoted much time to the consideration of the founders of *Punch*. He has given the world his views upon the originator of the title and the earliest composition of the staff. I do not wish to introduce any very contentious matter in this volume. My desire is to be faithful to its title, *The à Becketts of "Punch"—Memories of Father and Sons*. The late Gilbert Abbott à Beckett is the father, and I am a son. My father contributed to the first number of *Punch*, and wrote regularly without a week's break until the day of his death, August 30, 1856. I began to write for the paper some eighteen years later, and continued my work until June 4, 1902. My father was on *Punch* for fifteen years, I for eight-and-twenty ; so between us we were on the staff for forty-three years—a fairly long record for two generations. Then besides my father and myself, there was my brother Gilbert, who joined after I had been received at the table, and sent his last copy from his death-bed. And my elder brother, in the days of Mark Lemon's editorship, had sent a few articles to *Punch*, which appeared in the paper some time between 1856 and 1874, so that the connexion of the à Becketts with *Punch* was maintained in the pause between one

23

generation passing away and another growing up to take its place. But I repeat, I have no wish to introduce very contentious matter into this volume. I wish to show how my father came to join the staff of *Punch*, and do not desire to discuss whether he founded it. He certainly was a contributor to the first number, was the friend and school-fellow of Henry Mayhew, the co-editor with Sterling Coyne, and Mark Lemon and the printer Last. The printer I have named I met myself, and he spoke of my father with great respect. " He was a very clever man, sir, and brought out a lot of my papers," said he, when I, as Secretary of the Strand Printing and Publishing Company, Limited, was making arrangements for the production of the *Glowworm*. " And so you are his son, are you, sir ? Well, for the sake of your father, I wish you luck." And in this connexion I am reminded that my first and only chat with Henry Mayhew was in connexion with Last and the *Glowworm*. In its proper place I propose to tell the story (an amusing one) of the rise and fall of the *Glowworm*, but here it may be appropriate to mention under what circumstances I came across Henry Mayhew. Joseph Last had been engaged by the Directors of the Company to which I refer to print the paper. We were some months in making our preparations, and to fill up the time Last produced and published a periodical, *The Shops and Companies of Great Britain*. I am afraid that prompt payment to the contributors was not the order of the day, for continually our

Board Room (where I sat in state) was bombarded by angry authors demanding at any rate a cheque on account. I was then about twenty, and inclined to be conciliatory. I used to permit my angry visitors to say what they liked to my disparagement, and then explain that I and my Board had nothing to do with their grievances ; upon this they apologised. I replied, " Not at all," and then they withdrew in some confusion. However, the incidents were not absolutely of a pleasant character, so " my Board " gave directions that no one connected with *The Shops and Companies of Great Britain* was to be permitted on the premises of the Strand Printing and Publishing Company, Limited. I had noticed on my way to the Board Room a gentleman with very pronounced features standing behind the counter in the publishing department; full of zeal I asked the publisher for the name of this gentleman, and learned that he was connected with *The Shops and Companies of Great Britain.* " And what is his name ? " I asked. The reply was that he was the celebrated Mr. Henry Mayhew, whose work on *London Labour and the London Poor* was one of the books of the season. I approached my visitor, and asked him if he would kindly follow me to my room. Mr. Mayhew bowed his head, and allowed me to usher him into our Board Room. I begged him to take a chair. " Mr. Henry Mayhew," said I, " it is a great honour for me to have the pleasure of making your acquaintance, but unfortunately I have a painful duty to perform. I am the Secretary of the Strand Printing and Publishing Company, and have received orders from my Directors that no one connected with a publication called *The Shops and Companies of Great Britain* is to be permitted on the premises. Now, I know you wrote *London Labour and the London Poor*, a most admirable work, my dear sir, a most admirable work."

"You are very good," said Henry Mayhew, grimly.

"And I know what you did in *Punch*, and how you were connected with *Figaro in London*."

"Oh, you got that from Mr. Last, who was associated with both. But what do you want with me ? "

"Well, Mr. Mayhew, if you are connected with *The Shops and Companies of Great Britain*—for it's sake I hope you are, for ours I hope you are not—it is my painful duty to request you to retire, or, to quote the words of the resolution, ' to put you out.' "

I never in my life saw any one quite so angry. He anathematised me in English first, and then in a foreign language. I felt that he was calling down the vengeance of heaven on my devoted head. Then he suddenly asked for my name, I presume to give further emphasis to his denunciation. I gave it. He started and became quite silent.

"Not the son of Gilbert Abbott à Beckett ? "

"Yes, Mr. Mayhew, he was my father."

EARLY DAYS

" Your father was my dearest and oldest friend, and you want to order me off the premises."

" No, I don't, Mr. Mayhew ; I am only obeying the instructions of my directors."

" Well, yes, I see," said he. " You are very like your poor father." Then he shook hands with me, walked to the door, and opened it. Then he turned round. " Good-bye, my boy, and good luck. But give this answer to your Board— D——n your Directors ! "

To return to my father ; at the mature age of one-and-twenty he started *Figaro in London.* In this paper I think we can trace the germs of the coming *Punch.* It was suggested by a Parisian prototype. In his preface to the first volume for the year 1832, my father wrote : " On the completion of our first volume we cannot help deviating for a moment from our customary course of modesty, and congratulating ourselves on the success that up to this triumphant point has attended us. Ever since we first made our appearance in London we have been ' *Figaro* here ! *Figaro* there ! *Figaro* everywhere ! ' We did not hope for a more favourable reception than attended our prototype in Paris, but we have the pleasing satisfaction of knowing by a return lately made of the circulation of the French newspapers, that *Figaro in London* sells more than four times the number of its namesake in the French capital. For this proud pre-eminence we feel we are indebted chiefly to the zeal with which we have used our razor for the public good, and to the liberality of those for whom we have so fearlessly wielded our formidable little weapon. It would be indecent in us to exult over the demise of one, and all those innumerable imitators which our success tempted into ephemeral existence, but in a preface (our annual opportunity for indulging in egotism) we cannot refrain from thanking the public for the singularly elevated position its favour has awarded us."

Here we have the *Figaro in London* founded on the Paris *Figaro*, as nine years later we find the London *Charivari* founded on the Paris *Charivari*. Next the scheme of *Figaro in London* was the scheme of *Punch*, as it had for its chief feature the large cut which dealt with the politics of the week ; more than this, the editorial inspired the cartoonist of *Figaro in London* as the editorial inspired the cartoonist of *Punch*. Further, we have the common link of the printer who knew the staff of *Figaro in London* (in its later volumes) and the printer of *Punch* in its earliest. The editor of *Figaro in London* was my father, helped by Henry Mayhew, his schoolfellow at Westminster ; the editor of *Punch*, in conjunction with Mark Lemon and Sterling Coyne, was Henry Mayhew. *Figaro in London* closed its career in 1839 ; *Punch* began in 1841. My father severed his connexion with *Figaro in London* at the end of the third volume. For years it continued, but fell from its high estate into a rather obscure theatrical print. Quite at the close my father was invited to try to revive it. It was too late, but he was connected with it until 1839, on the best of terms with Henry Mayhew and in close touch with Joseph Last. It ceased. Then in 1841 out came *Punch*, associated with Last, Henry Mayhew and my father. I do not wish to introduce very contentious matter into this volume, but does this not tend to prove that my father was practically the originator of *Punch*? I venture to suggest that it is something more than filial piety that induces me to adopt this view.

The appearance and great success of *Figaro in London* produced a number of imitators, and I have seen it suggested that some of these rivals, for instance, *Punchinello in London*, was the original of *Punch*. However, this idea is negatived by a paragraph under the heading " Notice to Correspondents," which appeared on February 23, 1832. I quote it : " A new disease has lately sprung up in the periodical world, for which we hardly know how to find a name. It consists of a strange *goût* for imitating our work, and we shall therefore call it ' Figaro-mania.' Several cases have recently occurred, and of course a number of deaths, and though the disease is intended to be *catching*, it has not been found to *take*. It has lately grown to so great an extent that we think of giving a weekly report in imitation of the plan adopted by the papers with regard to the cholera. For example : Remaining at last report, 10. Deaths—*The Patriot, The Figaro in Birmingham, The Critical Figaro, The Literary Test*, and *The English Figaro*. New cases, 3.

29

All very desperate, and almost certain next week to be included among the deaths. Remaining up to this date, 8. Recoveries, *none*." After a pause of three weeks my father continued his report. After referring to a new case which he described as hasty and malignant, he wrote : " Remaining at last report, 8. New cases, 4. Deaths, *The Devil's Walk in London* and *Life in London*. Total from commencement, 18. Deaths from the commencement, 8. Remaining at the present date, 10. Recoveries, none." In the number for March 31, 1832, my father continues : " The Figaro-mania is, we are glad to see, on the decline. There has only been one new case, and that will we have no doubt meet with a speedy termination. There have been two deaths, one of which has all along been anticipated by us ; and indeed the poor thing has lingered much longer than could have been expected. Remaining at last report, 10. New cases, 1. Deaths, *Giovanni in London* and the *Illustrious Stranger*. Recoveries, none." On April 7, 1832, my father wrote : " We proceed to our report of the Figaro-mania, which is, we hope, the last with which our readers will be troubled. Remaining at last report, 9. New cases, 0. Deaths, *Punchinello*, *Weekly Visitor* and *New Figaro*. Recoveries, none. In closing our report, we have to state that we feel no unbecoming exultation over the defeat of a rival. Gross indelicacy we have already protested against, scurrility we despise, and want of culture we pity. We feel therefore no compassion for any of the works that are now deceased, with the exception of *Punchinello* and the *Weekly Visitor*, both of which were free at least from the two first imperfections." My father kept his word ; no further report was published, and an apology offered to the editor of the *Illustrious Stranger* for announcing the death of his periodical. But, as my father added, " the statement was only premature "—a fact that was proved in the event. I think we may take it from the above that *Figaro in London* was the original of its own class of publications, and its imitators came to grief.

As I consider *Figaro in London* the immediate precursor of *Punch*, I ask permission to say something more about this wonderful literary work. But here I may observe that it seems to me that the reason my father did not wish to venture upon the proprietorial side of *Punch* was because he preferred a small certainty to a large prospective profit. He was on the most excellent terms with his colleagues. Under these circumstances I think there is something in the suggestion that Gilbert Abbott à Beckett was the originator of *Punch*.

It is interesting to notice how a feud is carried on from paper to paper. I have already traced the attack upon Charles Kean in *Punch* to *Figaro in London*, and I find that the attack upon the poet Bunn which ended, so far as *Punch* was concerned, in a venomous *brochure*, had also its origin in the earlier paper. His initial description

THE à BECKETTS OF "PUNCH"

is "a small and raving mad amateur," and from time to time the references to him are the reverse of complimentary. But turning over the pages of *Figaro in London*, and remembering that they were written by a lad only one-and-twenty, one cannot but be struck by the absence of malice and the presence of good nature which characterises them. They are full of chaff—schoolboy chaff—but there is no offence in a line of them. They are absolutely pure. *Punch* has been able to boast that a girl might read it from cover to cover without hurt to her modesty. The same assertion might have been made by the editor of the first three volumes of *Figaro in London*. But while this can be said in his favour, I find that he pays off old scores. He goes for Preston, the second master of Westminster School. He gives a notice to the Westminser Play of 1833, and refers to the pedagogue as follows : " The second master, old Preston, whom we remember ever since we recollect the school itself, has been doing a bit of wit in the shape of an epilogue, in which he attempts to satirise criticism, but he should confine himself to his old trade of flogging boys, leaving the flagellation of critics to a more skilful wielder of the tomahawk. There is a great deal of merit due to a man who, at his time of life, tries to be funny ; for the utmost wit he ever was guilty of is the stale classic pun of *Caesar venit in Galliam summa diligentia*, which old P., with a self-important chuckle, used to translate thus : Caesar came into Gaul on the top of the diligence.

32

EARLY DAYS

This joke is nearly as old as Queen Elizabeth (whose health, by the bye, the sapient Westminsters still continue to drink once per annum), and Preston shows a facetious animus, and that must atone for the horrible antiquity of his witticisms." Here we have the scholar with recollections of probably. well-deserved punishments going for his at-one-time tyrant. He refers to him as ": old Preston" and his love of flogging boys, and the writer is scarcely out of his teens. But in spite of his absolutely irresponsible attacks upon those he singles out for censure, he has his friends whose work he chooses out for the heartiest commendation, and amongst them I am glad to find the name of Douglas Jerrold. I have seen it said that my father and his comrade on *Punch* were on bad terms at this period of their lives, and that the author of "Black-eyed Susan" actually ran a paper in opposition to *Figaro*. If he had, my father would certainly have chaffed him in his own paper. But all through the pages of *Figaro in London* there is but one tone about Douglas Jerrold—the key-note of praise and respect. Yes—"Douglas" and "Gil" were friends, in spite of an occasional passage of arms over the mahogany tree in Bouverie Street. My father and Thackeray were fast friends, and the latter did not get on with Douglas Jerrold. Thus it may have come to pass that my father did not keep up the old friendship that saw its origin in the days of "The Rent Day" and *Figaro in London*. But there was a complete reconciliation the year of my father's death. It was the only time I saw Douglas Jerrold to my recollection, although he may have been amongst those who were asked to 10, Hyde Park Gate, South, to meet Mr. Thackeray. It was the custom of my father and mother to take us children to Boulogne, leave us there with our nurses, and then start off for a short trip up the Rhine or into Switzerland or Italy, returning viâ Boulogne to take us home. My father and mother had returned rather earlier than their custom, so as to spend a week at the French watering-place. The heat had been terrible, and I remember that the sands in front of the Casino (then called the Etablisment des Bains) was the favourite meeting place. I remember seeing Douglas Jerrold chatting with my father, and I remember him addressing himself to me. In another page I have referred to this meeting. Here I may say it marked the perfect reconciliation between two old friends. Very shortly afterwards my father died from what was then known as " Boulogne sore throat," but which now is called diphtheria. Douglas Jerrold wrote the obituary notice in *Punch*, recording my father's service—a record that was placed on my father's tombstone in Highgate Cemetery. It is delightful for me to think that my father left no enemies. Of course I remember him at home as the most affectionate husband and father, but I had to trace him to Bouverie Street through other eyes and ears. Of all the men who sat round the Punch table with my father, but one

remains, my dear old friend Sir John Tenniel.
He has told me that my father was very quiet
and greatly liked. He pulled his weight in the
boat in the settlement of the cartoon, and generally said the best thing of the evening. But he
was very reserved and even nervous, in spite of
his long service, his close friendship with Lemon,
Leech and Thackeray. This description of my
friend Sir John has been confirmed by the only
original member of the *Punch* staff who survived
until recent times—Percival Leigh. He told me
before he died that from first to last my father
was loved. He quarrelled with no one, and speaking when the occasion needed, was generally
silent. Perhaps it may be a proof of heredity
that my brother Gilbert, when he joined the staff
on the invitation of the present editor of *Punch*,
was also reserved, silent and beloved. My brother,
however, was a great invalid, and unable to stand
the sometimes rude chaff that was frequently
the *specialité de la maison* in Bouverie Street.
Speaking for myself, I fancy I was cheerful
enough when I first joined the table, but as my
old friends died off and new ones took their places.
I found that I was not quite so cheerful. In the
absence of the present editor, it was my duty
to take his place, and then I used to pull myself
together, and try to lead the conversation, as
Tom Taylor did to my knowledge, and as I have
always heard did Shirley Brooks and Mark
Lemon. But in the later days there was something wanting. So found Charles Keene—so

THE à BECKETTS OF "PUNCH"

found du Maurier. I must confess that in the days of my father's old friend, Tom Taylor, the *esprit de corps* of the *Punch* table was unique. During the course of this volume I may perhaps say something about the decay of that *esprit de corps*, although I have the strongest desire to write nothing of a controversial character.

As I have referred to *Figaro in London*, it may be well to set at rest a discussion that has arisen about the cartoonist Richard Seymour. It has been said that this artist, whose illustrations to *Pickwick* were interrupted by his self-inflicted death, committed suicide on account of a quarrel he had with my father. Nothing could be more unfair or ridiculous than such a statement. Gilbert Abbott à Beckett severed his connexion with *Figaro in London* at the end of 1834. Seymour killed himself three years later, and the quarrel between my father and the cartoonist was a storm in a teacup. But first let me quote the preface of the third volume of *Figaro in London*, which records my father's connexion with the paper. Gilbert Abbott à Beckett writes : " This is the third volume, and closes the publication as far as the projector and original editor is concerned, who is no longer responsible for anything that may appear in any periodical bearing the title of *Figaro*. Our labours in this work comprise three volumes—it being little more than three years since the first number of *Figaro in London* was sent forth, without being preceded by even one solitary advertisement.

Its popularity was soon great, owing, however, more to the novelty of the plan and the opportunity given for ridicule by the position of political parties than to any merit the execution of the design could boast of. It is gratifying to the editor to feel that he abandons the work from none but a voluntary cause, and that the public still patronises the little paper to an extent that renders it in a pecuniary point of view a sacrifice to abandon it. The venomous, who are always sure to be idiotic, will very probably send forth a stupid cry of obvious and commonplace sarcasm. This ignorant howl will experience no contradiction from us. The *Figaro* is known to be at this time a very profitable work; and even if it were not generally known, the publication of the fact would be to us a matter of utter indifference. A thousand surmises cannot overturn one fact—which one fact is to us perfectly satisfactory. We have often alluded to rivals of this work. We need not say that they have all long ago departed. We now at once bid our readers one and all farewell." And with these last words my father's connexion with *Figaro in London* ceased—to be renewed for a brief interval some five years later, just before the first appearance of *Punch*.

And now as to my father's quarrel with Robert Seymour. Gilbert à Beckett, as I have said, was a youngster of one-and-twenty when he took up the reins of editorship. Seymour was considerably his senior. Accustomed to meet at his father's house people of (to quote Disraeli) "light and leading," he had not that awe for talent and age that Seymour would have liked him to possess ; moreover, he had come from Westminster with that contempt for those who were not public school men that young men possess until they have turned five-and-twenty. So unfortnuately from the first my father was inclined to treat Seymour in a kind of "Hail fellow, well met!" spirit that was distinctly repugnant to the artist's feelings. Probably Seymour allowed Gilbert à Beckett to see that this feeling of good-fellowship belonged exclusively to the editor, and consequently was not shared by the artist. My father evidently retaliated by praising Seymour's work in *Figaro in London* in the most extravagant fashion.

I find as I look through the pages of the paper that my father was always referring to his colleague's work as "magnificent," "splendid," and the like. When "the Birthday honours" were announced, my father said that Seymour would be in the next batch of peers, and so on, and so on. I can quite believe that this kind of praise, coming from a youngster just out of his teens, must have made Robert Seymour very angry. However, editor and cartoonist had to meet to arrange the weekly cartoon, and all went fairly well for a couple of years. At last Seymour could not stand this extravagant praise any longer, and there was a quarrel. He told the youngster that he would no longer discuss with him the subject of the cartoon, and would send in what he pleased. Gilbert à

EARLY DAYS

Beckett smiled, and waited to see the next drawing. It came, and I have it before me as I write.
It was published on the 30th day of August, 1834.
Lord Chancellor Brougham was represented with
an enormous nose, tearing with that organ a copy
of the *Times*. He was also snapping his fingers.
From the *Times* came hands holding pens and
wielding them as daggers. The sum total was
that Brougham was being attacked by the *Times*,
and did not mind the assault. Up to this date
my father had been writing up to the cartoon,
giving it a title and supporting with the pen the
meaning of the pencil. These attendant articles
had, however, been growing more and more
" chaffy " for some time. Of the cartoon published July 19, 1834, my father had written :
" We, however, refer our readers to the caricature
itself. It must be confessed Seymour delights in
exercising the imagination of the British public,
and with this view confines much of his genius
to the dark and shadowy region of hieroglyphic
mystery." This was scarcely kind. When my
father had the Brougham mystery thrust upon
him he wrote up to it in the following fashion :
He began without a heading, and then continued :
" The above caricature is so purely hieroglyphical
that we decline any attempt at explaining it.
The artist when he conceived it must have been
under some strange and baneful influence which
we cannot possibly attempt either to enter or
elucidate. We suspect that he was labouring
under some frightful stagnation of his vital

39

functions, and the result has been a vivid affair which we can only describe as a pictorial frenzy. The fact is that our caricaturist has been so long and deeply impregnated with the horrible aspect of political affairs that his mind has at last become in some degree impressed with a hectic extravagance that has now vented itself in a caricature, which must take its place by the side of the grand effect to make which an Italian painter crucified his own servant that he might the more forcibly represent the agony on the Cross, which he had selected for his subject. Seymour has, as it were, undergone a sort of mental crucifixion, and the result is the awful sketch which heads the present number of our periodical. It would be almost impiety in us to attempt a solution of the sacred mystery, and we can only pay a tribute of reverence to the artist's over-excited imagination and morbid fancy. If, however, any of our readers can solve the pious problem, and tell us what the deuce is the meaning of the above design, we would gladly bestow upon him a reward of £100, for he who solved the Sphinx would be but a fool in comparison with the gentleman who can make head or tail of the caricature that surmounts the present article." Naturally a row followed, and Seymour refused to send in further work to the paper. Now, strange to say, something very like this happened in *Punch* about a quarter of a century ago. My friend Mr. Linley Sambourne sent in a cartoon without an explanation, and the present editor

EARLY DAYS

" wrote up " to it in the same spirit as my father wrote up to Seymour's pious problem. But the chaff of the present editor of *Punch* was more genial than the chaff of my father. Linley Sambourne laughed and enjoyed the joke. Seymour frowned and had a quarrel. But it is simply ridiculous to suggest that three years afterwards this incident (which, by the way, ended with the resignation by my father of the editorship) so weighed upon his mind that he committed suicide. Seymour was pompous ; my father was not blessed with the organ of veneration. Had my father stood in awe of great personages, the *Comic Histories of England and Rome* would never have been written. Seymour hated chaff; my father loved it. The successful and pompous artist met the typical public school boy, not caring a jot for any one, and the result was a quarrel. If I had been Seymour I should have anticipated the precedent set by Mr. Linley Sambourne, and treated the incident as a good or even a bad joke. But always as a joke. Seymour went on his way, and picked out Charles Dickens as a suitable person to write up to his sporting adventures. My father busied himself with play-writing, and gave up *Figaro in London*. Then after three years' work Seymour commits suicide. A great many things had happened since August 30, 1834 (the death day of my father twenty-two years later), and much water had flowed under the Pont Neuf. I repeat, it is ridiculous, it is wicked to suggest that the incident in the *Figaro* in any

41

way led to Seymour's death. Of the dead, let
there be said nothing but good things, but I have
always felt that Seymour treated my father, the
boy of one-and-twenty, badly. The quarrel led
to my father's resignation of what was his livelihood. And what did he do? Why, he faced the
future bravely, worked his hardest as a stock
author for some of the minor theatres, and later
on for the St. James', and ultimately came up
smiling to help to found the successor of *Figaro
in London* : *Punch, or the London Charivari*. He
did not commit suicide, although I am afraid his
early, too early death, was to a large degree
attributable to over-work. He was within a week
of writing his last copy when he met Douglas
Jerrold early in August on the sands of Boulogne.
He was so pleased to think that he and " Douglas "
were good friends. It was a tradition in his days
that peace and brotherly love should reign round
the mahogany tree in Bouverie Street. " What
is the good of quarrelling with the fellow? "
exclaimed Thackeray with a smile after an en-
counter with Douglas Jerrold. " I shall have to
meet him next Wednesday at the *Punch* dinner."

As I shall have more to say about my father's
relations with Charles Dickens, with whom he
was on the most intimate terms of friendship,
I may here refer to his cordiality to Thackeray.
My father of course was his near neighbour at the
Punch table, and they invariably supported one
another. There was another bond of union :
they were both public school boys. And although

EARLY DAYS

I whisper it with bated breath in these days of universal equality, years ago the three colleges of royal foundation, Eton, Winchester and Westminster, ranked before Charterhouse. Thackeray, Silver and Leech had been educated at Charterhouse, and my father represented Westminster, the Westminster of the Eton-and-Westminster boat race, the Westminster that sent Queen's scholars to Christ Church and Trinity. In those days, to be a Westminster boy meant a good deal. Thackeray respected my father on account of his school, and also regarded him with a kind of comic awe as a Metropolitan Police Magistrate. I am fond of quoting from the *Ballads of Policeman X*, wherein my sire is called " à Beckett the beak " and "that respected Magistrate." Moreover, Thackeray had a great admiration for Fielding, and, it is said, always looked towards the Magisterial Bench where the author of the *History of Jonathan Wild* had sat, with envy. If Thackeray had ever practised at the Bar, I think he would have applied for a Magistrateship, and this was the opinion of my father, who laughingly referred to his colleague in one of our morning walks from Kensington to Southwark. So the friendship of the two men was founded on mutual respect. My father was quiet and very kind. I am happy to think at his death he did not leave an enemy, and he died in the prime of manhood before age had come to wipe off old scores and reconcile old enemies. Thackeray was cynical, and certainly had no wish to efface himself. My

43

father's relations with Dickens were of quite a different character. As a young man, as will be seen from my references to *Figaro in London*, my father was absolutely irresponsible. He bubbled over with good spirits, and laughed at everybody and everything. In Charles Dickens— pressman, actor and author—he had a man after his own heart. They could talk shop about the theatre and the newspaper office to their hearts' content. And throughout his short life he was friends to both, and when he died Thackeray and Dickens offered spontaneously to help the à Beckett family if there were need for assistance. If I had been a few years older I, a third son, might have gone to Oxford at the expense of the two greatest novelists of the nineteenth century. But I was not old enough, and my father's two friends, acting in unison, were able to show their kindness to the family of their dead friend in another manner. They both supported the application for a Government pension to my mother, and were able to be of the utmost service to my brother, a student at Christ Church, at the time of our father's death, when he was preparing to make his way in the world as a civil servant, and subsequently as a dramatist, an essayist and a journalist.

I consider that from 1834 until 1841 the way was being made clear for the appearance of *Punch*. There was a group of young men struggling to make ready the road for a worthy comic paper. *Figaro in London* was the advance guard.

EARLY DAYS

For the first time a humorous periodical rested upon something better and purer than vile personal abuse. The miserable scurrility of the *Satirist* and sheets of that class was abandoned for healthy genuine fun. I have said that my father was no respecter of persons, and he certainly " went for " one of the Royal Dukes pretty regularly. Every week he used to publish an article which he used to call " Gloucesteriana." In it the Duke of Gloucester was made to perpetrate a pun upon some topic of the day to the delight of his aide-de-camp, a most worthy gentleman of the name of Higgins. Here is a specimen : " The other day Higgins and the Duke were conversing on the subject of the Calthorp Street affair and the attack made by the police upon the public. Both were joking over the fun of smashing people's heads with staves. ' For,' said the Duke, ' such staves must have made the people sing out very enchantingly.' ' Yes,' replied Higgins, ' but one of the C Division of police is killed.' ' Is he ? ' responded Billy ; ' then it serves him right, for what could he have been doing on *land* if he belonged to the *sea* Division ? ' Higgins and his master tripped out of the apartment dancing the gallopade." This article was one of the features of the paper, and so my father supplemented it by publishing " Broughamiana," which related the jests of the Lord Chancellor. In both articles there was nothing offensive, only good-natured chaff. The mildest witticisms of the Royal Duke were received with delirious joy by the A.D.C. " Higgins loosened his cravat to prevent convulsions," " Higgins swallowed his pocket handkerchief at one gulp to check his risibility." At length the chaff grew too fast and furious, and Higgins called upon my father. The A.D.C. turned out to be a most amiable and accomplished gentleman. He brought a message from the Duke of Gloucester that he was a great admirer of *Figaro in London,* and therefore could not be such a donkey as it was the fashion to represent him. My father told me that he was taken aback ; if Colonel Higgins had threatened him, or even called him out, he would have been equal to the occasion. But for a good-natured soldier to " speak to him like a father," and gently suggest that it was too bad to talk about his dancing gallopades and the rest of it, was too much for him. As the result my father dropped " Gloucesteriana," and was ever afterwards on excellent terms with the Royal Duke and his faithful A.D.C.

During the three years of my father's connexion with *Figaro in London* he was continually starting other papers. He produced the *Wag* and the *Comic Magazine.* The first was on the lines of the *Figaro,* but was sold at a higher price ; then he produced a periodical which was made up of extracts from its contemporaries. Nowadays it has a successor in *Public Opinion,* and I produced something of the sort myself in connexion with the *Glowworm,* called the *Echo.* To this paper of his my father gave a title which would have rejoiced the hearts of the Institute of Journalists who object to "lifting"—he called it the *Thief*. In those days, as well as these, there was a good deal of interchange of printed copy, and my father, who, when he had views, never hesitated to express them, stigmatized the "lifting" with what he considered an appropriate appellation. The paper was made up of the work of others, so he called it the *Thief*. Later on, when Bunn made an attack upon his three enemies—Lemon, Jerrold and à Beckett—he gave a list of my father's literary failures. It was rather a long one, and proved that his energy must have been untiring. At the time of the production of these ephemeral periodicals he was also a playwright, and for a short time the manager of a London theatre. Besides this, he read for, was called to, and practised at the Bar. I am not surprised at his early death. The mind was too great for the body ; he killed himself with overwork.

I dwell upon these early days of my father's literary activity because I can see in them the collection of those men who were subsequently to become the initial staff of *Punch*. He was a journalist and a dramatic author, and the initial members of the staff of *Punch* were drawn from the world of the Press and the Stage. Lemon, whose early career—as Bunn suggested later on—was in a direction away from literature, was bitten with the desire to write for the theatre. This was no doubt the link of union between " Gil " and " Mark." I have a collection of my father's plays, and after a time I find they were written in collaboration with Lemon. During the *Figaro* period my father was writing without a colleague, but shortly after his rupture with the paper Lemon came on the scene to help him. My walks with my father enabled me to learn the nature of the collaboration. The scenario of the piece was prepared by both, and then my father set to work and wrote the play straight off. Then he gave it to Lemon to read, and suggest alterations if it so pleased him. Finished, he handed the play over to Lemon for production. My father absolutely loathed rehearsals, and by his collaboration with Mark Lemon he escaped them. As a boy he was immensely fond of the theatre. In the *Censor*, a publication to which I have referred, he possessed himself of the control of the dramatical critical department, and this he directed at the age of nineteen. As I have said, it has been a tradition in my family that Dickens drew the character of Nicholas Nickleby from his friend, my father. So Gilbert à Beckett was for ever seeing the prototypes of the Crummles family, and had been often called upon to write up to " the real pump and splendid tubs." My father was a very rapid worker. I find in *Figaro* of January 14, 1834, a notice written by himself of his first play. Here it is—

A new farce from our pen will have been produced here (the Fitzroy) before this number gets into the nation's hands, though we go to press too early (for the purpose of supplying the whole world) to know what reception it will experience. It is called " The King Incog," and anticipating a failure, we will be beforehand with our apology. The following history of the thing must be the excuse for its errors—

EARLY DAYS

Commenced on Friday,
Finished on Saturday,
Copied by Monday,
Parts distributed on Tuesday,
Rehearsed on Wednesday,
Acted on Thursday,
and, for what we know,
Dead and d——d by Friday,
which is about as concise a record as we are able to give of it.
Whatever may be its fate, we shan't care ; for it would be poor
philosophy in us not to bear a laugh at our own expense when
we indulge in so many at the expense of others. Whether
received with favour or the reverse " we bow (in the words
of an established clap-trap) to the decision of a British
audience."

As a matter of fact it was quite successful.
My father, in his preface to the published work,
wrote as follows—

ADVERTISEMENT.

" The King Incog," though received with great favour
when acted, may be in its printed form open to the detection
of many egregious errors, for *litera scripta manet*, that is to say,
" when they have you in black and white there is no escaping."
For the various anachronisms the author does not think it
worth while to apologize, and therefore does not attempt to
defend himself for having introduced " pink note-paper,"
" Jacob's *Law Dictionary*," and " the bump of benevolence "
into the time of Charles II. These matters are of small importance to a farce, and even critics seem tacitly to admit the
fact, for they have in their notices of " King Incog " abstained
from remarks on an error which they could not fail to have
detected. For other deficiencies the only plea that can
be offered is the fact of its being the first dramatic effort of
the author and its having been written in two days, as well
as produced so hastily that it was not even rehearsed till the
morning before the night of its performance !

These and all other obstacles were triumphantly

surmounted by the talents of the performers, and the author, equally grateful to all, acknowledges his obligation to the whole strength of the company.

The success of " The King Incog " ended in my father—with characteristic impetuosity—running the Fitzroy Theatre. In *Figaro in London* the venture can be traced in his notices. It is very amusing reading. My father became a prolific author, producing in rapid succession " The Son of the Sun," " The Revolt of the Workhouse," and many other burlesques. " The King Incog " was a farce in two acts, written in prose ; the others were in verse. The music had evidently been collected under the superintendence of my mother, who was a composer of two operas, " Little Red Riding Hood," played at the Surrey, and " Agnes Sorrel," the initial production at the St. James' Theatre under Braham's management, and here I trace my father's connexion with Henry Mayhew. " The Wandering Minstrel," in which later on Robson scored so heavily, was produced at the Fitzroy. Henry Mayhew wrote under the *nom de guerre* of " Ralph Rigmarole, Esq." No doubt this disguise was assumed to disarm the criticism of Henry Mayhew's father, who was a highly respectable solicitor, like my grandfather, and who might have joined in the crusade against " the boys." My father, with characteristic enthusiasm—for he was a very good friend to his friends, and a good fighting enemy to his enemies—wrote a criticism in advance as follows—

EARLY DAYS

A new farce, from the pen of Ralph Rigmarole, Esq.; was to be produced on Thursday, under the title of " The Wandering Minstrel." We can venture in advance to announce beforehand its triumphant success, for we know the piece to be admirable ; and though the part was, we understand, originally intended for Reeve, we are quite confident that Mitchell will do it more justice, for he is sure to be perfect in the character.

On referring to the caste of "The King Incog " I find that Mitchell played a part of secondary importance. So evidently there had been a quarrel. Reeve had thrown up his part, and Mitchell was promoted to " leading business." The management of the Fitzroy was scarcely suggestive of a couch of roses. I trace in the *Figaro* a quarrel about the retention of some money by a man who, "in a fit of extreme consequence, in fact in the very last stage of a severe attack of dignity, called himself sole manager of the Fitzroy." There seems to have been a struggle of some sort, for my father writes that some one had asserted that Ollier (the name of the official) would have been murdered but for a friend's interference. Says my father, "the idea of taking the trouble to murder Ollier is too rich to be entertained." But the worries of the management of the Fitzroy impaired his editorship of his paper, for on May 31, 1834, he addresses the " readers of *Figaro* all over the world," and tells them that during the last few weeks circumstances had arisen to absorb so much of his time and attention that he had occasionally neglected his duty to his first and best friends, the readers of that periodical. He says that the

51

neglect had not affected in the slightest degree the
sale of the paper. He wonders that it had not
occurred, for he merited it. Then he explains an
excess of other and various occupations has dis-
tracted him too much from his work, which has
often gone forth to the world full of imperfections,
and very late in publication. All this is to be
amended in the future. My father brought his
apology to a conclusion as follows—" The editor
hopes that the present number may not be taken
as a specimen of the intended reform which will
commence next week, and in the meantime he
claims the indulgence of his readers, which by the
bye is asking lenity at the hands of the whole
country." It is interesting to note the sympathy
existing between the editor and the public. My
father takes his readers into his confidence in
return for some very outspoken criticism, and here
again is an excuse for the quarrel with Seymour.
After praising up the artist as he praised all his
friends, Seymour turned round and complained of
his impertinence. It was not unnatural that my
father should have felt scornful annoyance.

It has been said that the easiest road to ruin is
by the copyright of a paper or the lease of a theatre,
My father was interested in the Fitzroy and editor
of *Figaro in London,* and ultimately was forced to
sever his connection with both. But now he was
writing, at express train speed, plays for what were
known as the minor theatres. Amongst the rest
he became stock author of the Royal Coburg,
built by Joseph Glossop. The lessee of this

property was the younger son of a Derbyshire lad of good family, who had made his fortune in London from a very limited capital as a commencement. All Joseph's brothers without exception were clergymen. The Derbyshire lad, the founder of the family (so far as London was concerned) was desirous to see all his sons parsons. But one of them, Joseph, refused to take orders. He was a friend of George IV, and Adjutant and Clerk of the Cheque of the Body Guard, and later on acted as King's Messenger. I never met him, because he died before my time. But from all accounts he seems to have been what is now known as a " good sort," with the additional disadvantage of being " no one's enemy but his own." He was keen about theatres, and induced his father the millionaire to help him to build the Royal Coburg. The title was selected in compliment to the Court. It was opened in state by a member of the Royal Family. Mr. Glossop was very anxious to make a good start, and provided what was called a looking-glass curtain. His original idea was to have the mirror made of one continuous sheet of glass, but of course this turned out to be impossible, so the screen was composed of squares, with frames in between. At its best the curtain looked " patchy," but when it was handled by the scene-shifters it was further adorned by the impress of dirty fingers. The eventful night arrived, and the glass, which had been largely advertised, was seen for the first time. The front of the house was faithfully reproduced, and caused

53

a roar of laughter. What with the panes and the dirty finger-marks, and a rather plebeian gallery, the picture was distinctly comical. When the merriment had subsided one of the gods cried out, " Well, that *is* pretty ; now show us something else." And then came a second roar of laughter. The Royal Coburg was the original of the Victoria Theatre, once famous for its blood-and-thunder dramas. It still exists close to the Waterloo terminus of the London and South Western Railway. Joseph Glossop had married the daughter of Count de Feron, who was a French *emigré* whose father had been guillotined in the Place de la Republique—afterwards and at present the Place de la Concorde—during the Revolution. The *emigré* had entered the British Army as a Surgeon, knowing something about medicine. He was in the 13th Light Dragoons, and changed his regiment so as never to fight his countrymen on the Calais side of the English Channel. His daughter, who subsequently became Mrs. Joseph Glossop, had a most lovely voice, and was a born musician. Miss Mary Anne Glossop, who inherited her mother's gifts, met my father at her father's house, and soon after (January 21, 1835) became Mrs. Gilbert Abbott à Beckett. My grandmother knew all musical London, and it was through her introduction that my father met Henry Braham, who was then building the Royal St. James' Theatre. He became a great friend of the famous tenor, and was appointed stock author; in that capacity he translated two or three of Auber's operas, and

54

wrote original farces by the dozen. But Braham, before falling back upon the foreigner, thought he would give native talent a chance. Would my mother write an opera for him ? My father answered without hesitation in the affirmative, and furnished the book. So it came to pass that the Royal St. James' Theatre commenced its fortunes in King Street with an opera called " Agnes Sorrel," written by my father and composed by my mother. It was proposed at the time that the lady should conduct in the orchestra the initial performance. But my dear mother, who was devoted to my father—she put him in a position to get called to the Bar without any assistance from Grandfather à Beckett—drew the line at an appearance in public. She did not mind singing for a charity if need be, but she had no taste for waving the bâton on the audience side of the footlights. I am afraid " the first opera written by a lady " was not a complete success, so Braham soon had something else. There still hang on the walls of the St. James' Theatre some old play bills showing that "The Postilion de Lonjumeaux" and " The Ambassadress" were produced there in the thirties. The librettos were provided by my father. At this time he was on the best of terms with Charles Dickens, and it was through my father's introduction " The Village Coquettes " was produced at the Theatre Royal, St. James'. And yet another link in the chain that bound my father to *Punch*. " The King Incog " was published by John Miller of Henrietta Street, Covent

THE à BECKETTS OF " PUNCH "

Garden, and described in 1834 as Agent to the
Dramatic Authors' Society. The first secretary
to that Society (of which I myself became a
member some eight-and-thirty years later) was
Stirling Coyne. So here we have, in close connexion with my father, Henry Mayhew and Stirling
Coyne, both of whom signed the original deed
creating *Punch*. I may have something more to
say about the Dramatic Authors' Society, to which
all the earlier literary members of the *Punch* staff
belonged, but it is sufficient for my purpose at the
present to show how close was the connexion
between those who signed the original deed of
creation, and even contributed to the initial
number, so early as 1834. My father was close
friends with Coyne, Henry Mayhew, Douglas
Jerrold, Mark Lemon, and Percival Leigh. The
two latter were medical students, who were friends
of my uncle, Arthur Martin à Beckett, the doctor
of the family. So the nucleus of the *Punch* staff
were ready for employment some half-dozen years
before the paper was started. The signal had
only to be given to commence. That signal, I
contend, was given by the ultimate decease of
Figaro in London in 1839. There was a short
interval, then the staff-in-waiting were collected,
and out came the first number of *Punch, or the
London Charivari*.

Besides the opera of " Agnes Sorrel," my father
wrote the libretto of, and my mother composed
the music for, " Little Red Riding Hood," produced in the Surrey Theatre on Monday, August 12,

EARLY DAYS

1842. It is interesting to note this date, as it shows my father was keeping in touch with the world of the theatre, associating with Douglas Jerrold from December, 1835 (the date of the production of " Agnes Sorrel " at the St. James' Theatre), until 1842, a year after the first appearance of *Punch*. Reading all my father's notices of Douglas Jerrold's pieces, I find nothing but praise, which negatives the suggestion that there was any ill-feeling existing between them caused by conflicting interests as newspaper proprietors. I write this as I have seen it stated that some of the early journals started in opposition to *Figaro* were edited by Douglas Jerrold. Be this as it may, those papers had disappeared before my father had resigned his editorship at the end of 1834. Later on, just before the final stage of *Figaro in London*, he was called in again to edit it. Although the paper still boasted of its uprightness, it had changed its character to a theatrical journal and little more. It had increased its size from four pages to eight, still retaining its original price of one penny. Its address to its subscribers on the occasion of the enlargement ran as follows—

Figaro in London will as usual possess the same portion of satire, or " folly as it flies " ; a larger portion will be devoted to theatrical critiques and intelligence throughout the country on a novel plan. A powerful article on any crying evil of the day—not an attack on private persons or property, for the purposes of extortion or such vile purposes, but the legitimate object of an honest journal—removal of the abuse for the benefit of the subscribers to *Figaro in London.* This journal, although it has created a sensation by the sharpness of its satire, never has debased itself by an attack on individuals for the purpose of blasting their character, or the infamous object of enforcing blood money for its silence : its object has been, as it always should be, pungently to portray the vices, improprieties and cant of the times, by fair and honest attack. The subject reprobated, the victim to the sharpness of the razor—not the individual.

These were brave words, but glancing through the eight volumes representing as many years I cannot gainsay them. It seems to me, with some knowledge as a journalist, that the first idea was to resuscitate *Figaro in London*, and then, as there was no vitality in it, to let it die and start another periodical. Henry Mayhew, Stirling Coyne, and Last were all interested in *Figaro in London*, and started *Punch*. My father was quite ready to help with his pen, but preferred to keep his purse unopened. He was in 1841 a young married man, not yet turned thirty, with three children—two boys and a girl. The elder boy and the daughter were both old enough for school bills. So my father, I consider, was wise to accept no pecuniary liability in the new venture, although quite prepared to give to it his best services with the pen. Thus it came that my father's signature did not appear to the original deed which Mr. Spielmann has produced in his book in *fac simile*. It is very probable that the original idea was to see if anything could be done to revive *Figaro in London*. But, as I have suggested, it was too late, and it was considered better to commence an entirely new journal. It is a painful labour to look through the last volume of this paper which began so well, and with the prospect of such a successful future. First, the proprietors declare that the number will be composed of entirely new matter. They give themselves the lie direct in the next issue by lifting columns and columns of matter that had already appeared in a previous number. Then the type is made larger, no doubt to save expense. Later on the few advertisements have their position altered. From the back page they are put in special position in the inside sheet next matter, to the experienced eye a proof that the canvasser has had to offer great attractions to secure a repeat. Then a sheet of " Places of Entertainment," with just here and there programmes given (no doubt for a suitable consideration), are represented only by a tariff of prices, which certainly could not have been sanctioned as " money's worth " by the acting manager. At length, on August 17, 1839, it came to an abrupt conclusion. It contained an advertisement repeated from the last issue, announcing something " next Saturday." The editor had not taken the trouble to alter it. To this volume there was no preface, and the date of its natural determination had been forgotten. It had every sign of decay and demoralization. So ended *Figaro in London*, after a career of eight years and eight months.

During the interval between the time of my father's connexion with the early satirical papers and his reappearance in the initial number of *Punch* he was keeping his hand in by writing topical burlesques. In the days of *Figaro in*

THE à BECKETTS OF "PUNCH"

London I have shown that he suggested a weekly cartoon to Seymour, with disastrous results, when that eccentric artist repudaited his assistance. When Robert Cruikshank took up Seymour's work my father schemed the cartoon for him. So his experience was valuable to *Punch* on its appearance. I have gone into the matter rather fully because my friend Mr. Spielmann observes in his excellent work the *History of Punch :*—" It has been worth while for the first time, and it is to be hoped the last, to collect and compare the various versions of the foundation of *Punch* and ascertain the facts as far as possible." Then he says—" Although Henry Mayhew was not the actual initiator of *Punch*, it was unquestionably he to whom the whole credit belongs of having developed Randall's specific idea of a 'Charivari' and of its conception in the form it took. Though not the absolute author of its existence, he was certainly the author of its literary and artistic being, and to that degree, as he was wont to claim, he was its founder." Unfortunately, Mr. Spielmann did not give me an opportunity of offering the evidence I have now prepared. My father edited and founded *Figaro in London*. I say that *Punch, or the London Charivari* was on the lines of *Figaro*. I claim for my father, Gilbert Abbott à Beckett, the merit of having helped to found *Punch*.

Chapter II

SOME NIGHTS AT ROUND TABLES

WILLIAM MAKEPEACE THACKERAY!
Yes, my first glimpse of the master who
half hid his identity under the name of Michael
Angelo Titmarsh and other *nommes de guerre*, was
obtained at a round table. Not the famous
" mahogany tree " in Bouverie Street on which
he carved his monogram side by side with the
initials of his old friend " à Beckett the beak "
and " that excellent magistrate's " two sons,
"G. à B." and "A. W. à B.;" but at No. 10, Hyde
Park Gate South, when Kensington was without
the postal " W."

I was a child in those distant days. I was *en
route* for " Dominie " Birch (by the way, did this
suggest the title to one of Thackeray's Christmas
books ?) who lived in Scarsdale Villas giving the
western boundary to the playground of Kensington Grammar School (three laps to the mile), now
the site of the High Street, Kensington, Station
on the Metropolitan Railway. Opposite our
house was the studio of Cope, the Royal Academi-
cian, next door to Redgrave. Our immediate
neighbour at No. 9 was Cook, also R.A., the marine

painter, who called his place the Ferns and denounced the side of our mansion as an eyesore. " I tell you what I will do," said he to my father, " I will paint Mount Blanc on the stucco." " Much better make it Vesuvius in eruption," replied the beak, " then you will be able to account for the smoke from the chimneys."

And I believed for some time that No. 11 belonged to Thackeray himself. The reason for my belief. Our parents were away on the Continent, and the control of affairs was in the hands of my eldest brother ("third election" at Westminster) and a sister a year older. We behaved very badly. We turned our small garden (afterwards to be converted into a studio by Corbould, the drawing master of his present Majesty) into a military camp, and besieged No. 11 with pea shooters. It was in the days of the Crimean War, when England, France, Turkey, and Sardinia were attempting to take Sebastopol. No. 11 —he later on became head of B.N.C., Oxford— said he would write to his landlord. My elder brother informed the reverend gentleman (who objected to the rattle of peas when he was composing his sermons) that it was no use complaining to Mr. Thackeray, as he was a great friend of our father. But recently my friend Mr. Henry Silver has told me that No. 11 belonged to his uncle, the Rev. Mr. Watson, the aforesaid head.

The occasion of a great dinner was the entertaining of my father's most intimate friends and colleagues from the " Bouverie Street mahogany tree," and a few of the beloved " outsiders." One of the latter was Balfe the composer. He was a jovial, amusing Irishman. He played the accompaniment to my mother's songs, " Ne'er think that I'll forget thee," and " Dear Italy " (words by G. A. à B.), when she subsequently sang them in the drawing room.

As I have said, facing 10, Hyde Park Gate South, was the studio of Cope the R.A. Coming home from school with his son Charley I used to know when the late Prince Consort was there by the horses walking up and down the street, which was only about three hundred to four hundred yards in length, and ended in a *cul de sac*. East of us were fields, now occupied by Queen's Gate. On the site of the Imperial Institute I remember a country fair. I was carried to it by my nurse somewhere about the earliest of the fifties, and remember the gingerbreads. The whole suburb was intensely literary and artistic. South Kensington was still Brompton with a slip then called Kensington New Town—due north of the last turnpike.

Thackeray must have been living in Kensington at the time of " The Great Dinner." The earliest arrival was Horace Mayhew, brother of Henry, author of *London Labour and the London Poor*, and one of my father's schoolfellows at Westminster. He was immensely fond of children, and was promptly captured by the olive branches and taken to the pantry to see the dessert. " We don't have this sort of thing every night,

THE à BECKETTS OF "PUNCH"

Mr. Mayhew," explained one of my brothers, "and those are our best decanters." I was returning, I fancy, from that visit to see the special dessert in the pantry with "Ponny" Mayhew when I came face to face with William Makepeace Thackeray. Ellerman, our man—on state occasions he was our butler, when we had auxiliary assistance from the ushers of my father's court at Southwark — was helping him to unwrap. When Ellerman had divested Mr. Thackeray of his coat, and left him revealed in the rather elaborate evening dress of the period, I have a recollection of silver white hair, gleaming glasses, and a fine mouth. He exchanged kindly greetings with his colleague "Ponny," did this tall, prosperous-looking gentleman. Then he peered at me, patted me on the head, put his finger and thumb in the pocket of his waistcoat (I fancy it was of velvet), and gave me a shilling. Then we exchanged smiles, and I knew intuitively that he loved children. For the remainder of the evening I held him in less fear than the rest of the company.

There were very pleasant gatherings in Bouverie Street round the "Mahogany Tree." As my father scarcely ever was away from the Wednesday feast, week after week, month after month, and year after year, and I was continually with him as a child, I learned (and remembered) a good deal that happened in the famous dining-room. Douglas Jerrold represented the extreme left, and Thackeray the most pronounced right. Mark Lemon—the best of editors—was neutral,

64

with a tendency to Radicalism. My father, especially after he had been appointed a Metropolitan Police Magistrate, was also neutral, with a tendency to follow the policy of the *Times*. He had been on the staff of that paper as a leader-writer for many years, and was a fast friend of the Walters and the Ingrams. Douglas Jerrold used to say that the paper to which he contributed the Caudle Lectures set its watch by the clock of the *Times*.

The " Mahogany Tree " had a magnetic attraction for those invited to the hospitable board. My father took a large part of his annual holiday at Boulogne, so as to be able to get back to town to the Wednesday council. True, " the across-the-Channel suburb of Folkestone " was very popular with the Bouverie Street Brotherhood. Dickens loved Boulogne, and was much honoured by the inhabitants. " Look at the way they treat him ! " exclaimed an envious writer. " He is met on the quay by the Mayor, and conducted to a banquet. When *I* go to Boulogne they don't let off fireworks in *my* honour ! " " No," replied my father, " for when *you* go to Boulogne, you take good care that no one shall learn your address ! " (Boulogne in those days was the sanctuary for those avoiding imprisonment for debt.)

My first meeting with Douglas Jerrold was at Boulogne, I repeat in the year of my father's death. I remember the little gentleman with the leonine head and the bright blue eyes talking and laughing with my father on the sands in front of

THE à BECKETTS OF " PUNCH "

the old *Etablisment,* a low-roofed building, the site of which is now occupied by a palatial casino. I was duly presented to the author of *Black-eyed Susan,* who graciously pinched my cheek, and, to the delight of my mother, approved of my Sunday-go-to-meeting hat and feathers. Later on I heard my father say that he was very glad to have met Douglas " away from the Table," as they were not always quite as friendly as he would wish to be in Bouverie Street. " à Beckett the Beak," as Thackeray called him, supported his neighbour in Kensington, and " W. M. T." and " D. J." belonged to opposite camps. But large-hearted Jerrold bore my father no malice. The obituary half-page that was printed in the paper they both served so well it will be seen furnished the copy for the tombstone in Highgate Cemetery.

And this reference to Douglas Jerrold and Thackeray in Bouverie Street brings me to the reason why the latter ceased to write for *Punch.* Thackeray was a patriot, and took the keenest interest in the politics of the hour. Dicky Doyle left Bouverie Street on account of the attack upon the spiritual powers of the Papacy. Thackeray ceased to write because he objected to the treatment of Louis Napoleon, subsequently Napoleon III, Emperor of the French.

The Table was never deserted by Thackeray, but he ceased to be a contributor. He may have wished still to have a voice in the composition of the cartoon. The first bone of contention was the appearance of " A Beggar on Horseback," in

SOME NIGHTS AT ROUND TABLES

which Louis Napoleon, in rags and tatters, was represented with gory sword riding over dead bodies to power. Then came a number of cartoons attacking the Prince President right and left. The climax was reached when the Emperor visited this country. Thackeray and my father strongly recommended a heroic cartoon, showing Britannia grasping hands with France. They both believed that the best interests of the Empire would be served by a firm alliance with our neighbours across the Channel. The opposition were in favour of the same line of chaff that had been the tradition of the paper since the appearance of " A Beggar on Horseback." Thackeray had shown in his *History of the Next Revolution* that he was willing to admire the new Emperor, so he resented the attack from two points of view—the personal and the politic. There was, as customary, a compromise. Instead of Britannia and France grasping hands appeared Louis Napoleon in Rotten Row attire simply ringing the visitors' bell of Buckingham Palace. A sentry was presenting arms, and the cartoon was labelled " Who would Have Thought It ? " But in spite of the compromise, the author of the *Book of Snobs* wrote no more for the paper to which, until then, he had been a constant contributor.

Another round table I remember was in Portland House, North End, Fulham. The house is still standing, and is within a stone's throw of the bridge on the King's highway overlooking the Addison Road Station. It belonged to my father,

67

THE à BECKETTS OF " PUNCH "

then Stipendiary Police Magistrate for Greenwich and Woolwich. As he was "beak" of two courts, the Government allowed him a horse to ride or drive from place to place. I remember one horse, " Polly," then when she died we had a second mare, " Polly the Second." I was a very small child in socks and a sash. But I remember that little table covered with books in my father's study, with the bright, cheery-looking gentleman talking to him in the candle-light. The bright, cheery-looking gentleman in the candle-light was the literary lion of the hour, the century, perchance the ages—Charles Dickens.

I am under the impression that Dickens had called to see my father about dramatizing one of his Christmas books. Charles had been a little disheartened by the trial trip at the St. James', and did not venture upon dramatic authorship until he joined hands with Wilkie Collins, and produced " No Thoroughfare " at the old Adelphi Theatre with Charles Fechter as Obenreizer. And again, the remuneration of dramatists was simply scandalous at the commencement of the nineteenth century. It is said that because Benjamin Webster declined to give Dion Boucicault the regulation remuneration—£100 an act— for " The Colleen Bawn," the playwright made his fortune. Dion accepted a percentage on the receipts in lieu of a sum down, and cleared £20,000 by the alteration. Again, it was scarcely worth Dickens' while to dramatize his own works, and so he got his two friends, G. à B. and Mark

SOME NIGHTS AT ROUND TABLES

Lemon, to convert " The Chimes " from a story to a play to outwit the pirates. My father and his editor on the paper they both assisted to found, worked in collaboration. My father—a busy man at the court all day—wrote the piece and Lemon rehearsed it. And as they were both doing very well with their pens in other directions, no doubt they were quite willing to help their colleague, Charles Dickens. Knocking up a piece was only child's play to them.

During the present year a Dickens Exhibition, organized by the Dickens Fellowship, was held at the Memorial Hall in Farringdon Street. It was deeply interesting, and was visited by hundreds of working men. One of the exhibits (1359) was a photograph of Charles Dickens, his family, and friends, at Gadshill. There are nine portraits of the novelist, his eldest son with his wife, his two daughters, and his sister-in-law, together with Fechter, the actor, and Charles and Wilkie Collins. " The tenth and last figure," says the catalogue, "is that of a Mr. Hamilton Hume, the photographer." Poor Hamilton Hume ! We were co-editors once on a time of a paper called *Black and White.* He had been an officer in the army, and served in the Crimea. An excellent journalist and a thoroughly good fellow. The photograph was published in a magazine of which Hamilton Hume was the editor. It caused some trouble, I remember, because it interfered with an arrangement that had been made by the great novelist to sit for his portrait to a firm of photographers. Hamilton Hume was a dramatist in a small way himself, and knew Charles Fechter. Hence the introduction. At the time the photograph was taken Fechter had retired from his Lyceum management, and was playing in "No Thoroughfare" at the Adelphi. Charles Dickens and Wilkie Collins were the authors, and Charles Fechter was the leading actor.

I can quite understand Dickens' objection to the pirate dramatist. "The Mystery of Edwin Drood" was left a fragment, but I saw at the Surrey Theatre a piece (in which I think Mr. Henry Neville played the principal character) which finished the work for the author. The secret of the death of the hero was the mystery left unsolved. The dramatist of the version to which I refer laid his last act in the crypt of Rochester Cathedral. He sent the comic man into a lower vault, and then brought Rose Budd (the heroine) and Jasper (the villain) together. The villain put his knife to Rose's throat. Then emerged the comic man from the vault below. "Why?" asked the villain, annoyed at being interrupted in his murder of the heroine, "Why this intrusion?"

After my father's death I met one of his colleagues, Richard, otherwise "Dicky" Doyle, in a club of which he was a member. The club was composed entirely of members of the Church of Rome. Subsequently the club was practically absorbed by the Junior Athenæum. I had come to see "Dicky"—every one called him by his little name—to ask him to join a paper I proposed to produce, which, annexing a title used thirty years earlier by my father, I intended to call *Figaro in London*. I was a lad of two-and-twenty, and " Dicky " was twice or thrice my age. Would he join my staff ? He smiled. Well, he was not doing very much work just then —only drawings of gnomes and the like for private friends who made the commissions a business matter—but he was pleased with the idea. He would consider it. I showed him the cover— we had got as far as a cover—and he approved of it. The last cover he had designed was for *The Owl*—did I remember it ? Of course I did, and I recalled the names of Borthwick, Ashley, and Thomas Gibson Bowles—the latter had been an occasional contributor.

Naturally we talked of other things. He had been a great friend of my father. He told me that he had illustrated *The Almanack of the Month* for him from cover to cover, and he spoke of Leech and Thackeray. The latter had been anxious to work with him, and through his instrumentality he had drawn a second series of " The Manners and Customs of the English " for Thackeray's publishers and Thackeray's magazine. The first series had appeared in a paper of which my father had been one of the founders and " Dicky " Doyle a very early contributor. He had severed his connexion with that paper for conscientious reasons. I asked him—for I had heard rumours to the effect—had the severance come as a surprise that had caused great

inconvenience to the proprietors ? " Not at all,"
said " Dicky," " I expressed my opinions very
strongly at the table from week to week, and when
the attacks on the spiritual Powers of the Papacy
became intolerable I tendered my resignation."
The table was an institution in Bouverie Street
which Thackeray had christened the " Mahogany
Tree." Round that table sat Doyle, Mark Lemon,
Percival Leigh, John Leech, and my father. I
understood " Dicky's " allusions. I could quite
believe the story of the surprise was without
foundation.

Then we spoke of *The Owl.* " Dicky " was not
on the staff, although a friend of most of its
members. *The Owl* had no illustrations, but
only a cover. It appeared only during the session.
" Why ? " I asked. " Because the contributors,
who were principally private secretaries to
Ministers, wanted a holiday quite as much as their
masters." But in spite of its intermittent appearance *The Owl* was a great success. The staff
(including the proprietor) had souls above filthy
lucre, and the profits were said to be absorbed by
boxes at Covent Garden and dinners at the *Star
and Garter.* Altogether a very agreeable arrangement. " A Richmond Edition of Bouverie Street ? "
I suggested, but Doyle did not answer my question.

I am sorry to say that my projected paper did
not appear, and consequently I did not have the
honour of numbering Richard Doyle as one of my
contributors. Before we parted that evening we
had a long chat about illustrations. I told him

SOME NIGHTS AT ROUND TABLES

that I had come across a " cartoon" from the
Figaro in London appearing as a headpiece to
a cheap comic song. He laughed, and told me
that my father in the days of his youth delighted
in adapting his blocks to all sorts of purposes. He
once illustrated a more or less serious novel with
blocks of a distinctly political character. I once
myself had to use old blocks to illustrate a story
I called *The Mystery of Mostyn Manor*. The
publisher provided me with some engravings—he
said he could afford nothing better—of a man with
a long beard breaking open a writing desk, a
fellow clean-shaven killing somebody, and a
person in a short moustache reading a letter in the
Tropics. The individual so treated was evidently
intended for my villain, so I used him—with his
beard at the commencement of my story, made
him an assassin—disguised without it towards
the end, and, saving him from the gallows by
procuring for him a commutation of the death
sentence to transportation for life, sent him (in the
last chapter) to repent—with his moustache—in
Australia.

" How will that do ? " I hear again. The
speaker is standing in front of my father in the
study of 10, Hyde Park Gate South. He is a
neighbour of ours who lives a little nearer Hammersmith than we do, and he has come over to chat
with my father on the latter's return from his
court at Southwark. He is showing him a drawing
is this tall sporting looking gentleman with the
scarf and the scarf-pin. I know him very well—

THE à BECKETTS OF "PUNCH"

Mr. Leech. He has been a fellow-student with my uncle and namesake, the doctor who won decorations on the medical staff of the expedition under Sir de Lacy Evans in Spain, and a contemporary of dear " Professor " Leigh, another of my father's oldest friends. I know Mr. John Leech very well. He is kindly and fond of boys. Why, his book about *Master Jacky's Holidays* was founded upon my brother Gilbert's mythical adventures on his return home from St. Peter's College, Westminster. I see him standing in the firelight talking to my father about the newest work they have in hand in collaboration. They have written and drawn together *The Comic Histories of England and Rome,* and are fast friends. It must have been something very urgent that brought Mr. Leech to Hyde Park Gate South, because he and my father were wont to meet one another every Wednesday round the Mahogany Table, in Bouverie Street. My father urges him to stay to dinner, fixed for the then regulation hour of six o'clock, but he cannot. He is engaged to another neighbour of theirs—Thackeray. In those days, Kensington, the old court suburb, was full of representatives of the pen and the pencil.

I am reminded by this recollection of Mr. Leech's visit to my father of the working day of a barrister-journalist in the early fifties. My father was up, dressed, and breakfasted by nine o'clock. Then for the sake of exercise walked over to Southwark. Then he spent six or eight hours in a badly-ventilated police-court dispensing justice, and drove home to arrive at Kensington by about half-past five. He dined at six ; slept from seven to eight. Then until two in the morning he was writing his daily articles for *The Times* and weekly contributions to the *Illustrated London News* and the paper he helped to found. He was very proud of his contributions to the latter, and pasted them in a book which I possess—it was saved from the fire that destroyed his library—and showed that he was a contributor from the day of its birth to the week of his death. On one occasion he wrote the whole of the leaders of the day's issue of *The Times* —a feat which, I believe, has been equalled by two living contributors to the great organ of Printing House Square. But all this varied work I fear was too much for him—he died before he had completed his forty-fifth year.

John Leech was very fond of sport, especially of hunting, and my father's delight was to object to the cruelty of killing a fox, unless to rid the country of vermin by shooting ! A famous successor to Leech at Bouverie Street, Sir John Tenniel, also loved the sound of the pack in full cry, and I carried on in my day the family tradition of laughingly denouncing the best-liked pastime of English country gentlemen. My father wrote *A Quiziology of the British Drama* (the cover was by John Leech), which contained parodies of the dramatists of the day. In a long sporting speech, burlesquing the famous description of a race by Lady Gay Spanker, my father described a fox being followed for ten miles down a high road,

75

and ultimately being killed by meeting face-to-face a sheep-dog ! Leech turned his experiences in the field to good account in his delightful illustrations to the Jorrocks' Series.

The drawings of John Leech are scarce and valuable. Unfortunately they are nearly all unfinished sketches, because the finished work appeared from the artists' hand on to the woodblock, and of course vanished in the engraving. The application of photography to the reproduction of pictures doubled the incomes of the leading draftsmen in chalk, lead, and ink. I remember that Mr. Mark Lemon took a deep interest in the subject—as he naturally would as an editor—and had some plan for reducing and enlarging blocks made of indiarubber. Then came the earliest development of process graphotype, which required the artist to draw with a fine brush on a chalk surface. But photography worked in the interest of the artist as process had come to the aid of the proprietor. Had photography reached full development in the days of John Leech the world would have been richer for scores and hundreds of finished original drawings in lieu of a few studies and tracings, the property of literary clubs or collectors in black-and-white.

Although Leech overflowed with humour in his drawings, there were very few " good stories " told about him. He was quiet and reserved, and perhaps that was the reason he was so closely associated in his work with my father, who after an adventurous boyhood, commencing with his

SOME NIGHTS AT ROUND TABLES

Westminster schooldays, sobered down at an exceptionally early age into a dignified ornament of the Bench. The two friends found a third in Thackeray. Thackeray, Leech, and my father lived in Kensington, and once a week for years travelled the same road home from Bouverie Street, although there may have been occasional visits to the Garrick Club—then in King Street— of which Thackeray and my father were both members. And here I may say that I have recently read in some magazine—I think it was in the *Pall Mall*—an article dealing rather harshly with the early days of the famous Table. As an antidote I quote—

> Here let us sport,
> Boys as we sit,
> Laughter and wit
> Flashing so free.
> Life is but short
> When we are gone,
> Let them sing on
> Round the old Tree.
>
> Evenings we knew
> Happy as this,
> Faces we miss
> Pleasant to see ;
> Kind hearts and true,
> Gentle and just ;
> Peace to your dust
> We sing round the Tree.

The lines are signed " W. M. Thackeray."

I have said that amongst other work my father contributed a daily leader to *The Times*. I give an experience in this connection.

THE à BECKETTS OF " PUNCH "

A small table in Serjeants' Inn. It is contained in a corner house of the square, and I have come to it with my father (who has business with his editor) from the Theatre Royal Adelphi, where there is being performed a piece by Buckstone, with a cast containing Webster, Wright, and Madame Celeste. I am a boy of eight, anxious to get back to the playhouse, and listen rather impatiently to the conversation carried on by my father and his editor, which turns on the subject of a leading article. When we left the house, my father bade me remember the occasion. " You have missed the farce," said he, " but you have had the honour of making the acquaintance of Mr. Delane, editor of *The Times*."

It was said of Delane that he controlled the writing of others, but seldom wrote himself. He was certainly devoted to the interests of the great paper of which he was the literary director. The leading journal, or as it used to call itself when advertizers wanted to quote it in its own columns, " a morning paper," was regarded with deep admiration by the general public, and absolute devotion by its regular staff. The Briton carried with him everywhere his sense of the power and justice of *The Times*. I remember once finding myself at Amiens in the time of the Franco-German war before a group of officers who wanted to kill me because my passport was marked with a German visé. Fortunately I got out of the awkward position by producing my commission. But I still have my doubts whether it would not have been better to have told those angry warriors " that if they dared to shoot me I would certainly write to *The Times.*"

The respect paid to the British journal abroad was merely a reflection of the honour in which it was held at home. To this day only one paper receives an invitation to be present at the Banquet in Burlington House, held on the eve of the opening of the Royal Academy. Read the list of guests and you will find " *Times* Reporter." Even that representative of the British Press was ignored by that august body, the Royal Academicians, until there was a difficulty about " taking " a speech of the late Prince Consort. One of the most important orations of the evening one year went wrong. It was decided to introduce the Press for the future. In other words, *The Times.*

Taking down from my bookshelves a volume of *The Mask*, edited by Alfred Thompson, ex-Carbineer, and one of the founders of the A.D.C. at Cambridge, and Leopold Lewis, solicitor and adapter (for Sir Henry Irving) of *Le Juif Polonais*, otherwise *The Bells*, I find a caricature of the staff of *The Times*. It appeared nearly forty years ago. I copy the key : Mr. Delane as Jupiter, the Thunderer of Printing House Square ; Dr. Dasent as Juno ; Mr. Mowbray Morris, Mercury ; Mr. John Forster, Vulcan ; Mr. Vernon Harcourt, Minerva ; Rev. Lord Sydney Godolphin Osborne (S.G.O.), Neptune ; Dr. Russell, Mars ; Mr. M. J. Higgins (" Jacob Omnium "), Hercules ; Mr. Davison, Apollo ; Mr. Tom Taylor, Cupid ;

THE à BECKETTS OF "PUNCH"

Mr. John Oxenford, Bacchus; and Mr. Walter, the Eagle (a bird with Proprietary Rights). I am particularly drawn to one caricature in that sketch in *The Mask*—John Oxenford represented as Bacchus, God of the Drama and Wine. He was the leading dramatic critic of the sixties, and the best of good fellows, excellent *confrère*, and kindly creature. I heard him say once when responding to his health, that when he wrote a critique, as a dramatist himself he never forgot the labour and anxiety represented by a first night, and objected to setting down scathing sentences about actors. "I didn't want any one," said he, "to have to hide away my notices from the wife and the children."

I am afraid there is but one survivor of all the brilliant company depicted in caricature by Alfred Thompson. But it may be said—remembering his services to his country—the greatest of them all. The first and best of War Specials—William Howard Russell—appears as Mars. To Sir William —known affectionately to his intimates as " Billy " —the country owes the reform of the Army dating from the dark days of the Crimean campaign. He represents the censorship of the Press. In the fifties that censorship was uncontrolled by the professional censorship recommended at a later date by Lord Wolseley in his *Soldiers' Pocket Book*. " Look here," was the final instructions of the Secretary of State for War to a trusted subordinate on the eve of his departure for the East to put things straight in Balaclava ; " mind you are very civil to Russell of *The Times*." But all the civility in the world did not influence the representatives of *The Times* in those days. And the situation of half a century ago remains to this moment unchanged. But if the third volume of à Beckett's *Comic History of England* has yet to appear (concerning which more anon), there was another of my father's works which I was able to bring up to date. My sire, in spite of his love for journalism and the drama, always possessed what I have seen termed a "legal mind." In his earliest contributions to *Punch* he took the Bar under his protection. He created the character of " Mr. Briefless," a gentleman that I have attempted to revive in the person of his son, " Mr. A. Briefless, Junr." My father, with delightful gravity, told of the comic struggles of poor luckless, cashless Briefless to keep the wolf from the door without losing his dignity. He had a supporter in another member of the Bar in " Mr. Dunup." The adventures of these two gentlemen used to be received with delight by both branches of the forensic profession, and I have reasons for believing that my own contributions with the signature of " A. Briefless, Junr.," were also very popular. At any rate, their popularity was sufficiently marked to cause Messrs. Bradbury & Agnew, Limited, to publish *Papers from Pump Handle Court, by A. Briefless, Junr.*," subsequently. My father, fond of his profession, published *The Comic Blackstone* in 1844, three years after the appearance of the initial number

THE à BECKETTS OF "PUNCH"

of *Punch*. Much of the matter, if not the whole, of this book appeared in the pages of the *London Charivari*. It had but two illustrations—one by George Cruikshank, and the other by John Leech. I see that it is asserted in Mr. Spielmann's excellent work that George Cruikshank only appeared once in *Punch*, and then only in the advertisement sheet. This no doubt must be the case, but it will be seen that he must have been on friendly terms with Messrs. Bradbury & Evans (the then proprietors of *Punch*), or he would not have been asked to illustrate my father's *Comic Blackstone*. I may here mention that I once had the pleasure of meeting George Cruikshank, and in—of all places in the world!—the Westminster Aquarium. But the old place of entertainment—now disappearing to make room for a building to be erected by Wesleyan enthusiasm—was on its best behaviour on the occasion to which I refer. It was its opening day, when the late Duke of Edinburgh (with my old friend Viscount Newry, now Earl of Kilmorey, in attendance) declared the Royal Westminster Aquarium at the service of the public. I sat opposite George Cruikshank at the following cold collation. We had the Royal Duke with his address taken as read, and " his gracious reply " handed over as read. Prince Alfred inspected the Royal Naval Artillery Volunteers, who furnished a guard of honour, and the fish that in the early days were swimming in the tanks of the Aquarium. Later on, both Volunteers and fishes disappeared.

SOME NIGHTS AT ROUND TABLES

The citizen sailors were not required by the Admiralty, and the fishes found little favour in the eyes of the sightseers of the Royal Aquarium. George Cruikshank looked at me for some few moments, and then repeated my name. " Any relation of Gilbert Abbott à Beckett ? " he asked. " I am his third son, Mr. Cruikshank," I replied. " Your father was a good man, sir," said he ; " you cannot do better than try to equal him." Then he relapsed into silence. Of course, he was a very intimate friend of my father, who edited *Cruikshank's Table Book* for him. George was the brother of the Robert Cruikshank who replaced Seymour on *Figaro in London.* No doubt my father's friendship dated from those early days. George Cruikshank illustrated my father's " Quizziology of the British Drama," which appeared in the *Table Book,* in company with that delightful parody, Thackeray's *A Legend of the Rhine.* By the way, I note here that the moment my father gets an editorial appointment he draws his staff from his colleagues at the *Punch* table. Thackeray, of course, was a star of the first magnitude, but there were minor lights as represented by Horace Mayhew. In 1887 the proprietors of *Punch* asked me to bring the *Comic Blackstone* up to date. I immediately saw the propriety. When I was reading for the Bar, some ten years earlier, my kindly "coach" had recommended me to prepare for the necessary examinations with the assistance of my father's *Comic Blackstone,* and I had practical experience of the

THE à BECKETTS OF "PUNCH"

value of such a text book. In like manner, when a schoolboy I had "floored" my exams. in English history with the assistance of my father's *Comic History*. So I undertook the commission, and with the help of Mr. Harry Furniss, who supplied some excellent illustrations, turned out a new edition that was not only passed by the professional papers as "all right," but extorted the admiration of my old uncle, Thomas Turner à Beckett, in Australia. This relative of mine had reached and passed his eightieth year, but still was able to write. He told me that he thought the work capital, and was sure that his younger brother (my father) would have approved of it. Of course, after a pause of thirty years, there was much to revise. But, strange to say, there was one subject in which I noted little change. The "Irish Question" was then almost at its worst. All I had to do to bring my father's volume thoroughly up to date was to substitute "Home Rule" for "Repeal," and the name of Charles Stuart Parnell for that of Daniel O'Connell. The work was a labour of love. My father delighted in puns—witticisms now entirely out of fashion—but his puns were of superior quality. I can't say that I am particularly fond of puns myself. Thank goodness they are now out of fashion, so it is unnecessary to summon a smile to greet these ancient subjects for merriment. From this it will be held I was not entirely out of sympathy with Dr. Johnson when he discovered

SOME NIGHTS AT ROUND TABLES

the connexion between pun-making and larceny. My recollections of the *Punch* staff, as inscribed on my memory by my father, are of the pleasantest. In spite of the " hard knocks " that occasionally were given at the table, there was a loving *camaraderie* that existed far beyond the walls of Bouverie Street. There were two men at the *Punch* table when I was called to that hospitable board who had sat there in the presence of my father. One has since that date, nearly thirty years ago, joined the great majority, but the other still, thank God, lives, and is as cheery and delightful as ever. The first was the late Percival Leigh, author of the *Comic Latin and English Grammars*, whose tribute to my father's kindly humour was grateful to his son's ears. The second was Sir John Tenniel, who also testified to my father's popularity. He quarrelled with no one, but loved his confreres. He was on the most intimate terms of friendship with the proprietors, the Bradburys and the Evans of the past. My dear friend, William Bradbury, about whom I have told the anecdote of my unexpected rise in salary, was the contemporary of my brother Gilbert, and my father took the two boys with him on one occasion to Paris. Under my father's guidance I grew up with a love of *Punch* that to this day I remember. The *Punch* of the mighty dead, of Thackeray, and Jerrold, and Leech, and Gilbert Abbott à Beckett. The echoes from the room that contained the table used to reach my ears when I was a small boy walking with my father to his court, or talking at the breakfast table before we started. And those echoes were always of a pleasant character. I cannot help thinking that the original staff were perhaps pleasanter companions than those of a later date, because they were personal friends; they (to use the old school phrase) "knew one another when they were at home." And I was sufficiently fortunate to join the staff at the invitation of Tom Taylor when some of the old staff, and all the old *esprit de corps*, remained. Later on I shall show how I came to join the board of the paper that my father helped to found.

Looking through the pages of *Punch*, it is interesting to note how the paper gradually changed its character from the journal of Bohemia to the mouthpiece of Mayfair. Taking the original staff, we have Henry Mayhew, journalist and dramatist; Gilbert Abbott à Beckett, dramatist and journalist; Stirling Coyne, ditto; Douglas Jerrold, ditto; Leech, medical student; Percival Leigh, young surgeon; and Mark Lemon, licensed victualler, with a soul high above hotels. So the fashion of the hour was "Bohemia." It was an affectation like the affectation of a celebrated literary club that, when I belonged to it forty years ago, rejoiced in "shirt sleeves, pewters, and churchwardens," and like the affectation of another distinguished comic paper still flourishing, which did its best, and still does its best, to persuade the public that the very clever staff were and are composed of earnest anti "blue

SOME NIGHTS AT ROUND TABLES

ribbandists." So when *Punch* started, the order
of the day was " the fun of Bohemia." My father,
whose hand was well in with his numberless
burlesques, wrote "Songs for the Sentimental"
and " Songs for the Seedy." They both went
well, and were very popular. I remember one
which was quoted to me when I was a schoolboy,
and the master who referred to it was trying to
get me to use my influence to get his own jokes
inserted in *Punch*. It was the story of a poor
fellow who had been thrown over by his lady love,
and who was anxious to return the presents that
she had given him in happier hours. He sends
back gifts of minor value, but when he comes to a
handsome scarfpin he explains that he cannot
return it, for he has it no longer in his possession—

But, base deceiver, here's the ticket!

Then comes the history of Briefless, to
which I have referred, showing the struggling side
of a barrister's life. In the politics of the paper I
easily note the influence of Douglas Jerrold. The
brilliant satirist was a democrat of democrats,
and his ideal was the perfect working man. He
had a feeling of respect for the representative of
labour which I do not think my father shared.
Then there was the tradition of the past that
spared neither the highest nor the lowest. Seeing
Mr. *Punch* now in his courtly attire, one almost
shudders at the daring of some of his earlier
cartoons. Loyalty to the Throne has been the
guiding star of all those, without an exception,

87

THE à BECKETTS OF "PUNCH"

who have ever sat at the *Punch* table, but for the first quarter of a century of his existence the sage of Fleet Street, as he used to call himself before he surrendered the historical "85," reserved to himself the right of criticizing the actions of even the most exalted personages. But from the first *Punch* was wholesome. In spite of his love for the pipes, shirt sleeves, and pewters, he appreciated talent and taste. The medical students at the table, as they grew older (and they matured quickly) had higher aspirations than those suggested by the removal of a knocker or a street row with the police. Then my father, as a member of the Bar, was not too pleased to be tied down to the level of the tavern. Freedom from the thraldom of fads came with Thackeray's appearance at the table. Thackeray was a strong man, and had the courage of his opinions. Those opinions were that *Punch* could be comic without descending to the jokes of the pawnshop and the public house. In these views he received the support of my father, Leech, Percival Leigh, and Mark Lemon. To put it concisely, *Punch* threw off his street rags to don evening dress of the best cut. Since the date to which I refer the London representative of the Parisian *Charivari* has been a consistent courtier and the most exemplary of men. It is true, as has been recently pointed out, he ventured to lecture her late Majesty for retiring from public life after the death of the lamented Prince Consort. Still, he was in good company. He followed the lead of *The Times*, and was in step with another comic publication of the period. But Thackeray gave the tone to the paper which has lasted to the present day. The old staff has completely passed away. Even Sir John Tenniel, who sat beside my father for five years, did not join *Punch* until the tenth year of its existence. I have ventured to join recollections of my father with my own. The *Punch* creed, as it was taught me by Gilbert Abbott à Beckett, was perfect loyalty to the paper, which included proprietors and staff. It was high treason to put anything before their interests. But the *Punch* creed included something in the interest of the disciple. It was the tradition of the *Punch* men—staff and proprietors—to stand shoulder to shoulder together. For my father's sake I revere the names of Thackeray, Jerrold, and Leech ; and I also, for his sake, honour the names of Evans and Bradbury.

As we live in an age of anecdotage, I might follow the precedent of my friend, Mr. M. H. Spielmann, and give stories of what happened at the *Punch* dinner in the earlier days of its existence. The old tradition was to keep the *vie intime* sacred, but with the appearance of *The History of Punch* (written with the full approbation of publishers and staff) the veil has been drawn aside to display the sanctuary. Save as regards my father's share in the founding of *Punch*, I am quite satisfied to leave the *History* with its picture of life at the table and other details uncriticized. No doubt the dinners of the past were as cheery and delightful as those of the present. I see that in his book Mr. Spielmann gives the description of a dinner in which Horace Mayhew and Professor Leigh are the chief conversationalists. I knew Horace Mayhew, as I have already written, very well. He was the godfather of my younger brother, Walter Horace Callender à Beckett, and the kindest of fellows. On my brother's birthday he always sent him a book of some kind. One was *The Peasant Boy Philosopher*, written, I fancy, by his brother, Henry Mayhew. I remember meeting him once at Evans', when he was chatting with Sydney Blanchard, who has been credited with the thought of wanting to start a *Comic 'Punch.'* "You know," said Sydney, who was proud of being a militiaman (by the way, he belonged with me to the same regiment, the King's Own Light Infantry), " I had a good deal to do, when I was in Calcutta, with the Indian Mutiny." "Of course you had, my boy," replied "Ponny." "Why, you were the cause of it!" But in spite of this repartee, I do not remember "Ponny" as much of a conversationalist, and as to the Professor he was certainly rather silent than otherwise. By the way, here again I can give a story that redounds to the credit of the proprietors of the past. From the year 1881, when I acted as *remplacement* to the present editor, it was my duty to serve as *locum tenens* during his absence. I performed the duties with a certain amount of reluctance, as dear old Professor had done the same service to Tom Taylor, the present editor's predecessor. But, truth to tell, the Professor was really not equal to the work, for his years were threescore and ten. I have been told by experts that a man, to be thoroughly efficient for the task, should be not more than five-and-fifty, and should be full of new ideas. Well, the first time I undertook the task of editing *Punch tout seul* my dear old friend, the Professor, wrote me the kindest letter congratulating me on my successful performance. Really and truly, my father's old friend had written himself out. He used to send in, week after week, the customary amount of copy—short articles, two-line paragraphs, nice little " junks " of verses. But his contributions were Dead Sea fruit, faded flowers ; they could only be most sparingly used. They were duly set up and added to the slips of the " overset." But not five per cent. of the matter was ever used. Still, in spite of the real impossibility of his copy, the then proprietors of *Punch* raised his salary a few years before his death, on account of his long service. He was the doctor of our staff, and gave Tom Taylor warning of that serious illness which ended in his death. Tom Taylor, who lived in Lavender Sweep, complained of a pain in his foot. Hurrying to catch the train to be in time for the *Punch* dinner, he injured his leg. The Professor examined it, and ordered his editor to go home at once and have the limb examined by his medical attendant. Percival Leigh was so peremptory

in his command that Tom Taylor obeyed. My
first editor took to the couch which proved to be
his deathbed. He had a varicose vein, from
which had escaped, during the running to catch
the train, a clot of blood. It was hoped that Tom
Taylor, by keeping on his back, would give the
clot time to be absorbed in the system. But Tom
Taylor, who was a man of great vitality and
energy, insisted upon getting up to fetch a book.
The clot reached my poor friend's heart, and he
died instantly. On another occasion the Professor was knocked down by a cab and carried to
a hospital. When he recovered consciousness, he
found himself in the hands of two young doctors.
They were treating him with contempt, for the
dear Professor was not what is technically known
as a "dressy man." He listened to their
diagnosis, and then suddenly observed : " Gentlemen, you are wrong," and gave a most elaborate
description of the injury, mostly with professional
terms. The young doctors were astonished
beyond measure. But their amazement was
exchanged for admiration when they found their
patient was an alumnus of " Bart's." And here,
by the way, when I once had to see Sir James
Paget, I spoke to him of my old Professor. "Percival Leigh," said Sir James, "was with me at
' Bart's.' as a brother student. He was the best
man of all of us. If he had stuck to surgery,
instead of writing for *Punch*, he would have
probably been far ahead of me." And the death
of Tom Taylor recalls to me an incident connected

with the death of another editor of *Punch*, his immediate predecessor, Shirley Brooks. I met Mr. Brooks many years before I had the honour of being called to the Table—which my friend Mr. Spielmann describes as the literary and artistic peerage of *Punch*—at the house of the present editor. Mr. Brooks was extremely kind, and had much to say in praise of my father. But, full of the traditions of the earlier days of the *London Charivari*, I had respect for him, but not that deepest respect that I reserved for original members. Mr. Shirley Brooks was comparatively, with the older of his colleagues, a new boy. Not very long after this meeting, Mr. Brooks went to the sea coast, and, feeling out of sorts, sent for his doctor, a well-known specialist. It is said that at this stage there was not much the matter with him. But the doctor drew a long face, and thoroughly frightened my father's friend. " Do you think I should make my will ? " asked Brooks. " Every one should make his will," was the significant reply. To make a long story short, Shirley Brooks sickened and died. Many years later I went to see the same doctor on my own account. I was accompanied by my wife. The doctor examined me. " My poor fellow," said he, " you will have broken health for the remainder of your life. You may linger on, but you should be prepared for the worst." " Then I had better not undertake to contest Kinsale ? " I was thinking of seeing if I could not get into Parliament. " Contest

THE à BECKETTS OF "PUNCH"

Kinsale ! " the doctor exclaimed. " Why, if you were returned, it would be in your coffin ! " I saw that this sort of thing was not exactly cheerful to my wife. " Look here, doctor," I said firmly, " I believe I shall live longer than you. I will stake five pounds that I shall be living when you will be dead." I won the bet, but the executor has never paid the five-pound note ; not that I blame the executor—no doubt the doctor had forgotten, or, at any rate, omitted to add the sum to the list of legacies. In these days of " suggestion " it is well to be careful. " Never say die " is a motto that should be particularly addressed to a doctor.

As my father had very hard work to get through, he used to avoid late hours at the *Punch* dinner, which in his day commenced at six o'clock. My friend, Sir John Tenniel, has told me that very often the staff enjoyed the highest spirits when the time for breaking up had been reached. On one occasion the Kensington contingent, which consisted of Leech and Thackeray and my father, determined to see the latter home to the house in which he resided, Portland House, North End, Fulham, or as it now would be called, West Kensington. On reaching their destination, an impromptu dance took place in the garden. " I will now tread a saraband," said my father. At this moment a voice was heard : " Gilbert ! " " Yes, dear," said my father, and without greeting his two friends, quietly disappeared. It is pleasant to me to hear that my

94

father would unbend on occasions, as he lives in my memory as the most genial, and yet the most dignified of men. He was abstemious to a degree, and cared nothing about wine, and never smoked. On one occasion he was given a glass of '24 port when that vintage had come to magnificent maturity. " You are drinking, sir," said the host, a rather pompous man, " some of my best '24 port." " Indeed," returned my father; " that works out at two shillings a bottle." The story got about, and my father insisted that he was absolutely unaware of the real value of the wine, and had no intention to lessen the importance of the boasting epicure. Filial piety makes me accept the assurance without question, the more especially as I know that my father's favourite beverage was tea, undiluted water, or lemonade.

Apropos of Portland House, the place of my birth, I can tell a story which has its interest in these days of metropolitan development. I have said that the proposed saraband which was to have been treaded was to have taken place in the garden. Portland House, North End, Fulham, half a century ago, had some very fine pleasure grounds. To-day, if you look at it, you find it the corner house of a terrace. In its front are a number of railway lines, as it is not two hundred yards distant from the Addison Road Station, Kensington. It was proposed to start a local line which, amongst other projects, was to annex our garden. My father, to use a colloquial

THE à BECKETTS OF "PUNCH"

expression, was "full against it," and did his utmost to prevent its execution. Week after week appeared attacks upon the objectionable line, until it came to be known as " *Punch's* Railway." My father described the erection of the station and the establishment of the cabstand. According to *Punch*, there was so little traffic that the station-master was wont to grow cabbages between the sleepers, and train vegetable marrows along the rails. Then one cab turned up with a horse and a driver. The next day the driver disappeared, and the horse stood in his place for twelve hours. The third day the horse had disappeared with the driver. Then the horseless cab stood on the cabstand deserted for a fortnight. At the end of that time the coachman appeared without a horse and dragged away the cab singlehanded. But the attacks were of no service to their author. The railway ultimately became what it now, I believe, still is, the most prosperous line in the world. If I have not been misinformed, that mile of railway in front of Portland House is leased by some of the leading English lines, and pays a dividend of enormous proportions on the original stock. My father made up his mind to give up his house, and removed further East, taking up his residence in the house to which I have already referred, No. 10, Hyde Park Gate, South.

Before turning from the memories of *Punch* left me by my father, I cannot help referring to the last scene of all, which was played in Boulogne-sur-Mer in August, 1856. It had been an exceptionally hot summer. My father and mother had left us children in the French watering-place while they took their customary trip in Switzerland. We had heard that my father had felt the heat, and it was determined that instead of going towards the mountains he should return to the seaside. My parents rejoined their younger children, and took up their residence in a house at the corner of the Rue Victor Hugo, which stands forth recalling painful memories whenever I visit Boulogne. In front of it is a water fountain that still remains in the same condition in which it existed half a century ago. I remember the passing of the grand religious procession in front of our house, and the decking of the windows with white and blue draperies. At that time my father was ailing, but well enough to see the procession, and afterwards to walk up to the *haut-ville* and look at the fair. On the Sunday before, we had met Douglas Jerrold, when the reconciliation between the two old friends was completed. In looking through the pages of Mr. Spielmann's colossal work on *Punch* I see that he suggests that Douglas Jerrold was not best pleased with the success of my father's comic histories. He had suggested that there might next be "a Comic Sermon on the Mount." But Mr Spielmann suggests that this proposal was made in connexion with Mr. Thackeray's *Miss Tickle-loby's Comic History,* and as Dickens agreed with him, I think there may be something in the suggestion. Wrote Jerrold to the rival of Michael Angelo Titmarsh : " *Punch*, I believe, holds its course. Nevertheless, I do not very cordially agree with its new spirit. I am convinced that the world will get tired (at least I hope so) of this eternal guffaw at all things. After all, life has something serious. It cannot all be a comic history of humanity. Some men would, I believe, write a comic Sermon on the Mount." And then he ventured to paint a number of pictures from English history that could be treated in the spirit of burlesque. As a matter of fact, neither of my father's comic histories appeared in *Punch*, but were published in monthly numbers after the fashion of the novels of Charles Dickens. It is not impossible that Douglas Jerrold may have not intended to attack my father, but wished to strike a blow at his lifelong opponent, William Makepeace Thackeray. But although I am glad to concede this consideration, still ? remember that my father took to heart that suggestion about a comic Sermon on the Mount. He was one of the most reverent and truly religious of men. Every Sunday in my life I used to march to All Saints', Ennismore Gardens, where we had a pew—my father, my sister, and my younger brother. My mother, who had been brought up in a convent at Avignon, was not always of the party. The incumbent was Mr. Harness, who was described as a friend of Byron. He had served in the navy, and then entered the Anglican Church. He was a charming old gentleman, but a little indistinct in his utterance. When reading the tenth commandment he used to refer to the wickedness of coveting "his sox and his sass." For years afterwards I used to be particularly careful to avoid looking at any one's socks, for fear of coveting them. Even to this day I think it safer to covet boots. Well, my father was terribly upset at the suggestion he could be thought capable of writing a comic Sermon on the Mount. Until I read Mr. Spielmann's book I fancied that the proposal appeared in a paper— in some review of my father's work. I have the distinctest recollection of hearing my father referring to it. In his preface, too, he was most careful to protest against the charge of writing irreverently. His idea was to test history with ridicule, so as to distinguish the gold from the tinsel. Be this as it may, whatever the cause of quarrel that had existed between my father and his dear old friend, it had disappeared at that meeting on the sands of Boulogne—a few days before my father's death. Douglas Jerrold returned to London, and my parents, my sister, my little brother, and myself were left at Boulogne. I recollect our visit to the fair. We entered one of the booths, where there was a very realistic representation, on a small scale, of " The Siege of Sebastopol," then the all-absorbing topic of the hour. Before it was over my little brother complained of headache, and we left the booth with our nurses. The next I remember was visiting my father's bedroom, and kissing him,

99

and crying when I found that his chin was rough
from want of shaving. My father tried to con-
sole me. He was taking his breakfast in bed ; he
did not feel very well. My tears increased in
volume. He smiled his well-remembered smile,
and told me I must not be stupid. Then I turned
round and found my godfather in the room :
William Gilbert, father of William Schwenk
Gilbert, was standing near me. He had
been staying, I think, at Folkestone, and had
run over to Boulogne to see my father. My
godfather was a doctor, and he looked at me
sharply. " He had better go away," he said as
he led me to the door. I turned round to say
good-bye, and once more met the face of my
father, with that well-remembered smile. It was
the last time I saw him. I was taken to my room.
I recollect feeling hot and ill. I remember seeing
the face of our old family doctor, who had been
present at my birth. He prided himself upon having the sternness of Abernethy, and was one of the
kindest men in the world. " Wrap him in a
blanket," said Dr. Nichols, " and send him to
London." I have a dim recollection of getting
back somehow to Hyde Park Gate South. And
then there comes a long blank. My first recollection after this blank is a number of copies of
Punch in their wrappers waiting to be opened on
the hall table. Then my elder sister told me
gently that my father was dead, my brother
was dead, that I had only narrowly escaped
death after running through the stages of typhus

fever. The wretched drains of Boulogne-sur Mer were responsible for a disease known as "Boulogne sore throat," now recognized as diphtheria. My father and brother succumbed to both. It was a terrible time, and I read the account of their deaths years later in *Douglas Jerrold's Life.* As I have said, Douglas Jerrold wrote my father's obituary notice in *Punch,* and it was copied on his tombstone at Highgate Cemetery. His merits as a magistrate, a scholar, and a gentleman were recognized. A reference was made to the *Punch* table at which he had sat. Said Douglas Jerrold, speaking of my father, " His place knows him not, but his memory is tenderly cherished."

Chapter III

THE WORK OF A BOY EDITOR

A ND now I will assume that Gilbert Abbott à
Beckett has joined the *Punch* table and passed
through the various adventures connected therewith recorded by Mr. M. H. Spielmann in his
excellent work, *A History of Punch*, to which
I have already referred. As I have said, my
father took a great pride in his contributions to
the *London Charivari*, and saw that they were
cut out and pasted in a book for future reference.
No doubt he intended, at the time, some day to
republish them. But they have remained in
their paper book for half a century, and I fear
may continue there to lie until the end of the
chapter. As scenes of the times they are no
doubt interesting, and as specimens of perfectly
good tempered and wholesome fun they have
also their value. But in these days event follows
event so rapidly, that the story of the near past
ceases to attract much attention. But the
collection proves to me, that my father was a
great believer in illustration. Most of his longer
articles are adorned with pictures. He does not
seem to have written up to cuts, but to have had
his work " drawn up to." There is one work

which has a worldwide celebrity that did not appear in *Punch*, but which was illustrated by a *Punch* man. I refer to the *Comic Histories of England and Rome*. After my father's death, when my eldest brother was looking over the MS. that had been left by him, he came across a batch of copy intended for Volume III of the *Comic History of England*. Neither Gilbert nor I were then on terms with Messrs. Bradbury & Agnew, the proprietors of *Punch*. Subsequently we were both called to the table and were interviewed by the late William Bradbury, into whose hands the MS. had passed. Our father had brought up the history to the end of the reign of George II, and the new copy dealt with the reign of George III. Mr. Bradbury suggested that we should take the history to the end of that monarch's tenure of power. But we were not to touch more than we could help upon the Regency, as we should then be nearing the time of living celebrities, or the immediate ancestors of men of the time. Gilbert and I undertook the commission, and supplemented our father's work to the extent of matter for a third volume. It was set up in type, and possibly still exists in proof in the office of Messrs. Bradbury & Agnew, Limited. It was pleasant work, and I found no difficulty in following my father's style, with the exception of turning out puns. My brother and I arranged to take point to point dates and to compare notes when our work was done. After a pause of twenty years it is a little difficult to recollect what one has written, still I remember that I had to deal with the Anglo American War, and was much struck with the history of the struggle. I discovered that had England shown a little more energy the American Colonies would not have been lost to us. At the last moment, Washington's militia were on the eve of disbanding themselves and scattering. They could not get their pay, and had not the slightest enthusiasm. At this critical moment Washington had his way, and the British Government capitulated. I went for my information to Bancroft's history, which I found in the excellent library of the Junior United Service Club. But most of my reading and writing took place in the British Museum. I was sufficiently . fortunate to obtain a "green ticket," which constitutes a life membership of the reading room. During the course of my investigations I came across *A Word with " Punch."* the scurrilous pamphlet which attacked my father and his two colleagues, Mark Lemon and Douglas Jerrold. I had known that my father had a feud with Bunn, from the date of *Figaro in London.* In the thirties, the poet was suffering from the chaff of the period. I am afraid it had grown into a second nature with Gilbert Abbott à Beckett to laugh at "the Poet Bunn." My father, as I have also shown, had written opera librettos himself, and the "words to songs" by the score for my mother, who was a prolific composer. So, added to a hearty contempt for

THE WORK OF A BOY EDITOR

the really absurd lyrics of Mr Bunn, there was just a *soupçon* of professional jealousy. So it was the tradition " to pitch into Bunn." The poet's retaliation was to publish an attack upon the three men he believed responsible for the chaff—à Beckett, Lemon, and Jerrold. He was not sufficiently clever to write the brochure himself, so he called to his aid the late George Augustus Sala, who refers to the authorship in his *Life and Adventures*. I had the pleasure of the late Mr. Sala's acquaintance, having had the honour of editing him when he contributed " Echoes of the Week" to the *Sunday Times*. Nay, more, when he was unable to write his quota in *Sala's Journal*, I took his place at the request of those responsible for that publication. So I was on fairly intimate terms with " G.A.S." When his *Life and Adventures* came out, and he owned up to writing *A Word with "Punch*," I took an opportunity of asking for "further and better particulars." My friend was apologetic, and pointed out to me the very flattering references he had made to my father in his *Life and Adventures*, and pleaded that he was quite a youngster at the time. " The young have their indiscretions," said Sala. " It was an indiscretion to have written *A Word with 'Punch'*." It was a kindly concession, and a great one too, from such a pugnacious writer as " G.A.S." I had felt very keenly the attack upon my father, as I remembered the effect it had upon him. It appeared at the time when he had been appointed to his

magistracy, of which I have shown he was very
proud. I recollect as a child his returning home
in a state of the deepest depression. He was
absolutely bowed down with sorrow and talked
about retirement. He felt the attack so deeply
that from that moment until I was engaged in
collecting materials for the third volume of the
Comic History of England, in the Reading Room
of the British Museum, I had never wished to see
A Word with " Punch."

But looking over the catalogue I found that
A Word with " Punch " was entered under the
names of Jerrold, Lemon, and à Beckett. I
immediately sent for it and read it. Well, all
that Sala, speaking for Bunn, had to say against
my respected sire, was that in the days of his
earliest manhood he had been financially un-
successful in connection with a theatre and several
papers. The information was given in as in-
sulting a manner as possible. I was disgusted
with such an attack—a blow levelled below the
belt. In some articles furnished to the *Pall Mall
Magazine* within the present year by Sir F. C.
Burnand, Editor of *Punch*, I read a reference
to *A Word with " Punch,"* with a caricature
of the three gentlemen abused reproduced. My
father was depicted as the worst enemy of man.
He was wearing the robes of a barrister, from
which were peeping the cloven hoof and the
Mephistophelian tail. However, I did not take
offence at this picture, as no doubt my father,
when he was in practice at the bar, had " devilled "

for some of his colleagues. But the letterpress of *A Word with " Punch "* filled me with disgust and indignation, that in the catalogue of the British Museum such a work should be ascribed to his authorship. The copy of *A Word with " Punch,"* that was brought to me contained, moreover, an introduction by some partizan giving a ridiculous account of the quarrel of Bunn with his three opponents. I left my work of writing the continuation of my father's history, and interviewed the secretary of the British Museum. He was most courteous, and described himself as a friend of my father, of whom he spoke in terms of the deepest respect. I appealed to him. " Is it fair," I asked, " that a black-guard brochure should be ascribed to my father and his two friends, Douglas Jerrold and Mark Lemon ? " " Well," he replied, " the brochure referred to his works." " If that is a reason," I returned, " I must ask you to be so kind as to put in every single notice of my father's works— I have hundreds of them (for he preserved them)— and shall be glad to see them referred to in the Museum catalogue. But if every author follows the example, I am afraid the catalogue of the British Museum, already a work of reference of large dimensions, will have to be considerably augmented." The secretary laughed, and asked " what he could do ? " " Well," I returned, " I hope you will do something. For after I had read the attacks upon my father and his two dearest friends, I was inclined to tear the book

in half, and write across the introduction the
truth, 'The author of this twaddle is a liar,' and
I am afraid both proceedings would have been
contrary to the regulations." Then it turned
out that it was impossible to withdraw or touch
any book accepted by the library. But the
secretary promised to correct the catalogue, and
to take steps that the lying introduction should
no longer be seen. No one could have been more
kind, courteous, and conciliatory than the secretary, whose place is now filled by an equally
worthy gentleman. If I had followed my own
feelings I would not have referred to *A Word
with "Punch,"* as I remember the deep distress
it caused that most sensitive of men, my dear
father; but as *A Word with "Punch"* has been
referred to within this last year, and may be
referred to again, I think it well to meet the
matter frankly.

I have given the history of my father's connexion with the Fitzroy Theatre, and some
publications that were equally unproductive of
wealth. Without entering into details it must
be patent to every one that the position he subsequently held as a magistrate was a proof that
any debt he may have contracted when he was
little more than a boy had been satisfied.

To return to my brother Gilbert's and my
continuation of the *Comic History of England.*
It was duly completed and handed to Messrs.
Bradbury & Agnew, with whom it remains.
During his lifetime, my valued friend, the late

THE WORK OF A BOY EDITOR

William Bradbury, was anxious to produce it ; but the difficulty was to find an artist to take the place of John Leech. That difficulty proved insurmountable. My own and honoured colleague, Sir John Tenniel—the sole survivor of those who sat at the *Punch* table with my father, and with whom I have enjoyed an uninterrupted friendship since I was a boy—was approached, but unfortunately could not see his way to accept the commission. There was practically no one else, for it not only wanted an artist with the spirit of John Leech, but an artist who had a "knowledge of colour," for the large illustrations. Sir John Tenniel, as all students of *Punch* know, furnished our paper (as I venture to call it, recollecting the *tête-à-têtes* we enjoyed when we were the solitary representatives of the *Punch* staff at the *Punch* table) with some splendid illustrations of Shakespeare adapted to topical events. These "illustrations of Shakespeare" were exactly in the spirit of Leech's drawings in the *Comic Histories,* and more than worthy to form a part of the series. But it was not to be so. The third volume of the *Comic History of England,* written by the late Gilbert à Beckett, the late Gilbert Arthur à Beckett, and the yet living Arthur William à Beckett, still awaits publication. Some day, it may be when "the late" can be prefixed to the survivor of the trio, the work may appear. If it does, I beg on behalf of my colleagues that our joint work may be properly revised. I can speak for the work of my father and brother. Their " stuff " (to use the technical term) was excellent. As to my own it was common form "comic copy." It is refreshing to be able to criticize one's own work before publication. And here, as the subject of employers and employed in works journalistic has attracted much attention I take the opportunity of referring to the late William Bradbury, whose father had been the friend of my father, and whose son was one of my hosts for many years at the *Punch* table. The reference recalls to me a memory.

I am sitting in the corner of a room in a restaurant (Durand's) overlooking the Madeleine. The host—for I am a guest—is a very good friend of mine. It is not so very many years ago—the date of the last Paris Exhibition but one. Only the other day our well-loved Sovereign passed close to the same window on his way from the Rue Royale to the Rue Faubourg St. Honoré. His Majesty was on the road to the British Embassy, which I used to know very well in the days of the Third Empire, when Lord Lyons was " His Excellency," and Sheffield, Clay Kerr Seymour, and Hubert Jerningham were members of his staff. Dear Paris ! Slightly expensive, but for all that, none the less dear Paris !

I had come over in very pleasant company. There were three in particular who will never be forgotten by me—George du Maurier ; my friend and colleague, on and off, for the last twenty years, Harry Furniss, and William H. Bradbury. Of the latter, I reiterate I cannot help telling a

THE WORK OF A BOY EDITOR

story—a story that it is wholesome to repeat in these days of sudden journalistic "surprises," when a life's labour is worth six months' purchase, without a remainder over. I had been working for a score of years or so for *Punch*, of which William Bradbury was a prominent proprietor. I wanted to go to Paris, and I " thought out " a book which would be worth the necessary sum to pay for the holiday. I told him frankly how matters stood—I wanted so much, and I would earn that money by producing the book. " I think your idea utterly absurd—your book won't do at all ! " I got up a little down-hearted, and said : " Well, I will think of something else." " But stop," said William Bradbury. " Did you not say you wanted a cheque? Look here, you have been worth more than we have been paying you. So we are going to raise your salary, and the cheque I shall send you up before you go this afternoon will be retrospective—to wipe off arrears ! " What would not a man do to serve such a proprietor ?

It was a very pleasant jaunt. We started in the early morning, lunched between Calais and Paris, and dined at the dinner to which I have referred in the restaurant overlooking the Madeleine. Then we lunched twice in the Exhibition— once on the second *étage* of the Tour Eiffel, and once at the Russian Restaurant. When we had returned my friend, Mr. Harry Furniss, drew a delightful caricature of those who had taken part in the expedition. I must confess that I

was a little reluctant to show this picture to one
of my sons, as I feared he might be a little hurt
at seeing the unceremonious manner in which
his parent's personal peculiarities had been
handled. But my mind was instantly relieved.
" My dear father," said my son, roaring with
laughter. " Why, it's exactly like you ! "

Of all the men I have ever known, George du
Maurier was the most accomplished. The first
time I met him was when he was singing in an
amateur performance of *Cox and Box*, a performance subsequently repeated at Moray Lodge,
then the residence of the late Arthur Lewis, who
was soon to become the husband of that most
charming of actresses, Miss Kate Terry. Later
on I sat next to " D.M." every Wednesday for
many years in Bouverie Street, and found him
the most delightful of companions. He could
draw, he could write, he could sing. His colleagues
were overjoyed with his success with *Trilby*.
The song I heard him sing, " Hush-a-bye, Bacon,"
had such a delightful setting by Arthur Sullivan
that the words were changed to those of a more
sentimental character. But I believe the second
version was scarcely a success—the odour of the
original bacon clung to it. And poor Arthur
Sullivan, I fancy, did not find the sale of his
sweet song, " Meet me once again," increase after
George du Maurier had published a " half page "
showing a tenor singing the refrain, to the evident
satisfaction of a " Tabby," who was recognizing
the cry of the cats' meat man. " Me—et me once

again, me—et me once again," was accepted by pussy as an invitation to dinner.

And now for a confession. In spite of the pleasant character of the holiday trip to Paris, I cannot recall a single good story connected therewith. That may have been the penalty of constant companionship. The ideal staff dinner is one that associates with the contributor the presence of the intellectual well-wisher and friend. I have been a member of many a staff dining club in my time, and that is my experience. A letter from the late Charles Keene, the artist, in which he spoke disparagingly of a staff dinner of which he was a member, attracted some attention years ago. It lives in my memory because it was published in a book which was kind enough to say I was dead. The report of my decease had already reached a Scotch paper of which, in years gone by, I had been the London correspondent. That journal very amiably said that I " was greatly respected and deeply regretted by a large circle of friends and acquaintances." But the biographer of Charles Keene simply gave my name, and added in a footnote, " Since dead." The announcement was not nearly such nice reading as the half-column in the *Perthshire Advertiser*, so I called the attention of the publishers to the fact of my continued existence. They most amiably stopped the press, and erased the premature announcement of my untimely—it will always, from my point of view, be untimely—decease. They also most courteously presented me with the impression of the revised work. But I regret that I did not have the " since dead " edition—it is now of far greater value than the later ones. Of course the earlier impressions of Keene's drawings are ear-marked by " since dead."

Chapter IV

CONCERNING THE "GLOWWORM"

I THINK I have suggested by what I have written that I was, so to speak, brought up upon *Punch*. From the days of my earliest childhood the chief topic I heard discussed was *Punch*. All the domestic arrangements of the household depended upon the requirements of *Punch*. My father's well deserved annual holiday was made to fit in with the exigencies of Bouverie Street. Every week I saw my elder sister, under the supervision of my father, pasting in his contributions to *Punch*. Most of my father's dearest friends (inclusive of the proprietors) were connected with *Punch* ; I lived in an atmosphere of *Punch*. Was it then unnatural that my greatest ambition should be some day in the distant future to myself write for *Punch* ? It never entered into my wildest dreams that I should sit at the same table that my father had attended, and, as chance would have it, at the very same place. And it seemed an absolute impossibility that I actually should be appointed assistant editor; and when the editor was yachting, or away without an address, I should positively edit *Punch* myself. And yet

in course of time all these pleasant things came to
pass. They seemed a dream in the days of my
boyhood, and they seem a dream now in the hour
of what I will call by stretching a point my middle
age. Yes ; my connection with *Punch* was and
is a dream. I do not propose to make this book
a volume of controversy. I merely desire to
record facts that I think may be interesting to
the general reader rather than to the large circle
of acquaintances it is my delight to believe take
a personal interest in my career.

My father was dead, and his death made, of
course, a great difference in our means. At the
moment he put off harness—it was the very last
moment, for contributions from his pen appeared
in *Punch* and the *Illustrated London News* on the
day of his first funeral—he was in the receipt of
an income of £2,500 or £3,000 a year. This was
made up as to half by his salary as a police magistrate, and as to the rest by the cash he received
as a contributor to *Punch*, the *News*, the *Times*
and the *Express*. Moreover, there was always
a decent income derivable from his stage works
on the list of the Dramatic Authors Society.
That income was expended on the household,
and those claims of the house to which I have
referred. Of course his death affected me. My
two brothers were some years my senior. One
was a midshipman in the Indian Navy, and the
other a student at Christ Church, Oxford. In
course of time the idea, I believe, had been that I
was to follow my elder brother to Oxford, and then

either become a clergyman or a barrister. I never went to the University, and although I was called to the Bar it was through my own exertions, much as in the same way it was through my father's exertions that he was called to the Bar. The assistance in each case was from the same source. We were both called to the Bar at Gray's Inn after our marriages ; and here I cannot help suggesting the strong resemblance that his career bears to my own. We both were editors before we were one-and-twenty. We both wrote for the stage, both worked our hardest on *Punch*. We both sat at the same place at the same table, and in each case our place knows us not, as I once told M. Zola. "I believe in heredity," I said to him. "I trace a resemblance between our namesake, St. Thomas of Canterbury, with whom we claim a blood kinship, and ourselves. Look at him, look at me. Eleven hundred years or twelve hundred years ago he wrote the best of books after waging war in France as a soldier. So the career of St. Thomas of Canterbury. Now my case ; I, too, have been a soldier, as an officer in the Militia, and I, too, have followed in the steps of the saint by being a constant contributor to *Punch*." M. Zola received my suggestion with profound respect.

Well, I had the fixed idea of some day contributing to *Punch*. I passed my school life in touch with my father's work. I remember at Honiton I carried off a prize for history, thanks to a close study of my father's *England*. Dr. Mackarness (subsequently Bishop of Oxford) was kind enough to compliment me on my literary style and my sense of the ridiculous. At Felstead, when I was a boy of fifteen, I first became a journalist. I wrote for the *Braintree Times* short articles about the school, and constituted myself the local representative of the district. At length I reached man's estate, and found myself a temporary clerk in the War Office. My eldest brother Gilbert and myself were sharing rooms in Hanover Square in the house which was the first home of the members of the Arts Club. We were thirsting to rush into print, and we started upon *A Comic Guide to the Royal Academy*. The idea had been given us by our father's criticism of the pictures of the Royal Academy in the *Almanack of the Month*, of which he was the editor. We worked at it with enthusiasm night and day for a week. When it was finished we carried it to the Messrs. Routledge, who consented to publish it. This we considered a great concession. We were to pay all the expenses, and give a commission of so much per cent. on the sales. The brochure duly came out, and was noticed by the Press. In those days there were no press agencies to send more or less laudatory paragraphs to authors and others whose names got into the newspapers ; so we used to frequent a reading room near Leicester Square, where we could see what was being said about us. As men unknown to Fleet Street, we "caught it." We had apparently been guilty of two faults—the first of rushing into print, the second of being sons of our father. "There was once an à Beckett honourably connected with comic literature," said the *Sunday Times*, to which my father had contributed, and which I subsequently edited, "but neither of these is the man." We were slated right and left. On one of our visits to the reading room to which I have referred, my brother came to me beaming, with a paper in his hand. "A good notice at last," he exclaimed. "They say we are 'superficially smart.' Come, that's better than nothing !" Thinking over the matter after these many years, I can see that we had not much chance with the Press of the period. As completely unknown men with the name of a distinguished author for an introduction, we were very unlikely to be popular. In those days the struggle for existence amongst journalists was acute. The papers were few, and the pressmen regarded outsiders with aversion. "What right had two fellows, of whom no one had hitherto heard, to take the bread out of the mouths of the regular members of the profession ? " In our preface there was a suggestion of the earlier style of our father. After attacking the critics—by the way, a pleasant plan for obtaining the goodwill of the Press !—we came to the exhibitors. We said : " Your true critic's task is often a painful one ! and as we have wielded the quill, not altogether without independence, it is to be feared that a wound may have been inflicted here and there among our more sensitive subjects.

THE à BECKETTS OF " PUNCH "

To these we offer a balm. We have prepared a neatly printed and ample apology, which will be forwarded to any part of the United Kingdom on the receipt of *name, address and seven postage stamps.*—THE AUTHORS." This little witticism was freely quoted to prove that we were " flippant," " humourless," and " lacking in critical acumen." Besides the " superficially smart " notice, there was a really favourable review in a paper called the *Press*, which half a century ago ranked with the *Athenaeum.* For this we were immensely grateful. Then I appealed to my friend, Sir (then Mr.) Norman Lockyier, who was at the time a colleague of mine in the War Office. He promised to notice our " Guide " in the *Reader*, to which he was a constant contributor. He wrote : " We hear that the *Comic Guide to the Royal Academy* is going into a second edition, a proof, if one were needed, of the humour that can be found in parts of the book." But perhaps the most mortifying of all the notices was one in which our brochure was called a "catchpenny production," for as a matter of fact we were out of pocket to the extent of something between fifty and a hundred pounds. So, take it all round, *" The Comic Guide to the Royal Academy for* 1863, by Gilbert A. and Arthur W. à Beckett, price sixpence ; London : Routledge, Warne and Routledge, Farringdon Street," might have been accepted by us as a " Warning by the Way " to have nothing further to do with literature, humorous or otherwise. Not at all. In 1864

CONCERNING THE "GLOWWORM"

we repeated the experiment. We brought out a *Comic Guide to the Royal Academy for* 1864, but this time wrote under the *nomme de guerre* of " The Gemini." Our publishers fought shy of us, so we got our printer of our initial number to " print and publish for us," which he kindly did at the Milton Steam Printing Offices, Chandos Street, Strand. " What does it matter about the publishers ? " said my brother Gilbert ; " no one will buy it ! " And so far as I can recollect no one did. On this occasion the Press were more kindly than they had been the year before—they good-naturedly ignored us ! And this assertion reminds me of a letter that was once addressed by a persistent would-be contributor to a brother editor. The scribe had written again and again to the editor, but had never received an answer. On each occasion he had made a genial excuse for the neglectful recipient of his correspondence. " No doubt you have been absent from town." " Presuming that once more the postal authorities have been to blame," and so on. My brother editor received the letter with the well-known superscription, and was about to cast it aside intact when by accident he opened it. " Encouraged by your courteous silence, I address you once again." This was too much for the editor, who was *au fond* a good fellow, and he gave the would-be contributor a chance. But I am not sure that was the best thing for our book—it is more useful to have a bad notice than to have no notice at all.

THE à BECKETTS OF "PUNCH"

It was about this time that I had the pleasure of meeting the present editor of *Punch,* with whom I worked for many years on the *London Charivari* and other papers. I had seen him for the first time at a fête given in the building of the Exhibition of 1862, in aid of the Royal Hospital for Incurables. The festival was under the immediate patronage of the Prince and Princess of Wales, who honoured it with their presence. There were the usual booths for barter and two distractions of a theatrical character. We had a Richardson's show with a " parade " in front of it, under the management of Lady Anne Sherson, the aunt of Lord Raynham, subsequently the Marquis Townsend, brother-in-law of the Duke of Fife. We gave two entertainments ; one was called "The Port Admiral," written by Mr. Thomas Gibson Bowles, and the other a burlesque, "The Brigand of Braganza," by F. A. Marshall, a younger son of the then Member for Sunderland. Both these gentlemen later on joined me on the staff of a paper of which I was elected editor. We had a parade according to the custom of the time round the building to assist the collection of an audience. I was only nineteen, so I was not entrusted with a part in the pieces—although subsequently promoted to play the heroine with Mr. Thomas Gibson Bowles as the hero before the Princess Louise at another charitable fête, and Mario and Grizi in the grounds of Campden House —but was allowed to dress as Richard III, and make myself generally useful. An elder brother of mine, who was more retiring than myself, appeared as the King of Hearts, and was told off to pair with me in the procession. He was highly indignant at what he was pleased to call my "confounded tomfoolery," because disguised and costumed as Richard III I attempted to keep up the character. The present editor of *Punch* was the life and soul of a companion booth, in which was being played at frequent intervals a military drama he had written for the occasion, called "The Siege of Seringapatam." The companion booth had its parade in rivalry of ours, and its procession crossed our procession. I need scarcely say that I knew every line that the author of "The Siege of Seringapatam" had written, and had a sincere admiration for his work. I was therefore very anxious to see him in the flesh. I was much impressed. He was dressed in a burlesque military uniform, no doubt used in "The Siege," and was at the head of a company that later on blossomed into many celebrities. Amongst his set I remember the late Sir (then Mr.) Charles Hall, the Recorder of London, and a man I was subsequently to know very well indeed, Mr. Matt Morgan. The latter was attired as a toreador. As I never had time to assist at "The Siege of Seringapatam" (much to my regret), I am unable to say whether Mr. Matt Morgan was in the play or not. As we passed I brandished my sword before the present editor of *Punch* to attract his favourable attention to my praiseworthy attempt to represent Richard III in all his wickedness.

THE à BECKETTS OF " PUNCH "

Again my elder brother was indignant. He had recognized friends in the crowd, and was anxious to be accepted by them as a gentlemanly and retiring King of Hearts, and how could he be gentlemanly and retiring " with a silly ass of a Richard III playing the fool like a confounded young idiot ? " or words to that effect. The present editor of *Punch* paused for a moment and saluted with the drum major's baton, which was an adjunct to his military uniform. Then the two processions continued their progress— one to take part in the " The Siege of Seringapatam," and the other to do their best in " The Port Admiral" and " The Brigand of Braganza."

My performance in the building of the Exhibition of 1862 led to a long friendship with Francis Albert Marshall, one of the best of fellows. He was quick tempered, and at times his enthusiasm carried him away to do things that in his wiser moments he would have certainly avoided. But for all that—eccentric as he undoubtedly was— he was the best of good fellows. In his father's (the Member's) house in St. George Road, within a hundred yards of my present residence, he entertained me to dinner. I had the pleasure of meeting at his hospitable board Mr. Alfred Wigan, the actor, Mr. Robins, nephew of the great auctioneer, my second brother (the retiring exponent of the King of Hearts), and last, and certainly first in my estimation at that time, the present editor of *Punch*. Our talk was about the approaching production of " Ixion," a burlesque that

CONCERNING THE "GLOWWORM"

was due at the Royalty, a little theatre for amateurs that had been transformed into a regular West End playhouse. Stories were told about those who had strutted their hour upon its stage in the days of Miss Kelly, the once proprietress. It now belonged to Mrs. Selby, the widow of Selby, the dramatic author and comedian. Mr. Robins had the history of the playhouse at his finger ends. Mr. Alfred Wigan, who was at the time the fashionable actor of the hour, was inclined to ignore burlesque, or at least—in consideration of the present company—to allow it, so to speak, to live. Of course, as quite the youngest of the company, I was expected to be seen more than heard, but I could not tolerate this implied aspersion upon my father's favourite work, burlesque. So I ventured to ask Mr. Alfred Wigan if he remembered "The Forty Thieves," written by Gilbert Abbott à Beckett in—and I mentioned the date ? Mr. Alfred Wigan did not remember it. Did I ? "No," I admitted, "I had never seen it. It was before my time. But I have the book, and in the cast the part of Hassarack is put down to Mr. Alfred Wigan. There can only be one Alfred Wigan—now do you remember it ? " Mr. Alfred Wigan suddenly recollected the play, owned up to the character, and was civil to me for the rest of the evening.

Thanks to my friendship with Frank Marshall I ran across a gentleman of great enterprise who, then a civil servant of the Crown, was anxious to start an evening paper. Thus it came about that

THE à BECKETTS OF " PUNCH "

I made the acquaintance of Mr. Last, printer of the *Squib* and first printer of *Punch*. He was appointed their manager by the Directors of the Strand Printing and Publishing Company, Limited. I was appointed their secretary. Our first object was to secure an appropriate name for the paper. A number were suggested. As it was to have a decided dramatic character, why not *The Harlequin ?* Then the promoter suggested *The Glowworm.* " Why ? " was the demand. " Because the *Glowworm* gives light like the *Evening Star,* which is a title taken by another paper." " Yes, that may be," insisted the objectors, " but then evening gives a proper distinction to the paper, it shows the public when it is expected to appear." " Quite so," answered the promoter triumphantly, " and so does the *Glowworm.* The glowworm can only be seen in the evening. Our *Glowworm* will only be seen in the evening." This argument was convincing, and we fixed upon the *Glowworm* as the title for our new evening paper. As a matter of fact the *Glowworm* was seen much earlier than the evening, for we brought out its second edition (we ignored a first edition) early in the afternoon.

The present editor of *Punch* was the original editor of the *Glowworm,* and amongst the earliest contributors were Mr. Thomas Gibson Bowles, Sir (then Mr.) Arthur Sullivan, Mr. Frederick Clay, and some of the editor's Cambridge friends— I fancy amongst the number Mr. Clarke, who had so much to do with the famous A.D.C. The promoter, who had become the managing director, was very energetic. We left the stocking of the newspaper office—the composing, the foundry and the machinery rooms—to our manager and printer, Mr. Last, who went to work on a grand scale. The site obtained was the land secured at the moment by a Judge and Jury Society. The ground is now occupied by the Vaudeville Theatre. We had some difficulty in getting rid of the Judge and Jury Society, an entertainment of a questionable character. The programme was a mock trial, usually connected with divorce, and the audience acted as the jury. The forms of the Law Courts were carefully reproduced, but some of the questions put in examination and cross-examination if permitted in Westminster, would have been directed to be heard *in camera.* We ultimately got rid of the Judge and Jury Society by taking down the premises before commencing rebuilding. When the site of the *Glowworm* was at length clear, Mr. Last entered into possession on behalf of the Strand Printing and Publishing Company, Limited. I have already referred to the *Shops and Companies of Great Britain* as one of his ventures. Besides this publication he had in his mind's eye the creation of a theatrical poster business. We found that he had purchased on behalf of the company an immense amount of wooden type that would scarcely be valuable to the *Glowworm.* Moreover he had large ideas about production. We had everything in duplicate—double engines, double boilers, and, unless we had interposed, double factory chimneys. We had several pleasant meetings of the staff, at which the present editor of *Punch* presided. We got a very effective poster of an old-time watchman in mediaeval costume, looking at what was intended to represent a *Glowworm*, with the legend, " What is this ? " However, the effect was somewhat marred by someone writing, " An oyster " as an answer. Then we hurriedly got out " *The Glow-worm*, an evening paper, price 1d." We decided to print the paper in two colours. Moreover, we had an idea that we might obtain a sale in the music halls by having an edition for each hall, giving on the front page a programme of the evening's entertainments. We proposed that this idea should be adopted by the theatres, but met with a rebuff, as the programmes were in the hands of the holders of the saloons, and they objected to substituting for their programmes, sold at sixpence, newspapers avowedly worth only a penny. Our managing director hit upon the idea of selling special editions at the doors of the theatres, but this was objected to on the score that the play bills were copyright. To avoid the contention, we then made each pro-gramme into a little story, in which the facts of the evening's entertainments were worked incidentally. But there was no sale for the *Glowworm* in this direction, and even the editions of the music halls went slowly. So our managing director gave a banquet to the proprietors of these places of entertainment, the ménu of which was one of the most luxurious character, and the oratory to consist of the greatest eloquence. He had prepared a speech commencing, " Gentlemen," in which he pointed out to the assembled throng expected to be present the enormous benefit that would accrue by the success of the *Glowworm*. He had learned this oration by heart and duly delivered it. But the effect was spoiled by the fact that instead of an assembled throng only one guest turned up, Mr. Charles Morton, who then represented the Oxford and Canterbury Music Halls. But still our managing director would insist upon addressing the " assembled throng " in spite of there being only a solitary representative of that expected multitude. I as secretary of the company was requested in an undertone " not to make an idiot of myself," because I giggled. But this took place some time after the *Glowworm* had made its first appearance.

The present editor of *Punch* had got together, as I have explained, a very brilliant staff. All that was wanted was a good publisher and manager. The sub-editor was Mr. Thomas Archer, who thoroughly understood his work, but was still, I think, better as a contributor than a sub-editor. On the day before the appearance of our initial number, our two engines both broke down and I, as secretary of the company, spent the night in trying to obtain auxiliary assistance. In the early hours of our opening day I rode into the Strand seated on what was known as a donkey engine, which I had been able to secure in the Blackfriars Road. Mr. Last was good enough to say that he thought it would do, and to a certain extent it did. As I write I have the initial number of the *Glowworm* before me. The two colours—red and black—are certainly rather blurred, and there is a not unpleasant eccentricity in the type. Mr. Last seemed to be working off some of his theatrical poster letters in various parts of the paper with startling effect. The letters were so large in some of the headings that even the most short-sighted must have seen them. One of the staff who looked in to see how we were getting on, suggested that we should advertise the *Worm*— the title of the paper was immediately thus affectionately abbreviated—" as a journal for the aged : one that could be read without glasses." The present editor of *Punch* was the most capable of conductors. If I may be permitted to be hypercritical, however, I fancy he was just a trifle too enthusiastic about reporting the fête day of his old school, Eton. If my memory does not play me false, he sent Mr. Thomas Gibson Bowles to Windsor to report the function. The now hon. Member for King's Lynn was a most charming writer, and he gave full vent to his poetical fancy. We were told, I think, of " the birds singing in the trees " and " the sun shining brightly on the water." But—and here I only speak to the best of my recollection—he had not made himself acquainted with the arrangements made for transmitting messages at a specially cheap rate for the Press, and paid at so much a word the sum demanded from the general public. This ignorance, too, of privileges conferred on the Press rather delayed the transmission of his copy and—again I speak under correction—I am under the impression that the final description of the scene on the Thames, "the birds singing and the sun shining," etc., reached the *Glowworm* somewhere about ten in the evening. Again the lack of organization in the managerial department, typified by a donkey engine acting as a substitute for two machines of enormous power, invaded the sub-editorial.

Mr. Thomas Archer, who was a most capable journalist from every point of view, was, I imagine, a little too trustful to the casual reporter, and consequently I fancy we published some copy that would have been better, from an aesthetic point of view, had it been subjected to stricter revision. But, as I am talking of what happened about forty years ago, I cannot speak by the card, but only give my impressions. I know that the present editor of *Punch* and I smiled very frequently during the day, being both blessed with a keen sense of humour. To the best of my recollection the present editor of *Punch* conducted the *Glowworm* for a few weeks, and then, finding the work uncongenial and too much a strain with his other engagements, tendered his resignation. It was accepted by the Board with regret, and then, having no one on the spot but myself, the directors ordered me to take up the duties. I have made it my rule of life to accept the situation whatever it may be, so when I was told to edit the *Glowworm*, I did as I was bid. I was fairly successful. After all, when a paper is in full swing it is not so very difficult to keep it going. The present editor of *Punch* had left the *Glowworm* as a going concern, and I continued the movement. I had just reached my majority, and I celebrated the occasion by getting the paper into an action for libel. Like my father, I was always very fond of the theatre, and when I was appointed editor of the *Glowworm*, and " was lord of all I surveyed with no one my right to dispute " (save perhaps the directors, who objected to all my actions), I constituted myself dramatic critic. In this capacity I visited the Lyceum and assisted at the production of the *Watch Cry*, an adaptation from the French, by J. Palgrave Simpson.

The play was a failure. Mr. Fetcher, the hero, appeared as a deaf and dumb personage, who was accepted into the confidence of the rest of the cast on account of his distressing infirmities. At the end of the second act he gave " the watch cry," which furnished the drama with its title. He threw open the windows of the Palace, and should have exclaimed, " Archers of the Guard watch ! " but in his excitement he mispronounced the last word, and " the cry " seemed to be a peremptory invitation to the swimming bath. The play had been hurriedly rehearsed, and, truth to tell, most of the performers were very imperfect in their

132

words. The father of one of the most charming
of our actresses had an important part. But I
still think that he would have done better had he
been a little more attentive to his book. Unfortunately, in criticising him I wrote, " Mr. So-and-So
was capital as Captain Thingamy, Mr. Such-a-
One conscientious as the Count of Chose, and the
part of Mr. Plaintiff subsequently in an action for
libel was efficiently spoken by the prompter."
A row followed. Within a day or two I got a
letter from Mr. Plaintiff's solicitor asking for an
immediate and ample apology, under pain of an
action for libel. I published the letter with an
editorial note, explaining what we considered to
be the duties we owed to our subscribers to nail
our flag to the mast and cry, " No surrender."
Those were not the exact words, but that was the
purport of our editorial. Of course, had the
incident happened nowadays, supposing I were in
command, it would have been at an end immediately. I would have apologised and been thank-
ful to the kind solicitor for giving me the opportunity. But half a century ago, more or less—
probably a decade less—I was enthusiastic and
conceited. I really believed I was performing a
noteworthy action in defending the independent
will of the Press. We duly went to trial, and the
present editor of *Punch* was our junior counsel.
I think we should have done better had we not
called the author the late Mr. Palgrave Simpson—
a most delightful man and then the secretary of
the Dramatic Authors' Society in succession to

THE à BECKETTS OF "PUNCH"

Sterling Coyne, of early *Punch* fame. Mr. Palgrave Simpson was disappointed and angry. His *Watch Cry* was a failure, and its discontinuance had ended a long friendship with Fechter. But he came as one of our witnesses for the defence. But when he got into the witness-box he " proved " a great deal too much. He duly approved of my criticism. The Plaintiff certainly did not know his words, and it might be fairly said that his part had been efficiently spoken by the prompter. So far so good. But when it came to his cross-examination by Sergeant Parry the matter took another turn. The Plaintiff did not know his part. Mr. Somebody Else did not know his part. Mr. Other Fellow did not know his part. Mr. Fechter did not know his part. The only man in the theatre perfect in his words was the prompter—and he only because he had the book before him. He proved a great deal too much. But perhaps the most amusing incident in the day's doings was the examination of myself, or rather the proceedings that led to my appearance in the witness-box. Our leader asked his junior (the present editor of *Punch*) what was the case about. The junior gave the necessary information. " Who was the dramatic critic of the paper ? " asked Mr. Leader. " Young à Beckett," replied Mr. Junior. " Any relation of the *Comic History* man ? " " Son." " Must be a young chap." " Yes, he is a young chap—only twenty or thereabouts." And at this moment our leader rose to open the case for the defence.

CONCERNING THE "GLOWWORM"

He began, of course, by describing the service we had rendered to the public by giving a fair criticism of a play, which had certainly failed to take the fancy of the public. Then he touched upon the necessity for a free Press. What would England have done if the treatment of our Press had not been a lesson to the world ? That kind of thing for five minutes or so. Then came the question about the selection of a dramatic critic to perform the responsibilities, the heavy responsibilities, of that most important office. It appeared that my board of directors had acted with singular discrimination. They had chosen a gentleman for the important post who had an hereditary knowledge of the stage. He was the son of the late Gilbert Abbott à Beckett ; and then I had the pleasure of listening to a very eloquent account of my father's qualities of head and heart. I was the lineal descendant of those qualities. But that " his learned friend " should not say that he had shirked meeting a possible weak point, he would admit that I was young. But then the gentlemen of the jury were requested to be so kind as to recollect that Hercules was still younger when he slew the two serpents in his cradle. They would not fail to remember that Napoleon was a young man when he did something or other heroic ; that Pitt was still a younger man when he did something or other statesmanlike ; that William, the hero of Hastings, as a yet younger man, gained the well-deserved title of the Conqueror. Call Mr. Arthur William

THE à BECKETTS OF " PUNCH "

à Beckett. And a very small boy with rather a pale face marched into the witness-box. I was so entirely unlike the popular conception of Hercules in his cradle, Napoleon, Pitt and William of Normandy, that there was a roar of laughter, in which I myself joined heartily. Before entering the box I had spoken to our junior (the present editor of *Punch*) to ask him whether I ought to try to be funny. " Certainly not," was the prompt reply of our junior, who may have been (I had no means of judging) more nervous than I myself. The present editor of *Punch* took my evidence very nicely and sat down with a sigh of relief. I did my best, but the evidence of Palgrave Simpson ruined us and we lost our case. We had to pay 40s. damages, a sum which carried with it costs. However, the trial did us no harm. The entire Press took up our case and supported us. For many years after the verdict very little was said about the successful plaintiff ; the dramatic critic by mentioning him had no wish to run the chance of an action for libel. But it was a lesson to me. It was my first and last action for libel. Stay, let me correct myself. I should have added that the plaudits of the Press had a bad effect upon me. I republished all the kind articles that were written in our favour. And the result, Mr. Solicitor for the plaintiff commenced a fresh action and again succeeded. But the second trial was really my last. Since that time I have been sufficiently fortunate to keep out of the libel court. Of course the paper,

CONCERNING THE "GLOWWORM"

through its publisher, and not the dramatic critic, was sued. Since that date I have had a good deal to do with the law of libel, as I was one of the committee appointed by the Newspaper Society to assist Lord Glenesk (then Sir Algernon Borthwick) in the passing of his Libel Bill. I do not say that I was prudent to a degree when I was editing the *Glowworm*, but I do say that there are many cases in which the client is a mere dummy and the speculative solicitor is the moving spirit. I have a case in my mind that proved to me that there was a speculative solicitor who saw his way to making an income out of every paper with which I was connected. I sent for him, expressed my admiration at his talent for scenting a libel and engaged him by paying a small retaining fee to act for the paper. If I ever had an article that I thought risky I would send it to him for his inspection. He should advise me. We struck the bargain and I never had another action for libel. I never employed him to give an opinion, but he was retained in readiness.

It may have occurred to the reader, what had the editorship of the *Glowworm* to do with the staff of *Punch*? Indirectly a great deal, for through the editorship I first became a worker with the present editor of *Punch*. Later on that comradeship in work was to stand me in good stead. My recollections of the editorship of the *Glowworm* are very pleasant ones. My Board was perfectly delightful. It was composed of three or four gentlemen, some of whom are still

137

living, so I must be careful not to give them away.
But one of the most influential of our body was a
captain of artillery who had given up following
the guns to watch races and card tables. He was
a very kind-hearted fellow, and ultimately became
somehow or other the sole proprietor of the
Glowworm. When we were struggling and our
resources were at their lowest he proposed at a
Board meeting that every sou at our disposal
should be put upon some outsider for the Cam-
bridgeshire at 50 to 1. The resolution was actually
carried, and I had really to invoke the aid of the
solicitors of the company to get the resolution
rescinded. Our articles of association gave us a
wide discretion, but our powers did not extend
to " fluttering " on the turf. But my chagrin
was great to hear afterwards that had we taken
the bet we should have multiplied our capital
fiftyfold. The outsider romped in. My friend
the captain, however, did not exult. " It wasn't
your fault, you young idiot," said he to me, " the
blame lay upon that beastly Limited Liability
Companies Act."

By degrees in the cause of economy I became
almost the entire staff of the *Glowworm*. I had
one assistant, the late Mr. Brockwell Dalton,
who was the best of sub-editors. But while it
was running its course the *Glowworm* had found
many distinguished contributors. For instance,
Mortimer Collins was one of our leader writers,
Andrew Halliday gave us a weekly letter, Dion
Boucicault furnished a feuilleton, and Tom

CONCERNING THE "GLOWWORM"

Robertson was an occasional contributor. But by degrees I was left single-handed. I had to write leaders, theatrical notices, reviews, even sporting prophecies. It was excellent practice, and made me a fairly ready writer during the rest—so far as it has gone—of my life. But before I came to the pass of writing everything myself I had the assistance of two of my dearest friends. One is still living, and after a brilliant career at the Bar and on the Bench, has returned to journalism. I refer to Mr. (now Sir) Douglas Straight; and the other was that brilliant humorist, Corney (otherwise Dick) Grain. These two friends of mine were of the greatest help to keep the *Glowworm* glowing for many a long day. Both were in active practice at the Bar. Later on Straight and I wrote a novel together, and Corney and I collaborated in a piece for German Reed's. I was to some extent at one time the stock author—with and without my brother Gilbert—at the St. George's Hall. It was quite a school for actors and dramatists. The firm of German Reed (of which at one time Mr. Parry was a member) turned out some actors and actresses. Amongst the authors figured W. S. Gilbert, Tom Robertson, Tom Taylor, Shirley Brooks, Arthur Law, and the present editor of *Punch*. When I was doing odd jobs for the firm I was asked to bring up to date "The Card Basket" written by Shirley Brooks. Having been assured that there was no objection on the part of the family of the author I set to work, proud of the idea of being associated (even as a ghost) with one of my father's *Punch* friends. When the time came for me to revise the play it was discovered that it had been lost, so I had to write the piece and rely upon the recollection of Mrs. German Reed, whose portrait, by the way, as Miss P. Horton, had been published in *Figaro in London*. I was immensely amused to read in the notices of the new version of the " Card Basket " that the old dialogue of Shirley Brooks (which I had supplied) was much better than the conversation of more modern plays. This idea was repeated when I re-wrote some of the more risky parts of " The Maske of Flowers," on its production at Gray's Inn in honour of Queen Victoria's Jubilee. I spoke of " Kawasha's crew," and " crew " was singled out as quite late Elizabethan or early Jacobean. As a matter of fact, it was pure à Beckettean. Before I quit the subject of the *Glowworm*, I may say that my engagement on the paper obtained me many pleasant acquaintanceships.

I recall one of these pleasant acquaintanceships.

I am sitting at a round table in a corner house of Stratford Place, Oxford Street. It is the dining-room of the Portland Club, where the table d'hôte system, peculiar to the old Coffee Houses of St. James's Street, still survives. I am talking of many years ago, before the days of " bridge," but when " humbug," or two-handed whist, was the vogue. My neighbour at the dinner of which I am writing played through the

CONCERNING THE "GLOWWORM"

night at "humbug," and two days later committed suicide. I was editing the *Glowworm*, as I have explained, at the time, and was asked to keep the inquest out of the paper. Looking round the board I noticed one old gentleman, who subsequently seemed to enjoy his rubber thoroughly. He spoke to no one and no one spoke to him. He was stone deaf. The name of the old member of the " Portland " was Sir Edward Bulwer Lytton—the butt of Thackeray in the past, and only the other day the hero of the literary hour. Cultured London was thinking of the centenary of the author of half-forgotten *Pelham*, and scarcely remembered *Money*, *Richelieu*, and " *The Lady of Lyons*. The last survives on account of the character of Claude Melnotte, whose garb as a French peasant in Act I makes an excellent costume for a fancy dress ball. You can dance in it, and in these khaki days it seems quite " possible."

One of the plays—now quite forgotten so far as a theatrical *repertoire* is concerned, was " Not so Bad as we Seem," written by Bulwer Lytton, in aid of his pet scheme, the Guild of Literature and Art. It was acted by amateurs selected from studies and studios. At the head of this dramatic company stood Charles Dickens, who subsequently made it the nucleus of the troupe who furnished the casts for " The Light House " and " The Frozen Deep " at Tavistock House. For the Boz theatricals the scenery was painted by Clarkson Stansfield. In August, 1865, a dinner

was given to celebrate the completion of the
three houses of the Guild, on ground given by Sir
Edward Bulwer Lytton, at Stevenage. And last
year, 1902, if I am not mistaken, a private act of
Parliament relieved the surviving trustees—Sir
John Robinson, and, I fancy, Mr. J. C. Parkinson
—of any further responsibility. From first to
last, sad to say, the Guild of Literature and Art
was a failure.

At the dinner to which I have referred, Bulwer
Lytton spoke of the three houses as " modest in
themselves, but of such a character that a gentleman may inhabit them with a small but well-
assured pension." In responding to the toast of
his health, Charles Dickens added—" The ladies
and gentlemen whom we shall invite to occupy
them will never be placed under any social disadvantage. They will always claim on equal
terms the hospitality of their generous neighbours." But it would not do, in spite of the
wishes and suggestions of Lytton and Dickens.
Authors and artists would not live in the Guild's
almshouses, and the charity has been wound up.
I fancy some of the proceeds went to the Royal
Literary Fund and some to the Artists' Benevolent
Fund. I am afraid that in the distribution the
claims of that most admirable of charities, or
rather provident organizations, the Newspaper
Press Fund, were either ignored or forgotten.

To return to the Portland Club. I do not
think that Lytton played heavily. He was satisfied with the stakes, and did not care for " outside

betting." Oh, those outside bets! I knew a man—who has since joined the majority—who never allowed a rubber to be played if he were standing out without staking £500 on the result. He said " it sounds terrible, as I lose or win thousands every night ; but at the end of the year it works out with something—not much—to the good." He told me his golden rule was to go on so long as he won, but the moment he had three losses in succession to cease playing for the day. After the second loss he turned his chair, and with the third was off.

I am afraid it is impossible to ignore the fact that Thackeray hated Bulwer Lytton—of course on his literary merits. There may possibly have been some personal reason which has never risen to the surface. At the very dinner to which I have referred, Lytton spoke of Dickens—who was not on the best of terms with Thackeray—as " the author whose writings are equally the delight of the scholar and the artisan, and who has united an unrivalled mastery over the laughter and the tears of millions with as sweet and genial a philosophy as ever made the passions move at the command of virtue." In reply, Dickens spoke in the handsomest terms of " the genius of their accomplished host." This " passing of compliments when gentlefolk meet " was scarcely likely to commend itself to W. M. T.

One of the last pieces written by Lytton was " The Rightful Heir." It was produced at the Lyceum by Herr Bandmann, a German actor, who spoke English with the accent of the Fatherland. It was immediately burlesqued under the title of " The Frightful Hair." And of all people in the world, that most accomplished actor, Mr. William Kendal, was cast for the principal character. As the hero, the creator of so many rôles of an entirely different kind, danced and sang admirably. And in this connexion it is well to remember that Mr. John Hare and Sir Charles Wyndham were both excellent in burlesque. Remembering their subsequent careers, the old saying might be revised : " There is but a step from the ridiculous to the sublime, and not a long one." A story is told that Lytton was invited to a trial of the heavy ordnance that was beginning to be adopted just before his death. He duly watched the preparations for loading and laying, and then turned his back upon the cannon. Finding himself enveloped in smoke, he said to his neighbour : " I suppose they have let it off ? " He had heard nothing ! Another story : Once, when he had spoken too long for the patience of his audience, they got out of hand, and conversation became general. When he had leisurely finished his peroration, he added, " And now, ladies and gentlemen, all I have left to do is to thank you for your kind attention ! " Lytton may have had faults—which raised the ire of Thackeray— but for all that he was a good friend, a kind father, and an excellent landlord.

Yet again I have a memory connected with the *Glowworm*.

CONCERNING THE "GLOWWORM"

I am seated at a table in the Thatched House Club (then the Civil Service), and there is a vacant place. Opposite me is a gaunt, grumpy man, twice my age—for it must be remembered I am only a youngster of two-and-twenty or thereabouts. He is as sulky as can be, and has responded to my attempts at conversation with a " Yes " or a " No." I had never seen him before, and I was to have been introduced to him by the non-arrived. Charles B. Stephenson, once of the Treasury, then of Lloyds, and always the bright and brilliant writer, has failed to put in an appearance, and consequently I am dining *tête-à-tête* with Charles Reade, the novelist with a purpose, and (on this occasion only) in a bad temper.

After we had got to the first entrée, I took the bull by the horns. " Please, sir," I say to my surly guest, in the tone of a would-be conciliatory schoolboy speaking to an unreasonable schoolmaster, " it is not my fault. Please, sir, I am a nervous young chap trying my best to make up for Mr. Charley Stephenson's absence. Please sir, you are a big and famous author, and I am only a young journalist, just quit of the Civil Service. Please, sir, don't be too hard upon me." Charles Reade looks at me for a moment, then he holds out his hand, shakes mine, bursts into a loud laugh, and from that moment becomes the most charming companion imaginable. He stays at the Thatched House Club (then the Civil Service), telling me amusing stories and drinking

cold tea, until three in the morning. I have never
had a more delightful evening.

I am afraid that in these days the works of
Charles Reade are scarcely ever read, and perchance half-forgotten. And yet in his time—not
so very long ago—he was a power in the land.
Charles Dickens " wrote down " abuses, and so
did Charles Reade. At this dinner to which I
have referred I spoke to him about a book he had
levelled at the system of cure for the mentally
afflicted. I told him that the antipathy he had
created to institutions for the cure of the insane
had ended, in a case that had come within my
knowledge, in a suicide. He was shocked. " I
wrote too strongly," said he. " I will write
another novel, and put the matter in another
light." And later on he kept his word. He
admitted that sometimes he was a little uncertain
about his dates. He produced a romance, supposed to be of the passing hour, when the Blue
Book, upon which " the abuse " treated was
founded, was a decade old, or even more antiquated.

Before I met him at the Civil Service Club he
had had a controversy in the pages of the *Glowworm*. He had written a book called *Griffith
Gaunt*, and I had severely criticised some of his
" facts " about the practices in the Church of
Rome. He had answered very angrily, " slating "
the critic in the heartiest style. Then a correspondent took up the cudgels on behalf of the
paper, and there was pretty sword play on both

sides. I owned up to Charles Reade. "Oh, you were the critic, were you?" cried my guest; "and who was the 'Constant Reader'?" "Archbishop Manning," I replied. "Just so," returned Charles Reade; "a far better man than you!" And I did not complain of his estimate of our respective characters.

I was reminded the other day by the controversy that arose relative to the refusal of admission to the *Times'* critic to the stalls of the Garrick Theatre on a certain first night, of a similar incident that had occurred in connexion with one of Charles Reade's pieces. "Never too Late to Mend" was produced at the Princess's, and George Guest Tomlin hissed it. George Vining presumed to address the critics seated in the stalls, and told them as they had not paid for their seats, they were in the theatre on sufferance. Tomlin called for an apology. He was backed up by the audience, and Vining had to "express his regret." Then I think we all left the theatre. I was in years the youngest dramatic critic present, and amongst my colleagues of those days there still survive Clement Scott, Sir Edward Russell, John Hollingshead, W. S. Gilbert, Moy Thomas, and Joseph Knight. The last is still well to the fore to this day. He was representing the *Athenaeum* at "Dante," at Drury Lane, a few weeks since.

We have no novelist with a purpose nowadays. Perhaps it is better as it is. Charles Reade, had he been amongst us, would certainly have turned out a romance touching upon Mr. Chamberlain's project for Home and Colonial Free Trade. He was the most impulsive scribe I ever met, and a brave defender of writers' rights. He would have made an admirable lieutenant of the late Sir Walter Besant, when first that excellent gentleman was establishing the Authors' Society. When he bade me good night at the door of the Thatched House Club on the occasion of our *tête-à-tête* meal, he said : " Well, my boy, writing is all very well, but I have a University Fellowship to fall back upon. If you think you can do better with a pen in Fleet Street than with one in a Government office further West, say in Pall Mall, that's your business. At any rate, I wish you heartily —good luck ! " On the whole, I think that wish has been fulfilled.

The prospects of the *Glowworm* could scarcely be ear-marked rose coloured. We had started with too small a capital, and were pressed for money. The directors had disappeared, and the proprietors were represented by the card-playing genius. He was very anxious to get rid of it, and what I considered at the time a brilliant idea occurred to me. There had been much talk of starting a daily in the interests of the Church of Rome. Already a weekly—called the *Westminster Gazette*—existed, in which Archbishop Manning was said to be interested. I sounded the proprietor of the *Glowworm* upon the subject.

" Have you any objection to my trying to get some sectarian party to take up the *Worm* ? "

CONCERNING THE "GLOWWORM"

I asked one day when we were considering ways and means.

" My dear fellow," he replied, " you can sell the paper to (and he mentioned the name of the traditional enemy of mankind) if you find him fool enough to buy it."

I considered this a sufficient permission to enter into negotiations with Archbishop Manning. I called at York Place, and was received most kindly. I was exceedingly nervous, as I had never had the honour of meeting the Archbishop before. Although a Catholic (a Papist, to use the old-fashioned description), I was a little uncertain about the proper title I should confer upon him. Should I call him " My Lord " or " Your Grace " ? While I was considering the matter the door opened suddenly, and I was within an ace of bending down to ask the blessing of a footman. I was told that the Archbishop would see me directly. In due course he appeared, and seeing my nervousness — for I knocked over a chair in my greeting—put me at my ease at once by saying that he was very pleased to see me, and knew the works of my father, *The Comic Histories of England and Rome*, intimately. Thus encouraged, I began. I told the Archbishop that I was the editor of the *Glow-worm*—no doubt he had seen it ?

" Well, I confess I have not," said the Archbishop.

" You will see, my Lord," I said, producing a bundle, " that it has a dual advantage. Some of the copies are sold in the streets, and get as largely circulated as the *Evening Standard*—a paper which I venture to suggest, your Grace, is estimated at an exaggerated value."

I was very bitter about the *Evening Standard*, as its " Last Edition " was the rival to the *Worm's* " Final Extra Special."

" Yes," assented the Archbishop ; " yes."

" Our coloured edition, my Lord," I continued, " you see we publish in two colours. Here we have a special edition intended for sale in the Alhambra. Of course, your Grace has heard of the Alhambra ? "

" Oh, certainly," was the response, although on consideration afterwards I imagined that the thoughts of the Archbishop were in Spain rather than in Leicester Square.

" You see it is a very attractive programme. The features are in red, the remainder of the matter in black. The Bounding Brothers of Bohemia—some say they are as good as Leotard —are in red, and so on."

" Yes ? " was once more the response of the Archbishop, in a tone of gentle inquiry.

" Then again "—and here I was carried away by my enthusiasm—" I have ventured to bring, for the sake of comparison, the final edition of the *Evening Standard* and the Latest Extra Special of the *Glowworm*. You will see, my Lord, the superiority, the distinct superiority, of the latter over the former. See, your Grace, we give in this column the names of the jockeys and the prices at starting. Take the same race in the pages of the *Evening Standard*, and both pieces of information are conspicuous by their absence."

" Yes ? "

" Well, your Grace, it has occurred to me that under all the circumstances of the case, it would be a magnificent move to acquire the *Glowworm* to represent the interests of what Protestants call the Church of Rome in England."

The Archbishop smiled, patted me on the shoulder as I stood before him, and asked me a question.

" Don't you think, Mr. à Beckett, there would be something rather incongruous between 'latest sporting' and 'latest ecclesiastical' ? "

Not at all. I was prepared to argue the point. Then I offered to throw over the music hall editions, after suggesting to the Archbishop that the sporting characters who (with others) patronized these places would be none the worse for a sermon disguised in the shape of a leader. But it was not to be. Archbishop Manning was most kind and sympathetic, but he did not see his way to giving his patronage to my scheme. Any influence he had he wanted to bestow upon the *Westminster Gazette*, which he considered a very excellent paper.

" Although," he admitted with a smile, " it has not yet turned its attention—seriously—to sporting. But you must make allowances, Mr. à Beckett, the *Westminster Gazette* is in its infancy."

THE à BECKETTS OF "PUNCH"

I felt that the Archbishop was chaffing me, so I collected my papers and prepared to go.

"My dear boy," said the Archbishop, "I admire your enthusiasm, but you must keep it under control. Seriously, I do not think the *Glowworm* —to which I wish every success—is quite the sort of periodical for what we will call, using the technical sense, a religious paper. But of course I may be mistaken."

Then, in bidding me farewell, he told me, according to his custom, "to persevere." Acting upon the suggestion in this command, I called upon Sir George Bowyer, who at that time took a leading part in the sectarian politics of the hour. He was enthusiastic. Certainly a very admirable idea. Had I seen the Archbishop? I replied in the affirmative, and gave a brief account of our interview. His face fell.

"Oh, if the Archbishop said that, we must abandon the scheme. We cannot act in opposition to his wishes."

"Surely we have the right of appeal to the Pope?"

Then Sir George fairly roared with laughter. The idea of having a serious quarrel with our Archbishop because he would not push the *Glowworm* appealed to his sense of the ridiculous, as it did to mine. So I joined him in his merriment. But even after this long pause, I still think the *Glowworm*, properly handled, would have been a power in the land. My scheme embraced morning editions of (to be established) daily local papers. We were to have the *Bath News*, the *Plymouth Pioneer*, and so on. But there, the scheme is a memory of the past. I frequently saw Archbishop Manning afterwards, and he often referred to our initial interview.

" Well, Mr. à Beckett," he used to say, " have you come to tempt me with another sporting paper ? "

And so I had to tell the ex-gunner captain that my negotiations had come to naught. It was about this time, or it may be a little earlier, that I ventured to call upon my father's old friend, Mark Lemon. The post of dramatic critic of the *Sunday Times* was vacant, and I was given to understand that the then editor of *Punch* had considerable influence in the selection of the successful candidate for the appointment. I had not seen Mark Lemon since I was a child, and only knew him by repute as a gentleman who, for some unaccountable reason, had taken offence at a letter my elder brother Gilbert had once written to him. My brother had sent some small articles to *Punch*, which Mr. Lemon had accepted, and also some charming verses (my brother was a poet, and carried off the prize for English verse open to the whole school when he was a junior at Westminster) about the marriage of the Prince and Princess of Wales, for *Once a Week*. Encouraged by his success in the more serious line, he sent some verses to *Punch* of a graver character than those usually published in a comic paper. " I am afraid they are not quite what you want, but I hope you will give them your kind consideration," wrote my brother. They were returned with a note calling my brother "Young Sir," and advising him not to sneer at his father's oldest friends. Why Mark Lemon should have taken offence neither my brother nor I could understand. It is still a mystery to me. But I made up my mind to call, and was duly ushered into the editorial sanctum at Bouverie Street. Mark Lemon was courteous to a degree. He bowed to me as he offered me a chair, and his face was beaming with smiles. But for all that, I did not quite like the look of him. I told my story. I had had rather a hard struggle since my father's death, and was trying to make my living out of journalism. Could he help me ?

" No," said he promptly ; " he could not."

I told him of the vacant post on the *Sunday Times*. I had heard he had influence in that direction. Could he exert it in my favour ?

" No," came the reply promptly ; " he could not."

He said he wanted all his influence—if he had any—for his own family. Then he looked at the door. I got up to go, and shook hands with him. I expected him to call me " Young Sir." But no, he did not. Still I was greatly irritated. So when I got to the open door I turned round and addressed him.

" Mr. Lemon," said I, " I suppose there is not a chance of my getting work on *Punch* ? "

" Well, we always consider anything that is sent

to us, but you, with your knowledge of *Punch*, for I suppose you are old enough to have heard your father speak about his connexion with *Punch* ? "

" Yes, I have heard my father speak about *Punch*."

" Quite so. Then you will know that the staff of *Punch* is a very close one, and there is not much chance for outsiders."

" Then you don't think I have much chance of getting work on *Punch* ? "

" To be frank with you, I don't think you have any chance." And he bowed me out.

When I was once more on the flags of the pavement of Bouverie Street I thought the matter over. I have always hated to be beaten—a peculiarity I share with a very large number of my fellow countrymen—and I did not like the tone of Mark Lemon about *Punch*. Why should *Punch* be barred to me ? An idea suddenly occurred to me.

" By jove ! " I exclaimed, " I will have a *Punch* of my own ! "

And from this interview grew the *Tomahawk*, a paper which I have heard described in these later days as one of the cleverest of the period. Last year the Lord Chief Justice of England had to propose the toast of the Newspaper Press. This he associated with my name, and he spoke of reading the *Tomahawk* with the greatest pleasure, and wanted to refer to it. But I had edited the paper when I was literally a mere boy—when I was no older than my father when my father edited *Figaro in London*—and I wished no allusion to be made to it. So the Lord Chief Justice of England very kindly referred to me in general terms as a gentleman they all knew and all respected. Throughout my career I have ignored my connexion with the *Tomahawk*, and I have ventured to think that I have made my name— if I have made my name—in works in other fields of industry. Still, as I have seen references to the staff and editorship of the *Tomahawk* made not in the kindliest fashion, it may be advisable for me to tell my own story in my own way.

" Yes," I kept thinking, " why should I not have a *Punch* of my own ? " I thought of it more and more when the *Glowworm* became rather shaky. Of course, I had the formation of the staff of *Punch* at my finger ends. All I had to do was to get a printer and a staff. If I secured the last, it would not be so difficult to get the first. The idea grew upon me, and when Mark Lemon snubbed me I determined to defy him. But I made one condition—the new paper was not to be like *Punch*. We wanted something newer ! *L'audace, l'audace, toujours l'audace!*

My first object was to secure a good title. Shortly after the production of the *Glowworm* the *Pall Mall Gazette* had made its appearance. It was soon a success, owing chiefly to the support of the *Times* and a clever series of articles which attracted much attention at the moment, by " The Amateur Casual," otherwise Mr. Greenwood. The contributor to the *Pall Mall Gazette* gave his experiences in the casual ward of a workhouse. They were continued from day to day for several evenings, and caused a sensation. They even formed the subject of a drama, in which "the original Daddy," an official connected with the ward, took part. Of course, we of the *Worm*—a staff that included the present editor of the *Pall Mall Gazette*—were envious of the progress of our rival. The rival in question was described in its original cover as "an evening newspaper and review," and in its earliest days had an editorial soul far, far above sport. So it was our pleasure to refer to it whenever there was occasion as "our sporting contemporary." In those days we were particularly independent, and inclined, I fear, for chaff. An evening paper called the *Firefly* was started in opposition to us (I use the editorial "we" of the *Worm*), and greatly annoyed us by challenging our sporting pre-eminence. However, although we condescended to refer to the *Pall Mall Gazette*, we hadn't the smallest intention of advertising the *Firefly*. So we treated it with absolute contempt until the first evening after its non-publication. Then we published an obituary notice of it, surrounded by a black border and headed, " Death of an Evening Paper this Day."

So, having the *Pall Mall Gazette* very much in my mind, I went to the works of Thackeray for another title. I came across the *Tomahawk*, and that seemed a suitable heading. My father, in his *Figaro in London*, had talked of wielding "the critical tomahawk," and here was the germ of

the idea. Subsequently I heard the title had
been anticipated—what title has not ? I myself
have edited the *Echo* and *Black and White* long
before the present papers of those titles came
into existence—in a paper called the *Liverpool
Tomahawk*. So I fixed upon the *Tomahawk* as
the name of the paper that was to appear as a
rival of *Punch*, with the policy of being as little
like *Punch* as possible.

I formed my staff. I went to the earliest of
my friends, Francis Albert Marshall, who then
was a clerk in the Record Office. Next I approached Thomas Gibson Bowles, who had written
for the *Worm* and also contributed to the *Owl* as
an outsider, when it was produced by Sir Algernon
Borthwick, now Lord Glenesk. They both were
most kind and sympathetic. Frank Marshall
was enthusiastic, and subsequently invited us
to the first " *Tomahawk* dinner," in his own house.
Next I ran across F. C. Clay, the son of the
Member for Hull, whose father was one of the
original shareholders of the Strand Printing and
Publishing Company, the proprietors of the
Glowworm. He was a splendid musician, and
had been musical critic of the *Worm*. He assented, saying that he wasn't exactly comic, but
he thought "writing for the *Tomahawk* would
be greater fun than noticing music halls." Then
I asked Alfred Thompson to join us. He had
been in Cambridge, where he had helped to found
the A.D.C., and then joined the Carabineers just
before the Crimean war. He rather wanted to

CONCERNING THE "GLOWWORM"

be cartoonist, but I explained that I had already got a very clever artist on the staff, and, " to be unlike *Punch,*" we proposed confining our drawings to one picture. He consented, but on the understanding that if we produced an almanack he should share the pictures with the other man. I consented, and with my brothers and myself, the literary staff of the paper was complete. I must not omit, however, Mr. T. H. S. Escott, who succeeded me in the editorship of the *Glowworm*, and who wrote some very excellent copy, and Mr. Alfred Austin, who joined our regular staff after the completion of our first volume. I have left to the last a member of our body who certainly even then had made a distinguished name as a portrait painter, a scenic artist, and a draughtsman in black and white—Matt Morgan. I had seen him for the first time in the *cortège* of the present editor of *Punch* in the Exhibition Buildings of 1862. Then I had met him behind the scenes of the opera at Covent Garden, where Mr. Augustus Harris (father of the knight of that ilk) was the stage manager. Finally, he was intimate with another friend of mine, the late Charles Hambro, Member for Weymouth and Colonel of the Dorsetshire Yeomanry. We had a meeting, and we determined that the *Tomahawk* should be conducted on these lines. I was to be the nominal editor, but the cartoons were to be decided (as it is on *Punch*) by the staff. The real matter of importance was how we were to find the money to start it. All of us were fairly well off, but none of us saw our way beyond becoming the host (at our own expense) of one of the *Tomahawk* dinners.

" That would be a great saving," we all agreed, and Frank Marshall immediately commenced to rough out a suitable ménu.

" But how about the printing paper and the rest of it ? " I asked.

" Oh, that you must see to. If you are to be editor, behave as such."

So I had to take that department under my protection. I was fortunate enough to find a gentleman who had been befriended by my father when he was a boy at school. He was the son of an Anglo-Indian, who had been at school with my brothers. On account of the absence of his parents in India, he was left at the school for the holidays, when my father used to invite him to our house. This gentleman undertook to furnish the sinews of war for the production— printer, paper, publishing, office, and engraving —if I would find the literary staff. We were to leave matters undecided for a month or two, and then we were to come to a definite arrangement. For the moment all the work was being done free, gratis and for nothing. We were to divide the profits later on, when we had earned them.

Chapter V

A SATURDAY JOURNAL OF SATIRE

A T our first meeting we discussed the policy of
the *Tomahawk*. It was to be fearless, im-
partial, and to show in every line it was written
by scholars and gentlemen. It was to have one
cartoon ; that, like the cartoon in *Punch*, was to
be settled by the staff in consultation. We decided to do without smaller cuts, as it was difficult
to get any one to supply them. Its price was
threepence—a price subsequently changed after
a few numbers to twopence. And above all, it
was not to be a slavish copy of *Punch*. At the
time the *London Charivari* was going very strong,
thanks to the excellent work supplied by the
present editor. Very willingly, had it been possible, we should have secured his assistance in our
work, but of course he belonged to another camp.
However, shortly afterwards, when I started the
Britannia Magazine, with the assistance of Charles
Hamko and the Earl of Kilmorey (then Lord
Newry), the present editor of *Punch* wrote a most
excellent serial for us, called " The Adventures of
Major Blake," illustrated by our friend in common,
Matt Morgan. But as the *Tomahawk*, under the
circumstances of its production, could not be

exactly described as a supporter of *Punch*, we
could scarcely expect to be joined by the best man
on the literary staff of the *London Charivari*. I
should have been very willing to have served under
him—as I had on the *Glowworm*—as he was several
years my senior. But it was not to be, although
I am glad to remember that during the career of
the *Tomahawk* our friendship was close, in spite of
our belonging to different camps. After all, when
barristers contend in the Courts, as if they personally were the bitterest enemies, they very frequently return to their homes walking arm in arm
together. I have heard, too, that the pleasantest
dining club in London is one called the " Cabinet,"
consisting of members of Cabinet rank of the Crown
of both sides of the House. At this dining club,
I believe, politics are taboo. So when we chaffed
Punch, as we did rather unmercifully, the present
editor of that worthy periodical took it very
kindly. It was only chaff, and good-natured chaff.
It was in the day's work, and set down without
malice. So the present editor of *Punch* and the
editor of the *Tomahawk* remained excellent friends.
We shared the same rooms in Garrick Street, next
door to the Garrick Club, and when we had a short
holiday ran over to Paris together. Accustomed
to " amateur soldiering " as I was, I looked up to
the present editor of *Punch*—a decade my senior—
as the sub does to his captain, a recollection that
will remain always a pleasant memory.

A first number is always an important and
anxious event. The precedent was followed in the

case of the *Tomahawk*. Of course, the cartoon
had to be thought out a week in advance of the
publication of the paper. The staff had met in
consultation, and it had been decided that Britannia should be shown with a birch in her hand,
ready to punish a Mr. Beales, who at the head of a
riotous crowd had pulled down the railings sur-
rounding the Park. The Government were standing to their guns, and refusing to be coerced by
mob rule. We all thought the cut a very good
one, and Matt Morgan said that he agreed, so the
cartoon was drawn and delivered. Just as we
were going to press, to our great chagrin, Mr. Walpole, the Home Minister, surrendered. He saw
Mr. Beales and, trembling with emotion, told that
turbulent gentleman that he would not oppose any
further his desire to hold a meeting in the Park—
he could go there with his thousands without any
further opposition so far as he was concerned. So
we were launched with an absolutely inappropriate
cartoon for our first number. Here was Mr. Walpole—the representative of Britannia—patting
Mr. Beales on the back, and here (in our cartoon)
was Britannia (the representative of Mr. Walpole)
about to administer chastisement. In our cartoon
Beales was represented in an agony of grief when,
according to report, Mr. Walpole was the gentleman who had been moved to tears. There was
but one thing to be done, and I, as editor, did it.
I saved the situation by changing the title that
had been selected by the staff. I put under the
cartoon " But for Walpole." All this punishment

THE à BECKETTS OF " PUNCH "

was to have been meted out to Mr. Beales had
not the Home Secretary intervened. Britannia
was ready with the birch, but Mr. Walpole would
not let her use it.

But, as I have said, we could not have altered
the cartoon, for in those days " process " was
practically undiscovered, and the picture had to
be drawn on the block direct and then distributed
in cubes to the wood engravers. We could come
to the rescue in the letterpress. We took advantage of the situation, and published a set of
verses, supposed to have been written by the hero
of the hour, addressed to the Home Secretary.
They ran as follows—

> What statesman most my fancy charms ?
> Who saved me from my dread alarms
> From smarting in Britannia's arms ?
>   My Walpole !
>
> My foolish bray had almost taught
> A lesson I had little thought—
> Who shielded me from being caught ?
>   My Walpole !
>
> Who saved me by his timorous tears
> From all my fancy's idle fears ?
> We'll greet him with ten thousand cheers—
>   My Walpole !
>
> Who sported pleasantly with law ?
> Who placed the town within the jaw
> Of civic discord void of awe ?
>   My Walpole !
>
> Who kindly said, " Your little game,
> If played or not, was all the same
> To him "—Heaven bless his good old name—
>   My Walpole !

164

A SATURDAY JOURNAL OF SATIRE

Looking through the pages of the initial number of the *Tomahawk*, published on May 11, 1867, more than thirty-six years ago, it seems to me a very good one. It commenced with some special official information, evidently suggested by the same kind of paragraphs that used to appear in the *Owl* when " the brilliant private secretaries " were on the staff of that most excellent paper. Then there is an article upon "Criticism à la Mode," which satirized " log rolling." Then comes a very pretty little poem headed " Linda," which concludes with these lines—

> Linda when I praise her graces
> Tells me that there are
> Others fairer far,
> So I tried strange lands and faces :
> Find where'er I roam
> Fairer spots than home ;
> Yet shall home and Linda be
> Ever best beloved by me.

Then comes an " Extraordinary Meeting at the Royal Academy," in which the subjects of the pictures discuss the merits of the artists' production. The portraits all insisted upon being "speaking likenesses." The Dean of Westminster, for instance, objected to art advertisements. To quote from the article : " A little Miss Millais interrupted her minuet to request that the Bishop of London would prevent Mr. Walker's little boys from splashing her bright dress. His lordship patted the little thing on the head, in spite of her scarlet vestments, but gave her to understand that the little boys were worth a hundred red petticoats, and could not well be found fault with." Then an article, "Low Art in High Quarters," calls attention to the growing popularity of the music hall and the decreasing prestige of the opera. "Definitions for the Ball Room" describe "evening costume for men full dress, and for women undress." "Our own correspondent, with echoes from the Continent," burlesques the style of the Paris papers, in which the most commonplace incidents were reported with absurd exclamations of admiration, horror and cynicism thrown in to render them more appetizing. Then came a series of inquiries about the whereabouts of Mr. John Bright on the day of the riot in Hyde Park. The Emperor Napoleon is advised to mind his own business, and is informed that the assertion of the *Moniteur* that "the Member of Parliament for Hyde Park (Sir Bright) is in Paris; he has fled from his native land, Birmingham, disguised as a special constable, and pursued by the English aristocracy under the direction of Milor Maire," is absolutely without foundation. Then "Our Preliminary War Hoop" announces the paper's policy, which is summed up in the words, "If any one wants to know our opinions, we may say generally that we are bitter enemies to the whole tribe of shams." Then comes an article, "At the Council before Mr. Tom à Hawk, the presiding Magistrate," dealing with "a cruel case of torturing an audience." Mr. Dion Boucicault "(name and emblems registered, sole patentee

A SATURDAY JOURNAL OF SATIRE

of the personal pronoun I)" is charged with ill-treating a British public in the neighbourhood of the Haymarket by means of an instrument of torture technically known as "A Wild Goose." The prisoner is found guilty. The magistrate delivers the sentence : "Prisoner at the bar, I sentence you to be present at the second act of 'A Wild Goose' on three distinct occasions." " The prisoner burst into tears, and was removed from the court weeping bitterly." I have seen some articles not unlike the one from which I have quoted quite recently. Comic history repeats itself. Then came the "Money Market," a parody of City reports. The remainder of the number was made up of "*Tomahawk's* Preference Shares," "Couplets for Likes and Dislikes," a charade in common form, a most admirable criticism of the production of Gounod's "Romeo and Juliet " in Paris, evidently written by F. C. Clay, and "Les Mysteries d'Isis," in which I trace my brother Gilbert's hand. He gives the rules of the "Paris International Regatta — French Official Programme, authorized by Government." Here is the last regulation—

CLASSES F TO Z (VARIOUS):

Grand Prix International Five Thousand Francs.—Open to all nations. Fourteen heats. French boats to carry their own winning posts and to have half a mile start (see Rule 54 as passed by the Imperial Committee of Management). Breakfast (with meat or eggs), eighteen pence. This race will be rowed with topgallants, royals set and steam tugs in tow. An ironclad with the committee on board will lead each boat. No smoking or life buoys allowed. *Uniform* staff officer in the Marines, or from chorus in "Masaniello."

167

THE à BECKETTS OF "PUNCH"

seems to have occurred to the editor and staff of
the *Tomahawk* that something more emphatic
than two laudatory cartoons in the way of making
amends was demanded of them, and so when it
was expected that Her Majesty would reappear in
public, the *Tomahawk*, in a cartoon called ' God
save the Queen; or, the past, the present and the
future,' welcomed in anticipation the return of
Her Majesty to public life after her long and sad
retirement, and tried its very best to atone for
the attitude previously adopted.   In this cartoon
Morgan drew a figure of *Punch* (after Tenniel),
placing him beside the representative of the
Tomahawk, of course in an inferior position, and
showing both as making obeisance to the Queen.
The idea of coupling Mr. *Punch* with the representative figure of the *Tomahawk* was decidedly art-
ful."   I do not see where the artfulness comes in.
As a matter of fact the retirement of her late
Majesty from public life, to which the writer refers,
had been commented upon in the *Times* in severer
terms than those adopted by the *Tomahawk*, and
Punch had backed up the leading London paper
with a cartoon founded upon an incident in the
" Winter's Tale." Britannia was bidding Her
Majesty, represented as a statue, to be no longer
stone. And as to placing *Punch* and the *Tomahawk*
side by side, I am sure the artist had no intention
of putting the former in an " inferior position."
Were not the editor of the *Tomahawk* and the
future editor of *Punch* then on the best possible
terms, and was there any real ill-feeling (only a

little professional jealousy, nothing more) between
the staff of the *Tomahawk* and the staff of *Punch* ?
I venture to answer, although I have to go back
thirty-six years, in the negative. Dear me !
What ancient history ! Thirty-six years ago,
when I had not enjoyed for many months the
honour of having reached my twenty-first birthday ! But I reply to my critic.

For the first three months of the life of the
Tomahawk I was editing the *Glowworm*. During
those three months the editor, cartoonist and staff
were working gratuitously, as an equivalent to
the paper and printing and other incidental expenses incurred by the Anglo-Indian, to whom I
have referred. At the end of that period the
paper was an established success. Then there was
a terrible row—the Anglo-Indian wished to take
the paper as his own. For some time relations
were very strained. There was a prospect of two
Tomahawks or none. The staff held together,
and ultimately a compromise was arranged. We
gave up our proprietorial rights—save in the
Almanac, which was to remain our exclusive
property—on the condition that the Anglo-Indian,
to whom we made over the copyright, paid us each
a fixed salary. This agreement was to last for
a period of years, which period was never reached,
because the Anglo-Indian disappeared long before
the time arrived for its completion. The quarrel,
however, had one good effect. The staff became
their own masters. Until the strained relationship period the Anglo-Indian had had a voice in

our council, which was lifted up very often in
direct opposition to four-fifths of his colleagues.
When he became sole, instead of part, proprietor
we assumed the entire management, and to emphasize the fact my name appeared as editor on the
frontispiece. I may add that the staff in accept-
ing the situation were kind enough to say that
I had looked after their interests with greater zeal
than that with which I had watched my own.

On the completion of the various arrangements
which constituted me a salary-receiving member
of the staff of the *Tomahawk*, I resigned my
position as editor of the *Glowworm*. I found in
those days that the work was too much for me,
although some twenty years later I was able to
assist to edit *Punch*, and at the same time to
wholly edit the *Sunday Times*. In this connexion
I may tell an amusing story. On Saturdays my
work commenced without exaggeration at 4 a.m.,
and without a break—for I was reading proofs
during my meals—continued until 4 a.m. the next
morning. At that time the final revisions of the
Punch proofs were prepared for press at 8 a.m.
on Sunday morning. When the editor was away
that duty devolved upon me. Upon one occasion
it was fortunate. It was during the General Election, and Gladstone, as the warder, was represented as looking on at the fight. When I left
the *Sunday Times*—I had obtained the printing of
the paper for Messrs. Bradbury and Agnew—I heard
that Sir William Vernon Harcourt had lost his
election. Armed with this knowledge I was able

to put into the mouth of Gladstone, looking anxiously towards the struggle, " What has become of Harcourt ? " which amused the world very much on the following Wednesday. But to return, after filling up odd corners—two lines here, three there, and so on—with jokes made on the spur of the moment, I completed the pages of *Punch* and sent them back to Bouverie Street by the waiting messenger. When there were no suitable jokes in the overset I supplied them, and this further exercise of my brain fairly exhausted me. The pages generally took until 10 a.m., and then it was time to go to church. I was bound by my creed to go to church, unless there was some valid reason for abstaining from that duty. So I managed to go, until it occurred to me that sleeping through the sermon, and possibly snoring, was creating a scandal.

To return to the *Tomahawk,* the staff were a gay company. Nearly all of us at the time were members of the Civil Service, as had been the bulk of the staff of our predecessor, the *Owl*. We were pretty free and open in our opinions, but really not unkindly. Alfred Thompson was well up in the literature of the Continent, and was detective-in-chief of adaptations pretending to be original productions. For instance, we brought to book Charles Reade, who had claimed novelty for a piece produced at the Queen's under the title of " White Lies, or the Double Marriage." " Original," said Alfred Thompson, " stop a bit. We remember—and there are few plays that have

appeared during the last twenty years in Paris
which we have not seen—we remember a certain
drama in five acts which appeared in the Gaiety
early in the year 1852. The drama was written
by M. Auguste Macquet, and was called ' Le
Chateau de Trantier.' " And then Mr. Thompson,
or rather Captain Thompson, as he used to be
called on account of his severed connexion with
the Army, pointed out the resemblance between
the two productions. In the number in which
this article appeared there were two notices which
interest me. The first was an announcement
" that in consequence of the immense success
achieved by the *Tomahawk*, and its rapidly increasing circulation (already reaching 50,000
copies weekly), it has been resolved to enlarge
it from twelve pages, its present size, to sixteen
pages. We shall then be able to secure adver-
tisers from those disappointments which a limited
space has hitherto sometimes unavoidably oc-
casioned. So soon therefore as the machinery
necessary for printing this journal sufficiently
rapidly to meet the enormous demand shall be
fixed and in operation the enlargement will be
made. With the still larger circulation expected
from this important alteration in size the scale of
charges for advertisements will be increased to
£25 per page and 1s. 6d. per line." The second
notice in this number was one of the *London
Charivari*—" It is said that Mr. *Punch* has called
the censor of the *Evening Star* ' a silly and vulgar
person,' and it is known that the *Tomahawk* has

corroborated the words of his friend Mr. *Punch* in every particular." "Friend Mr. *Punch*" does not sound like any ill-feeling towards the Bouverie Street contemporary. This reference to Mr. *Punch's* estimation of the censor got the paper into trouble. A week later, under an appropriate heading, the following appeared—

" The staff of the *Tomahawk* insist that they cannot fight the censor on his own ground. He wants us evidently to advertise his own writings, and believes (we suppose) that he has paid us in advance for our puff by thanking Providence that we are about to enlarge ourselves ! *Eh bien !* not to be outdone in generosity we take up our pen once more to answer him (in spite of what he may hereafter be writing about) for *the last time*. We will try our hand at Billingsgate.

He called us	We call HIM
A liar.	A naughty story-teller.
A literary toadstool.	An illiterate Truffle.
A rat.	A sad dog.
A skunk.	A perfumed poet.
Weak and scurrilous.	Elegant and powerful.
Poison.	Milk and water.
An emetic.	A soothing syrup.

There ! we thought so—our friend has got the better of it."

The year ends with a good wish to every one. The musical critic (Freddy Clay) praised " La Contrabandista," written by our friends, Arthur Sullivan and the present editor of *Punch*—"The words of the book are rhythmical and fluent, and the fun is buoyant from beginning to end." This is the Christmas greeting. " The best wishes of the season," says *Tomahawk*. " The noblest precedence of all is precedence in good works, while there is no republic so honourable as the republic of brotherly friendship and charity. Let our list then be alphabetical while we run over the names of a dozen of the many charities appealing to us for help and succour." And then we gave a list of charities, inclusive of the Rescue Society, of which association more anon.

And up to this date there had been not one word of disparagement in the *Tomahawk* of *Punch or The London Charivari*, and the policy of the two papers (*e.g.* the desire to procure the presence of the Court in London) had been usually the same.

I have called attention to the Rescue Society, as this recalls to me the fact that I was in touch with the philanthropical Earl of Shaftesbury to see if something could not be done to remove a crying scandal which has now for many years been a memory of the past. We were terribly in earnest in the *Tomahawk*, and we tried hard to stamp out vice. There was one crying scandal, the site of which is now occupied by the London Pavilion Music Hall, which the editors of the *Lancet*, the *Guardian* and I tried to write down. I suggested to my two editorial friends that we should try to organize a body of editors and proprietors in London to consult and decide upon concerted action in certain press matters of importance.

A SATURDAY JOURNAL OF SATIRE

The late Mr. Wakley of the *Lancet* approved of the idea, but assured me that it was utterly impossible to do anything in the desired direction. Strange to say that many years afterwards, when I was called to a meeting of the Provincial Newspaper Society, and other proprietors, editors and managers were admitted to the gathering, my very proposal was adopted. But the Newspaper Society was founded (absorbing in its body the Provincial Newspaper Society) to protect the Press from the pernicious law of libel. Before Sir Algernon Borthwick, the present Lord Glenesk, took the matter in hand the case of the journalists was a hard one. However, thanks to his tact and energy—backed up with all the force of the Newspaper Society—a Bill was passed which has made matters better. But still there is plenty of room for improvement in the law of libel.

Looking at the *Tomahawk* Almanac for 1868, I find that Alfred Thompson was rather hard upon Tom Taylor, suggesting in one of his illustrations that the author of " A Ticket of Leave Man " and Charles Reade went to French sources for their inspiration. This may possibly have caused ill-feeling between the staffs of the two papers, as I find in the volumes of the Saturday journal of Satire a direct attack upon *Punch* on April 11, 1868, some eight months after the establishment of the new paper. Says the *Tomahawk* : " The *London Charivari* is decidedly improving. Its last number had one page full of the most perfect fun. We never so saw many good things together.

THE à BECKETTS OF " PUNCH "

We allude to the full-page advertisement of Du Barry's Delicious Revalenta Arabian Food. If the food is as rich as the testimonials, no wonder the consumers of it get fat." I am afraid that now and again the recollection of Mark Lemon's treatment of the younger generation of à Becketts came to the surface, as I find in the *Tomahawk* of June 20 of the same year : " Our innocuous old friend *Punch*, whose garrulous egotism sometimes does succeed in making one smile, talks with that dry affectation of waggish juvenility which so well becomes him of ' the baton of Field Marshal Costa.' The joke is rather above the usual *Mark*, and suggests another pleasing little jest (which our old friend is free to repeat as his own) about the last commander-in-chief being Field Marshal Costa. ' Ah, I see it ! ' says the intelligent tax-payer, ' and feel it too.' " Then there is a pause until July 25, when again reference is made to the famous sage of Fleet Street. Says the *Tomahawk* : " Our good friend *Punch* evidently reads his *Tomahawk* devoutly, for he continually produces jokes in his current numbers which have appeared in our pages the week before. Mr. *Punch* is quite welcome. It would be hard if we could not afford to lend now and then to an acquaintance who had lost all his capital." Not very savage, and rather suggestive of annoyance at not having drawn Mr. *Punch*. And I find this spirit running through the whole six volumes of the *Tomahawk*. An occasional little chaff about the imprint being the brightest thing in the number, and the illustrations of the advertisements being superior to anything artistic in the body of the paper and so on, but nothing really vicious. In the meantime the *Tomahawk* (irrespective of its occasional chaff of *Punch*) was doing really good work. Comparing volume with volume, the two papers seemed to be on the same lines. About one matter it was very decided. It did its utmost to suppress Fenianism, calling upon Rome—from a Catholic point of view—to put down that pernicious secret society. What the *Tomahawk* advocated was carried out in later years when Monsignor Persico, by order of the late Pope, visited Ireland and reported to him the condition of that country. Within a very short time of the visit Fenianism practically disappeared. One of the traditions of the paper was to oppose the Emperor Napoleon III. I am afraid that, although the policy was sound *au fond*, there was a tendency to select His Majesty Louis, because Matt Morgan, our cartoonist, was first-rate at a likeness of " the nephew of his uncle." Personally I was always pleased when the subject was chosen, because I knew we were safe for a thoroughly effective picture. And it was really wonderful how prophetic we were. We foretold that the commencement of the war 1870–71 would end in the fall of the Empire. Napoleon III was represented as the modern Curtius leaping into the gulf labelled " War," which was destined to destroy him. In this the *Tomahawk* was on all fours with *Punch*, which produced about this time Tenniel's admirable drawing

THE à BECKETTS OF " PUNCH "

of " The Warning on the Way," in which the great Napoleon was shown waving back to his nephew and the heir of the dynasty. Again, there was a picture in the *Tomahawk* long before the event showing the destruction of Paris by the fire of the Revolution. In its Almanac of 1869 the *Tomahawk* published the following—

CURIOUS DOCUMENT
posted up in every town in England.
To a paper
which has for years
supported a policy of perfect fairness
to all things and everybody
which has become the hope of the Weak
the terror of the wicked
the particular horror of
H. I. M.
Napoleon III
Emperor of the French
and all who support his policy
which has put down quacks
of all kinds and every denomination
in fact
TO TOMAHAWK
the wonder of the age
the gift of
an enormous circulation
is presented
by a
Grateful People.

This was scarcely exaggerated praise, although self. I have been led into this disquisition about the *Tomahawk* by reading the article to which I have referred in the *Pall Mall Magazine*. The paper was published when I was in my early twenties, and during a busy life I have not had too much leisure for reading documents of the distant past. But I thought it well to see if there was a joint in my armour exposed to a sabre thrust. Well, no, I can see nothing in the *Tomahawk* from my pen that I would not have written to-day. The chaff of *Punch* was good natured but regrettable, for my father had been known as " à Beckett of *Punch* " and was proud of the title. My *confrères* Frank Marshall and Alfred Thompson were a little too enthusiastic, perhaps, in pressing their views, but my brother Gilbert, Alfred Austin and myself were calm and dispassionate. I have never been too fond of politics, as a man who is by nature a Tory finds it a little difficult to row in the same boat with Radicals. That I belonged to the Radical boat gratitude demanded, as the Radicals for many years were the champions of Catholic Emancipation. But when my old chief—I was for some years his private secretary—the Duke of Norfolk joined Lord Salisbury's Ministry I felt that I was at last at liberty to become an official of the Primrose League. So during my connexion with the *Tomahawk* my work was in the direction of domestic reform with one great political object in view—the maintenance of the inviolability of the British Empire.

My friend Mr. M. H. Spielmann, in his excellent *History of Punch*, to which I have frequently referred, speaks of the *Tomahawk* as follows :—
" Mr. Arthur à Beckett started a satirico-humorous

paper of great ability and promise, the staff including himself and his brother, Matt Morgan, Frederick Clay and Frank Marshall, with Messrs. Alfred Thompson, Austin, T. G. Bowles and T. H. Escott—most of them civil servants. But in the first tide of its success its commercial foundations were weakened by one in the managerial department and the whole thing came to the ground." This very concisely tells the story. The Anglo-Indian proprietor disappeared, and after a gallant fight the paper followed his example. Fortunately all the staff—like the present staff of *Punch*—were not absolutely dependent upon their pens for their livelihood. So we bade one another good-bye, to meet again soon afterwards. As for myself, I thought I would see what they were doing in France and Germany, and started as special correspondent to the *Standard* and the *Globe*, and after spending the autumn and winter round and about Amiens and then at Cologne and the Rhine during the war of 1870–71, came back to England, first to be Secretary of the National Chamber of Trade and next to exchange that post for the private secretaryship of the Duke of Norfolk.

So ended my connexion with the *Tomahawk*. It was wielded wisely or unwisely in the days of my early manhood. When the hatchet was buried I was friends with all my staff and knew most of the contributors of *Punch*, which in truth had never been a rival publication. So the hatchet was buried in peace.

Chapter VI

MY EXPERIENCE OF THE "PUNCH" TABLE

I HAVE to thank the present editor of *Punch* for my appearance at the *Punch* Table. From the time of our working together on the *Glowworm*, during the season I was connected with the *Tomahawk* (a periodical which gave his portrait as one of the distinguished contributors to *Britannia*, my magazine), until 1874, my first appearance in *Punch*, our friendship remained uninterrupted. Early in this year he had brought up my name at the *Punch* Table. Tom Taylor, the then editor, had objected to one of the articles that had appeared in the *Tomahawk*. In this article, published a good six years before, the writer was supposed to have turned into ridicule a marriage of two celebrities. My friend asked for an explanation and I turned up the article. On inspection the article was found to be absolutely inoffensive to the celebrities. It was a skit upon the practices of certain of the public, rushing to see sights and treating a church as if it were a theatre. On the occasion to which the article referred, the clergyman conducting the marriage ceremony had absolutely to remonstrate with the congregation, who were standing on the seats of pews and using opera glasses. My friend arranged to carry down a volume of the *Tomahawk* with the alleged wicked article and challenge criticism. He again brought my name forward and once more the objection was raised. " How about that marriage article ?" asked Tom Taylor. The volume was produced, the paper was read, and found to be absolutely without offence.

" It is the kind of article his father would have written," said good old Professor Leigh, and I understand that the suggestion was adopted by the two men who could confirm it, Tom Taylor and John Tenniel. A revulsion of feeling followed. Tom Taylor was the most generous of men—his kindness of heart was proverbial. Very shortly after that *Punch* Dinner, I was invited by the editor to call upon him in Bouverie Street. Strange to say I had about this time received a letter from my old friend Matt Morgan, then settled in America, inviting me to resuscitate the *Tomahawk*. I showed this letter to Frank Marshall, who was enthusiastic on the subject and wanted to recommence the publication at once. But it was too late. I was now fairly on the road to the staff of *Punch*. I called upon Tom Taylor by appointment on May 13, 1874. I have an entry in my diary for that day—" Saw Tom Taylor about *Punch*. He was very civil." Yes, he was indeed. Our interview was a sharp contrast to that I had enjoyed some ten years before. Everything was changed—even I think the room. Tom Taylor spoke to me of my father and said how pleased he was to greet his son. He had seen some of my work and thought I could turn out the kind of thing that they wanted.

" Would I like to write for *Punch ?* "

I absolutely beamed with pleasure. " Would I ? Wouldn't I ! "

Tom Taylor smiled at my genuine enthusiasm and told me I might send in what I pleased. I would know doubtless the sort of stuff needed.

" Of course there is only one Mr. *Punch*, and he has no rival," said Tom Taylor with a kindly smile. " But I think you are not entirely unfamiliar with comic copy." Of course, this was a reference to the *Tomahawk*, and I smiled too and assured him I would do my best.

" Whatever you do, keep it short. All of us are tired of long screeds, and if you can only keep your matter down to half a column, you will be invaluable to us. And mind, write legibly—you can't imagine what a difference it makes to the compositor when the copy is legible."

He spoke quite seriously and I was also grave. I found out subsequently that there was no more illegible writer in the world than Tom Taylor. On referring to my diary I see that on one occasion I actually had to take him his letter so that he might read it to me himself.

" What ! not understand this ! " he exclaimed. " Oh ! you are joking ! " He handed the note back to me. I am convinced he could not read it himself. Pleased as Punch I left Bouverie Street and set to work at once to provide comic copy. According to Mr. Spielmann : " A curious success attended his opening chapters. His first paper on ' A Public Office ' (p. 226, vol. lxvi). as well as the twelve following, that is to say, his contributions to thirteen consecutive numbers, were all of them quoted in the *Times*." True enough, but why call it a curious success ? Mr. Spielmann says that "I was put on the salaried staff after my fourth number, and asked to the Table in August, 1875." Again yes, but this is a prosaic way of recording what was to me an event of gigantic importance. My diary is full of notes of exclamation about this time. On Monday, September 27, I have this entry in my diary : "Did some of my copy. Found on my return home an *invitation to the Punch Dinner ! ! !* Hurrah ! ! ! ! Wrote to Taylor and Bradbury thanking them." Then, two days later, I find this entry : " Wednesday, September 29. In *Punch* as usual—my seventy-first appearance therein. Unsettled all day on account of the *Punch* Dinner. *Went for the first time to the Punch Dinner ! ! ! ! !* I was received most cordially. My health was drunk and I think I made a very favourable impression. There were present Tom Taylor, Tenniel, Sambourne, F. Burnand, Sketchley and Bradbury. As I said in returning thanks : *It was the proudest moment of my life !* Hurrah ! ! ! !"

Dear me ! how pleased I was ! But I have this excuse for my genuine delight. I had been brought up upon *Punch*. My father was à Beckett of *Punch*. And I could wish for no prouder distinction than to succeed to his title. Yes, it was indeed—up to that date—the happiest moment of my life.

So far as I can remember—unfortunately my diary is silent on the subject—I dined for the first time with my *Punch* colleagues at the *Bedford Hotel*. I was not quite sure of the costume, so I appeared in evening dress, which I subsequently found was optional. As it happened there were only a portion—a small portion—of the staff present. I knew them all with the exception of Mr. Sketchley, who was a recruit in the days of Mark Lemon. According to custom Tom Taylor drank my health, but my speech in reply was quite superfluous. Fortunately for me I had not the full strength of the company present or I might have had to fear any amount of good natured chaff. And, as it happened, I had scarcely the brightest possible specimens of the *Punch* men to welcome me. Of course the present editor was a host in himself. He was writing his best, and always amusing company. But Tom ,Taylor was a little heavy, and I was rather afraid of Tenniel. Naturally I stood in awe of him, as the contemporary and personal friend of my father. But he did his best to put me at my ease. He insisted upon dropping the "Mr." which I wished to bestow upon him, as the intimate of a senior generation. I had not met Mr. Sketchley before, and, excellent fellow as he was, he was scarcely an amusing rattle. William Bradbury I knew as an exceedingly kind man,

who had already given me two commissions :
one *The Doom of St. Quirec*, to be concocted with
the present editor, the other a *Scotch Holiday Book*,
to be illustrated by my friend, Linley Sambourne.
So I can quite understand why I suddenly rose
in my place and made a speech. As my intro-
ducer, the present editor of *Punch* naturally held
his peace and let me down gently ; Tom Taylor,
at the head of the table, did not refuse to hear
me. Tenniel listened with unmoved attention
and Sketchley and Bradbury cheered courteously.
But I do not think I should have been allowed
to continue very long had Du Maurier been there,
and I think Sambourne, and even Charles Keene,
would have interrupted the flow of my eloquence.
However, I was treated with extreme courtesy,
and my suggestion for the cartoon of the week—
which I had already discussed with the present
editor—was received with much respect. I was
intensely delighted at having at length reached
the summit of my ambition, so everything was
couleur de rose. Had I not experienced the
glamour of success I think I should have come
to the conclusion that the proceedings at the
Punch Table were of a sedater character than I
had anticipated. But as will be seen by my
diary—" I thought I had made a good impression."

Here I interpolate a word about diary keeping,
for the benefit of my friends of the pen. For
nearly forty years I have kept a record of my
doings day by day, but only the briefest record.

EXPERIENCE OF THE "PUNCH" TABLE

My diary has been a very small one, allowing about two inches to each day, and those two inches I have filled regularly. Had I had more to fill I should have no doubt neglected the duty and got into arrears, and once in arrears it is all up with a diary. In this diary of mine I merely jot down the briefest notes. I have been to a theatre and seen a piece. Down go the name of house and play. Now comes criticism—" feeble," " not bad," " good," " excellent." I go to a place and stay at an hotel—criticism on hotel : " Fairly comfortable," " dear," " to be avoided," " first rate," and so on. As a specimen I give an extract from the diary in 1875, for a date immediately before my call to the *Punch* Table. I was writing my *Scotch Holiday Book* for Bradbury and Agnew. " Saturday, September 4. At Edinburgh. Linley Sambourne spent the whole morning in the cold, sketching Edinburgh from the National Monument. Paid our bill at the *Royal*, not a heavy one, and came on to Stirling. Put up at the *Royal*. Comfortable. Wrote two articles for *Punch* but did not post them as Sambourne said he would illustrate one of them. Met Charley Collette opposite the Post Office, Edinburgh." Now this was written eight and twenty years ago, and in a moment I remember every detail. I see my friend hard at work with his drawing for our book. As I was not wanted for " a figure in the foreground," I took a stroll now and again, coming back to him to see how he was getting on. Then I remember that we were both a little surprised

THE à BECKETTS OF " PUNCH "

about Scotch prices, which we had heard before
starting were sure to be high and mighty. I
record my relief: " Paid our bill at the *Royal*,
which was not a heavy one, and came on to Stirling." The arrival at Stirling comes back to
me—the old fashioned hotels with " slappers "
—slippers—provided for any guest who wanted to
take off his boots, and then at the end of the day's
doings the reference to Charley Collette. In a
moment my old friend of the 3rd Dragoon Guards,
now popular actor and entertainer, rises before me.
I had been very pleased to meet him again after
a long pause. The last time we had met had been
at Colchester, where his regiment was stationed. We
had been playing in amateur theatricals. The piece,
"Under False Colours," was by Mrs. Steele, the
sister of Lady Barrett Leonard, who, with her
husband, Sir Thomas, high sheriff of the county,
had taken part in the performances. The cast
had also contained Augustus Spalding, then in the
Admiralty, as I then was in the War Office. As
luck would have it, I had to play in the piece a
War Office clerk. Spalding, who had an idea that
it rather lowered the dignity of the Service to use
his own name, always appeared on the boards
under the *nom de theatre* of Mr. Montague. He
ventured on some gag about the War Office and
asked me what was doing in town.

"Nothing," I replied, "the only sign of real
hard work is Spalding snoring at the Admiralty."

Of course this little retort met with a roar,
as my dear old friend Augustus Spalding was well

190

EXPERIENCE OF THE "PUNCH" TABLE

known minus his incognito to " our friends in front." Then, between the acts, who should march in to greet his sister the authoress and Lady Barrett Leonard but Captain Evelyn Wood! The gallant soldier has been promoted since those distant days; he is now a field marshal. All this is conjured up by reading the short extract in my diary. So my advice to literary men and, in fact, to everybody, is " keep a diary "—the smaller the better—but always a diary. It has been invaluable to me in composing this volume. Here are another couple of entries. " Thursday, September 30. Wrote and posted three articles to *Punch*. Received civil letter from Cowen. Wrote to Joe Hatton about papa's connexion with *Punch*. Went to bed early. Dining at the *Punch* Table before I am one and thirty—on the staff before I was thirty! Papa would have been pleased to have known this." " Friday, October 1. Worked away at *Punch's Pocket Book* and posted it. In the evening Frank Burnand dined with me at the *Raleigh* and we went afterwards to see Irving in 'Macbeth.' He was good." Then on October 3 I come to another entry: ' Eighty-seventh letter to the *Perthshire Advertiser*. In *Punch* as usual; my seventy-third appearance therein. Wrote and posted an article for *Punch*. Was introduced by Dick Grain to a French novelist who knew me as the ' Foe of the Emperor.' Dined at the *Punch* Dinner. Present : Tom Taylor, Du Maurier, Tenniel, Frank Burnand, C. Keene, Percival Leigh, Sketchley, Sambourne,

191

and Bradbury. The full staff. Heard that R. Doyle was coming back to *Punch*, very pleased. Made a mistake in the time of the dinner. The next week I found my suggestion for the cartoon adopted." Now the allusion to Dick (Corney) Grain immediately recalls the incident to which I refer. We lived in chambers in 4, Pall Mall Place, I on the third *étage*, he on the fourth. I remember when I was hard at work upon my article for *Punch*, he rushed down to tell me that I must come upstairs to be introduced to a Frenchman who had insisted upon seeing me. He said that the attacks on the Emperor Napoleon in the *Tomahawk* had overthrown the Empire—had saved France ! He was enthusiastic, so Dick said, about my power, my iron will, my magnificent enmity to one who had betrayed France ! I must come up ! I was wearing a dressing gown and looking anything rather than pugnacious. In fact my general appearance was suggestive of mildness at its mildest. But I came up. Dick threw open the door and ushered me in to the most desperate looking desperado I have ever met, with the words : " Behold the foe of the Emperor ! " Upon which the desperado seized both my hands and went down on his knees before me ! I was never more startled in my life, and my embarrassment was increased when he insisted upon hailing me " as the saviour of La Belle France ! " All I could do was to say, " Not at all," and that he was " very good."

Then the reference to R. Doyle takes me by

surprise. As I have said, I had seen Dicky Doyle in the early days of the *Tomahawk*. It was at the time when the Anglo-Indian became possessed of the property and the staff were contemplating starting an opposition. The name of the new paper was to have been *Figaro*, and I hoped to add to the existing staff of the *Tomahawk* Doyle and one or two others. This was ten years earlier than my record in my diary. And the matter was mentioned at a meeting of the full staff. I wonder how the matter came about. Evidently the idea was favourably received. Practically, the place occupied by Doyle had never been filled up. Shortly after his secession from *Punch* his work had been taken up to some degree by Tenniel. The great cartoonist could, and, I venture to add, can turn his hand to anything. It was as easy for him to draw the gnomes and fairies that delighted Richard Doyle, as to compose the cartoons for the House of Lords, contribute to the Royal Institute of Painters in Water Colours, or supply the *Punch* cartoon. Now, for a time, Linley Sambourne to some extent took up the running, but there was no real successor to the quaintness of Doyle, until Bennett joined the staff. He died young, and then the post of artist in the beautiful and grotesque to *Punch* became vacant. So it is interesting to note that on October 13, 1875, there was a rumour in the air at the *Punch* Table that Richard Doyle was reconciled to his old friends and thought of returning to his old allegiance—an allegiance which was as absolute as any of his colleagues until the *force majeure* of religion made him hand in his resignation.

From the date I have given I was a constant attendant at the *Punch* Table, until June 4, 1902. Following the precedent set by my father I was seldom absent from the Council Room. During the editorship of Tom Taylor I had comparatively an easy time. In 1887 I even managed to get away for a month's or five weeks' holiday, which I spent in a trip to Switzerland and Italy. But when I was enjoying myself in Venice I got a kindly reminder from Tom Taylor that the cuts for the Almanac would be settled early in October and would I get back as soon as I could. Of course obedience was the first law of *Punch's* service, and post haste I travelled back to Bouverie Street, leaving my wife and her mother to follow me more leisurely. But in the days of Tom Taylor it was a pleasant servitude. All the members of the staff took part in the discussion of the cartoon. The subject was nearly invariably started by the editor. Then the ball commenced and every one had his say. As a rule, especially on any subject connected with Russia, the editor's proposal was severely criticised. Tom Taylor, however, took the strictures in perfectly good part, merely remarking every now and again. " My dear fellows," he used to say confidentially, " do you know that you are talking strong-expressioned nonsense ? " At this declaration of opinion we all laughed, and then renewed our objections.

When I took my place at the *Punch* Table in the

historic quarters in Bouverie Street, all the staff were known to me, with the exception of Keene and Du Maurier, whose acquaintance I then made. Linley Sambourne, as will be seen from the extract I have given from my diary, had taken share in a tour in the Highlands of Scotland in the last autumn, so we met as travelling companions. But I had known my friend for many a year before we paid our visit in common to North Britain. He had come on behalf of *Punch* to Aldershot during the first autumn manœuvres when I was doing wonders with a company of militia. My regiment, now the Seventh Battalion of the Prince Consort's Own Rifle Brigade, has been immortalized by Charles Keene. The artist very kindly presented me with the original drawing in exchange for the joke. Keene drew himself as an adjutant in an orderly room, interviewing a rather undersized militiaman.

" And who may you be ? " asked the adjutant.

" Please, sir, I am the Seventh Battalion of the Prince Consort's Own Rifle Brigade, better known as the Tower 'Amlets Milishy." And we were better known by the latter territorial title.

When Sambourne joined me—he found me, I hope, no end of a soldier. I was delighted with my men, every one a good sort. They were nearly all costermongers in private life and could march on for ever. I was in command of a company, and it was my duty to see that my men were safely under canvas before I looked after my own comforts. So on one occasion when we had to pitch our tents I found that the supply of pegs was exhausted before my own modest shelter was put up. " Never mind, capting," said one of my men, " don't you worry yourself—wait till its dark and we will see to *your* tent." They were as good as their word. When I returned to my quarters I found them a mass of pegs. I did not inquire too severely from whence the supports came. I have no further knowledge of the matter, save I was told later on that many of the tents in the lines near our battalion had come to grief. The general opinion was that in the hurry of pitching the canvas it had been underpegged.

As General Opinion was evidently my superior officer, I thought it strict discipline to adopt his view rather than to accept my own private judgment.

Sambourne and I had thoroughly enjoyed ourselves. I managed to get away with a brother officer to dine with my future *Punch* colleague at a local inn. Truth to tell, as we were in the enemies' country, if we had been taken prisoners we should have been liable to all sorts of imaginary punishments. When we bade our host good-bye we had to run the enemies' sentries.

" Who goes there ? " said one of these guardians.

" A friend ! "

" Pass friend and give the countersign."

" Don't know it," returned my comrade, imagining that our next moment would be our last of liberty ! " Don't know it ! "

" But I do ! " replied the sentry, a volunteer,

"it's 'Windsor.'" And then we got home safely, very much impressed with the thorough efficiency of one of our citizen soldiers, or, as some one has called them, " our twenty-third line of defence."

During our trip in the Highlands, Sambourne had collected a number of most admirable drawings. He never lost a chance. Once when we were in Gareloch, on the Sabbath, he would make a drawing that nearly incensed the entire fisherman population to lynch us. My poor friend was suffering from faceache, but still stuck to his easel in spite of a murmur of indignation. He got rid of me by insisting that I would improve the composition by standing in the foreground. I was regarded as a heathen because, according to my drawing, I was unable to go to church (kirk), and the population thought I was as bad as the other man. Fortunately, before we had furnished the subject for a paragraph under the heading of " Popular Murder of Two Writers for *Punch*," the faceache drove Sambourne within and I followed him. So I repeat my friend Sambourne (who sat beside me for many years at the *Punch* Table), was no stranger to me when the publishers of *Punch* entertained me for the first time in Bouverie Street. The Professor was in constant correspondence with me when Tom Taylor was away, as his *locum tenens*. A few years later, when the present editor succeeded to the chair I acted for him as Leigh had acted for Taylor. I have spoken of my friendship with Mr. Tenniel. The last time I had seen him in town before meet-

ing him in Bouverie Street, was at the Egyptian
Hall, where we were in company with the present
editor of *Punch*, and Mr. George Rose, who wrote
and entertained under the title of " Mrs. Brown."
On that occasion a conjuror who called himself
Dr. Lynn, was contributing a trick. He asked
for somebody's hat. George Rose promptly offered
his own.

" Are you sure it is quite empty ? "

" Think so ! "

" Why, what is this ? " and the doctor produced a loaf and some cheese.

" That is my lunch," promptly replied George
Rose. " I forgot to tell you that I had left it
there. And if you look more closely you will find
my wig. Please give it to me at once, as I am in
a draught and can't get on without it."

Dr. Lynn promptly returned George Rose his
hat and asked for another from some other member
of the audience.

The two men who were quite new to me
were Du Maurier and Charles Keene. One sat
next to me and the other opposite to me. I was
delighted with Du Maurier, to whom I have referred
in another part of this work. He was as kind as
could be, and although he seldom started the subject of a cartoon himself, always supported the
suggestions of others and proposed a detail that
added strength to the picture. He was the missing
link between the writer and the artist, the pen and
the pencil. Although towards the close of his
life he came rarer and rarer to the *Punch* Table, he

was always glad to see his colleagues at either Hampstead or Stanhope Terrace, Hyde Park. Almost the last time I saw him he was hard at work on his illustrations for his own novel, *The Martian*. I had to see him about some editorial matter and was shown up to his studio.

" My dear boy ! " he cried, " you are just the fellow I want. Turn the back of your head to me and it will do nicely for my Cardinal's." Then he apologized for choosing the back of .my head. " Of course your face is preferable, but there is more force of character in the back of the head. So think your hardest, because remember you are a cardinal."

He was the most charming of companions and delighted to hear all the chit-chat of Bouverie Street. Moreover, he was very sympathetic—I hold many valued letters that he sent me. When I was married, and when I lost my eldest son, when I had to mourn my brother's death—the first note of congratulation or sympathy came from Du Maurier. He was fond of the Army, and knowing my foible used to draw me out. But he was immensely pleased when his eldest son got his commission, and it would have been a delight to have learned that that son had become a D.S.O. Sometimes we spoke of serious things as we sat at the *Punch* Table. He said he wished to believe, but did not know. But I feel that his was the nature that belonged to the best of men—those men who obtain most readily the mercy we all require.

THE à BECKETTS OF " PUNCH "

Charles Keene was very reserved. When I joined the *Punch* Table he was quieter than the rest. He seemed to enjoy the jokes that flew about in more or less profusion. But he was ailing. He had been a most active and enthusiastic volunteer but had retired from the service. He was a constant smoker, and the cruellest deprivation was to give up, under doctor's orders, tobacco. I copy a letter I received from him shortly before he died.

> " 112, Hammersmith Road,
> " West Kensington.
>
> " Dear à Beckett,
> " Thank you for your kind note. I would like very much to come to the dinner to-morrow, but I don't feel well enough. I enjoyed the meeting last Wednesday week and the dinner. But careful as I was, the healthy profusion of the feast tempted me and I suffered afterwards ! Commend me to all who turn up, and I hope I may get my tobacco taste back again, and be able to ply a better knife and fork than I can do now. I noticed the change in the cut, but editors are an obstinate sort !
> " Yours ever,
> " Charles S. Keene."

I had written to him during the dead season when I was *locum tenens* for the present editor, and I fancy, too, that I must have had to smooth him down about an alteration in the legend to one of his cuts. Charles Keene was sometimes a little mysterious in his jokes. There was one about Westminster, which to this day remains unsolved. When he was asked for an explanation—quite in earnest—he used to laugh and take it for our joke that we did not understand him.

Of course the letter I have quoted from Charles Keene was written several years after our first meeting. But to use a colloquialism he " was out of it " with the other contributors. When I joined he told me by request his favourite story about a Bakewell pudding. The point of it was that a man said that no one knew the secret of its con-coction.

" Well, I eat one the other day."

" Impossible ! How was it made ? "

" First there was a layer of toast."

" Yes," with indifference.

" And then a layer of marmalade."

" Yes "—still uninterested.

" Then a layer of bread crumbs."

" Yes," deigning to pay attention.

" Then a layer of blackberry jam."

" Yes," awakening.

" Then a layer of junket."

" Yes," really interested.

" Then a layer of eggs mixed with treacle."

" Yes," much interested.

" Then a covering of blancmange and raspberry jam."

" Yes," excited.

" Then a tomato stuffed with brown sugar."

" No ! "

THE à BECKETTS OF "PUNCH"

"And boiled for an hour with a black pudding and served piping hot on a saucepan lid!"

A pause, and then in a tone of awe—

"By Jove! it *was* a Bakewell pudding!"

I may say that this version of the story is imperfect—I have been forced to imagine the ingredients of the celebrated comestible.

Well, for the next six years I was a constant attendant at the *Punch* Table under the kind and considerate editorship of Tom Taylor. He was full of hints and was for ever writing to the younger of his contributors. About this time I had a passage of arms with Edmund Yates, who at that period was always attacking the *Punch* men. I had crossed swords before when I had defended Hatton in the pages of the *Edinburgh Courant*, of which I had been the London correspondent. "E. Y." would insist upon calling my editor "Tum Taylor," which was neither pretty nor appropriate. "The Celebrities at Home" were making the fortunes of the *World*, so I tried my hand at them. Tom Taylor, who took a deep interest in them, touched them up and wrote one of them out of all recognition. They irritated Edmund Yates, and he went for "Tum" and myself, calling me "O'Buckett," which I do not think was a much better joke than the other.

Well, the warfare went on until one day I was asked (July 3, 1879) out by a friend in common, when I met "E. Y." face to face. We were perfectly civil, but of course behaved as if we had never met before. It was my pleasure to have to take down

EXPERIENCE OF THE "PUNCH" TABLE

Mrs. Yates to dinner. We talked much for a course
or two and then got back into the easy terms of
not so long ago. Our host was a Government
official who was fond of entertaining celebrities,
and I have a suspicion he knew something about
the feud and wished to see an end to it. The
Government official was very proud of his cook,
and used always to make a point of asking one of
his juniors to act as an assistant exhibitor.

" Jones," he said on this occasion, " you have
seen that piece of plate that was given to me when
I left the Blank Office for the Dash Department ? "

" Yes, sir."

" Would you kindly read the inscription ? "

Inscription read.

" And now what did you think of that new
entrée my chef introduced ? I mean the one with
truffles, oysters, ortolans and caviare. What did
you think of it ? "

" Well, sir," said the poor man, blushing with
nervousness at finding that he had the ear of the
table, " I thought it tasted like periwinkles."

" E. Y." exchanged glances with me, smiled and
five minutes afterwards shook hands never to
quarrel again. I entered the occasion in my diary.
" I made it up with Yates. Very pleased."

He was always amused at my reminiscences,
saying that he would never be surprised to find me
turning up anywhere, either as a commander of a
fleet or a leader of an army. Not long before his
death I had been writing a series of articles for the
Sunday Times called " How things are done," and

had drawn upon my recollections of the Bar. He
wrote to me as follows—

> "HOTEL METROPOLE,
> "CANNES,
> "*January* 5, 1894.

"MY DEAR ARTHUR,

"Tell us more about when you were in practice
at the Bar and cross-examined the man about that
diary. Meantime both of you take our love and
best wishes for '94.

> "Always yours sincerely,
> "EDMUND YATES.

"Blowing two gales and cold as Ramsgate."

I have already referred to Tom Taylor's illness
and death. Before the six years of his reign were
over I was doing a good deal of work of various
kinds. The present editor of *Punch*, before I
had joined the staff, had secured for ourselves a
commission from Messrs. Bradbury and Agnew to
write a Christmas Annual. It was to be called the
Doom of St. Querec. Our idea was the transmi-
gration of souls. We started with a legend
invented for the purpose of attracting public
attention. We laid the scene of "the doom" in
Brittany, to which agreeable country we had paid
a visit. The idea was that the Evil One could take
possession of a vacant body and restore it to life.
He gets hold of the body of a very good young man
and "plays the deuce" with the rest of the
characters. The good young man's body, before

the commencement of the evil One's tenancy has married a religious peasant girl. The good young man's body—plus the Evil One—appears and fails to recognize his wife. Ultimately all ends happily by the Evil One getting smashed in a fall of masonry, while the good young girl marries an equally good young man. It was a very thrilling story and worked out well. We christened it the *Doom of St. Querec*. We did not get the Saint's name from the calendar, unless it were from the Racing Calendar, as " St. Querec " was suggested by Dorling's Correct pronounced " creckt " Card.

After this we wrote another story called *The Shadow Witness*. Both of these have been dramatized, but have never seen the light, or rather the footlights.

When I joined the *Punch* Table the relations between the proprietors and the members were perfectly delightful. William Bradbury was never so happy as when he was entertaining his colleagues of Bouverie Street, and in the character of host was perfect. I have before me a letter from him in which, asking us to dinner, he writes—" Excuse brevity, levity, and bring your own jollity.— Yours, W. H. BRADBURY. Arthur à Beckett, Esq." The first idea of our stories was to bring them out in monthly numbers to continue for some time, as my edition of my father's *Comic Blackstone* was produced, but ultimately the book complete in itself was decided upon.

It is not so very difficult to write in the " to be

continued in our next " style. Not very long ago
the enterprising editor of a well-known ladies'
paper hit upon the idea of getting twelve authors
and twelve authoresses to write a story to be published week by week between them. It was to be
called *The Fate of Fenella,* and the men and
the ladies were to take a chapter apiece alternately.
I think it was Miss Helen Mathers who led off and
painted the heroine as a very unpleasant young
person. Then came Mr. Justin M'Carthy, who
defended her. Then Mrs. Trollope, who pulled
her down. To poor Fenella's defence hurried (in
the next chapter) Dr. A. Conan Doyle, and so on,
and so on. From chapter to chapter, the fight
went on until, about half way, poor Fenella reached
me partly saint, partly sinner. It was my very
agreeable duty to read the story up to date, and
add a chapter of my own. I need scarcely say it
was a delightful toil to peruse the admirable work
of my colleagues. I read my quantum, added my
chapter, giving the story a lift on its way, and
then left my eight successors to follow my example.
I do not know how the tale ended, as I never read
anything after my (the sixteenth) chapter. And
I was not singular in this, as I have reason for
believing that none of my colleagues ever read a
line later than the final ten words of their own
contributions. In spite of this rather casual
method of turning out our work *The Fate of
Fenella,* I have been given to understand, was a
great success.

A propos of writing in collaboration, this very

EXPERIENCE OF THE "PUNCH" TABLE

Doom of St. Querec had for its initial chapter a rather heavy opening. Wrote my partner— "Brittany was all superstition till Christianity appeared. The Bretons are of the same race as the Cornishmen and the Welsh. They have the same characteristics. For age after age the Devil ruled in Brittany. He was worshipped with cruel pagan rites." William Bradbury wanted something "a little more catchy," so I furnished an introduction as follows : "'He died here, sir!' I shuddered. 'In that very chair,' continued the withered old creature, who was addressing me, 'I came in in the morning, and there I found him sitting in that very chair. He was stark and cold. His jaw had fallen, and his eyes were staring up at the ceiling. I shuddered again, and I regarded the chair with horror." This commencement was voted entirely satisfactory, and with it we went to press. When *The Silent Witness* was produced I was called upon to undertake similar work. "Something that will attract attention," said William Bradbury. "Quite so," I replied, and I began : "The murderer paused in his horrible work!" Again voted quite to the taste of the public, and passed by acclamation.

During the editorship of Tom Taylor I received nothing but kindness and consideration. He used to look upon me as one near at hand to help him in any emergency. For instance, when Mortimer Collins died he wrote to me to represent with him and the Professor the staff of *Punch*. I had known poor Mortimer Collins well when I was editing the *Glowworm*. He had been our principal leader writer in the days of our prosperity. He was a delightful companion, but rather too fond of invading the editorial sanctum in the hours that should have been sacred to proof reading. I found that he was not averse to a glass of wine, although not by any means a devoted votary of Bacchus. As it happened, we had taken some awful stuff in exchange for an advertisement. I will not mention the brand (besides it may have matured during the passing of thirty years) as I have a wholesome fear of the law of libel. When Mortimer Collins turned up one day at twelve noon to tell me in verse of the beauties of the river I insisted upon his joining me in a glass of (shall I call it) nectar in honour of the Thames. He enthusiastically pledged me, but put down the glass after a mouthful.

" What on earth is this ? " he asked, pulling a wry face. " Where on earth did you get it ? "

I told him from whence it came and said that it was largely drunk at our board meetings.

" Then I will never become one of your directors. For if they can drink this they must be dangerous lunatics."

Mortimer Collins had strong opinions and was in favour of the execution of would-be regicides if they were sane or not. " If they are mad," he used to argue, " they will be happier in another world." He wrote excellent leaderettes and usually dropped into verse before he got to the

peroration. Here is a specimen which appeared
in the *Glowworm* of July 7, 1866.

" We quite agree with the *Times* that people
who want a pleasant holiday trip and would like
to avoid battlefields cannot do better than go to
Ireland this autumn. Its scenery is full of variety,
and its people, with all their little peculiarities of
Ribbonism, Orangeism, Fenianism and the like,
are uncommonly pleasant and hospitable. Peg
of Limaverody is dead or married we fear, for a
good many years have slipped away since Mr.
Thackeray fell in love with her ; but at many a
wayside inn you may see just such a maiden.

> Bare her rounded arm,
>   Bare her little legges,
> Vestris never showed
>   Ankles like to Peggy's,
> Braided is her hair,
>   Soft her look and modest,
> Slim her little waist,
>   Comfortably bodiced.

Take a trip to Ireland by all means."

Then when town was empty and most of the
staff were away on their holidays, either winter or
summer, Tom Taylor used to look to me to come
and help him with the cartoon of the week.

Here is one of his notes, written on a
half-page of paper and all but undecipherable
except by the compositor, assisted by " the
reader."

THE à BECKETTS OF "PUNCH"

LAVENDER SWEEP,
WANDSWORTH,
January 4, 1876.

" DEAR à BECKETT,

" I am prevented from coming out by a bronchial attack.   I have written to ask them to put off the dinner at the *Bedford* and to ask Tenniel to dine here at seven instead.   Will you come and settle the l.c. (large cut).   Many happy new years.

" Very truly yours,

" TOM TAYLOR.

" A. à Beckett, Esq."

The reference to the *Bedford* showed that Bouverie Street was either under repair or the dinner was expected to be so small that it was considered better to hold it at the hotel in Covent Garden then patronized by Mr. *Punch*.   It was at that hotel that I was received as a new boy the year before.   There had been a long pause between my appearance and " the new boy " who preceded me ; Mr. R. F. Sketchley had been called to the Mahogany Tree in 1868.   But in 1877 there was to be another " new boy " in the person of my friend the late Mr. E. J. Milliken, who was a great addition to our little party.   When he first appeared he was silent and apparently nervous.   He took very little part in the composition of the cartoons for a while, but only for a while.   He evidently was taking stock of the company.   Professionally, from a *Punch* point of view, he was considerably our junior. There were the veterans which ended with the present editor, and even "the new boy" (myself) was a son of his father, one of the founders of the paper. But soon the quiet Mr. E. J. Milliken, who created early in his Bouverie Street career the character of 'Arry, began to make his mark. His verse was better than his prose (although many of his prefaces were polished performances) and he had a natural talent for the designing of cartoons. When everybody was lazy (of course *never* the case) the custom was to fall back upon Milliken. He used to wait until there was a pause in the rather frivolous conversation and then suggest something that was exactly "right." There was an amused silence when he took out his notebook and leisurely read from its pages.

"Capital!" cried every one, with a sigh of relief, especially Kiki Du Maurier, who was glad to "cut the cackle and get to the 'osses," as Du Crow was reported to have suggested when one of his equestrian company got permission to put up "Hamlet" for his benefit. Kiki liked to know that business was over and the time for pleasure, otherwise conversation, had been reached. But E. J. M. was more than a cartoon concocter and an author of 'Arry verse. He was equal to poetry. I happen to have some verses that he wrote especially for a song composed by my wife. Here they are—

THE à BECKETTS OF "PUNCH"

SUNSHINE IN SONGLAND.

Sunshine in Songland, roses are red,
Melody's with us, mists now are fled—
Melody quickens, Hope beateth high
Shadowless under a shadowless sky.
Philomel pipes in the flowering grove,
The lark trills lyrics of dauntless love—
Who says the world's a round of wrong ?
Whilst life has sunshine and summer has song ?

Sunshine in Songland—there we will dwell
With radiant rose and the brave bluebell—
In golden June whilst the blood runs warm
And fears not winter and fears not storm.

Melody liveth in Memory still
When skies grow clouded, hearts grow chill,
True love is deathless, faithful, strong,
Who dream with summer and dwell with song—
Echoes of all the heart holds fair,
Whisper in Songland's mystical air—
True love is deathless, faithful, strong,
In that sweet dreamland of summer and song.

(This poem is copyright and may not be reprinted without permission.)

Here is another specimen, hitherto unpublished, written for an autograph book—

EN PASSANT.

Muse ? What will you for my lady's book,
    Which should glow with beauty and gleam with wit ?
Bright should it be as the babbling brook,
    Light as the swallows that wheel and flit.
That pen whose point would these pages press
    Not here, my Muse, may you flame or flow,
Just touch the leaf with a light caress
    With lips like Dian's that kiss—and go.

But genial William Bradbury, backed up by his brothers-in-law, William, Thomas and John Henry Agnew, believed that all work and no play made Jack a dull boy, and in the interests of the paper it was advisable to keep all the staff in good spirits. So during the editorship of Tom Taylor we had delightful outings. On one occasion the entire staff went to the Derby on the top of a coach. The other day I came across a rough photograph taken on the course. It had nearly faded away for it had never been properly fixed. But in it I could see the faces of the Agnews, Bradbury, Tom Taylor, Tenniel, the present editor, Sambourne, Milliken and myself, and seated on the top dear old Professor Leigh. We had a very pleasant time, and the early snack before the more substantial lunch that was to follow after the big race was a dream that still floats before my eyes unassociated with a subsequent nightmare. We had a sweep, and I remember I won it. The Wednesday before the Derby there is always a sweep in Bouverie Street, and on several occasions I have been the fortunate recipient of the first prize. Then there were garden parties in Nightingale Lane (where William Bradbury lived) and Lavender Sweep, the headquarters of Tom Taylor. These *alfresco* entertainments were very popular, because it gave the wives of the staff (known in Bouverie Street as the " *Punch* ladies ") the opportunity of foregathering. Thinking over the first six or seven years of my connexion with *Punch*, I feel that the memory is cloudless. I can understand the devotion of my father to the paper he helped to found. I can appreciate the reason that caused him to hold dear the title of " à

THE à BECKETTS OF "PUNCH"

Beckett of *Punch*," as Thackeray was proud to be known as a writer for *Punch*, as Douglas Jerrold wished to be associated with *Punch*. My father used to call *Punch* the blue riband of the Press, and the title has found an echo in Fleet Street. But I am talking of *The London Charivari* of 1880, when Tom Taylor, William Bradbury, Percival Leigh, John Henry Agnew, Thomas Agnew, Charles Keene, George Du Maurier and E. J. Milliken were alive and the world was nearly a quarter of a century younger. But on July 12, 1880, I received the following letter—

> " WHITEFRIARS,
> " LONDON,
> " *Monday night.*
>
> " MY DEAR à BECKETT,
> " I am grieved to inform you that our dear friend and leader, Tom Taylor, died to-day.
> " Sincerely yours,
> " WILLIAM AGNEW.
> " A. à Beckett, Esq."

My diary has an entry two days later : " Dined at the *Punch* Table. Present : P. Leigh, Tenniel, F.C.B., Du Maurier and Milliken. Heard that poor Tom Taylor had died at seven o'clock on Monday morning. He had been well on the Sunday, but got out of bed to get a book, complained of faintness and was dead in five minutes. The clot of blood got to the heart. General sorrow at his loss." Then on the Saturday following I received a summons to dine on the coming Wednesday at the *Bedford Hotel* at a dinner at which only Percival Leigh, the present editor, Tenniel and myself had been invited to attend. I was present at the meeting—the editorship of *Punch* was in commission. On July 28 the present editor occupied the vacant chair.

Chapter VII

TWENTY-FIVE YEARS AT THE TABLE

I MUST confess that I was not a little flattered at being summoned to the special interregnum dinner. Not that it was entirely unexpected. The appointment of the editor was naturally by precedent considered by the literary members of the staff, so the artists were missed out, with the exception of the principal cartoonist, who of necessity must be present. Percival Leigh had acted as *locum tenens* during the absence of Tom Taylor for years, and the present editor, the senior member of the literary staff, was of course present. It may be that I was possibly selected from the other three members of the staff as I represented the traditions of the paper as the son of my father. It was not by my claim to seniority that I was present, for, although I was senior to Milliken, I was junior to Sketchley. However, I came, and my diary records my presence. At the meeting Professor Leigh made it clear to us that he did not wish to continue the part of *locum tenens,* and I have it recorded in my diary that the matter was subsequently discussed by the present editor and myself, how that vacancy should be filled in the case of his expected succession. A correspondence of a satisfactory character followed, and on October 9 the newly appointed editor informed me that he would look to me to take his place when he was absent, at an increased salary. So from October 9, 1880, to December 31, 1901, I occupied the position of *locum tenens*, an appointment that was subsequently described, when my rooms had to be ear-marked in the new building, as " Assistant Editor." So after one-and-twenty years my position attained its majority! I was on the editorial staff of *Punch*, as the " literary books of reference " put it. Very shortly after the present editor assumed the reins of leadership, Mr. Sketchley, who was not too strong and had a great deal to do as a Government official, resigned, and dear Professor Leigh continued his work as usual of sending in his quantum of copy, which I have shown was not always available for publication. And here let me say there was no one more generous or helpful than the Professor, who did all in his power to make the path smooth in my new position. Here is one of his letters he wrote to me after his accident, and when the arrangement had been for years in force—

" OAK COTTAGE,
" 201, HAMMERSMITH ROAD, W.

" MY DEAR à BECKETT,
" Accept many thanks for your kind note. You

will be glad to hear that I am getting on tolerably well, though still too lame to attempt getting into a 'bus, and, as you surmise, the late bitterly cold weather has retarded my recovery, but I hope the change will hasten it. I am glad Frank Burnand has had a better climate in Paris. I noticed in the *Times* a death that I thought might be that of a relation of Guthrie's.

"With kindest regards to my lady your wife and congratulations on your management of *Punch* in Frank's absence,

"Believe me always,

"Yours truly,

"February 10, 1889." " PERCIVAL LEIGH."

I have gone rather fully into the question of the control of *Punch* after the death of Tom Taylor. From that date until 1902 it will be seen I had occasionally direct control. I venture to believe the subject is of considerable importance. There is no paper in the world that has —I will not say had—greater influence in the creation of public opinion than *Punch*. I am proud to know that for over twenty-one years I was able to give my best energies to advance the interests of that periodical—a paper my father loved so well as the child of his brain and the originator of his title, " à Beckett of *Punch*."

In Mr. Spielmann's admirable *History of Punch*, which must always be of great assistance to those who require information on the subject of *The London Charivari*, appears this passage—

218

TWENTY-FIVE YEARS AT THE TABLE

" In August, 1880, after the death of Tom Taylor, Mr. Burnand, who had been acting-editor in his last illness, was called upon to take up the task of restoring to *Punch* its ancient reputation for liveliness and fun."

⸗ In my annotations to Mr. Spielmann's amusing volume I say : " This attack upon Taylor's editorship is scarcely fair. *Punch's* reputation for liveliness and fun did not require restoration. During Tom Taylor's editorship F.C.B. contributed his best work to the paper." I might have added that Tenniel, Du Maurier, Sambourne and Keene were also in their prime, and that the literary staff, besides the present editor—then a host in himself—had the advantage of Milliken's 'Arry papers, and a mass of matter contributed by Sketchley (a very polished writer), and several promising outsiders. With appropriate modesty I refrain from referring to my own copy, which extended to an average couple of columns a week. My work was continually quoted in the *Times* —on one occasion for thirteen consecutive weeks —and therefore seemed to be appreciated not only in Bouverie Street but in Printing House Square. The two earliest appointments to the table under the new editorship were my brother Gilbert, who was one of those promising outsiders on Tom Taylor's list, and the other after Milliken had ﾤied his hand as a Parliamentary reporter with no great success to a trained gentleman of the gallery, Mr. H. W. Lucy. Later on the literary staff was greatly strengthened after the death of my

brother by the invitation to join the table addressed to my friends, R. C. Lehmann (editor of
the *Granta*) and Anstey Guthrie, the author of
Vice Versa. But certainly the pictorial side of
the paper received a great accession in strength
by the appointment of Mr. Harry Furniss to the
table. He illustrated Mr. Lucy's amusing contributions signed " Toby, M.P."—a succession to
the "Essence of Parliament" created by Shirley
Brooks—and was very helpful.

Looking over old letters, I found one the other
day addressed to myself shortly after his appointment. He seemed from it to be most
industrious. His connexion with the paper (fourteen years) was too brief. As we sat near one
another for so long a spell, it is pleasant to me to
have my old colleague associated with me in the
chief work on the newest of the comic papers.
I refer to the paper I founded on Coronation Day
(1902) under the title of *John Bull*.

I feel sure that Mr. Spielmann will forgive me
for this note upon his important book, but Tom
Taylor was a friend of my father, and called me
to the *Punch* Table. Moreover, I honestly believe that *Punch* was quite as prosperous in 1880
as in 1903, and had as great a reputation for
liveliness and fun then as it enjoys to-day.

And here, as I have referred to Mr. Spielmann's
book, I may note that he calls attention to the
present editor's power of pun making. Says
Mr. Spielmann, " When a fictitious dinner of the
Punch staff at Lord Rothschild's was reported in

the Press, Mr. Burnand briefly dismissed the matter with the remark that the only dish was *canard.*" The Press had only mistaken one brother for another. The dinner was given by Mr. Alfred de Rothschild, of whose hospitality I have a grateful recollection. It conjures up a memory.

A very large round table indeed. I am present as a member of the staff of a paper my father had helped to found, and I am meeting my host in that capacity (like most of my colleagues) for the first time. But my host is a most charming person. He has sent good things for our columns, and is altogether a delightful companion—excellent fellow—*bon enfant.* I am quite pleased to think that the fact that I happen to be on the staff of a paper that my father helped to found has gained for me the invitation to be present on this occasion. Round about me are a Right Hon. Member of the Cabinet, an eminent physician, an influential member of the Lower House (on the road to a peerage), and above all and before all, Lord Randolph Churchill. It was the first time I had met one of the brightest intellects of the age, and, as it happened, it was the last. The occasion of our meeting was towards the close of his career. I was told that he was not in his best form, but for all that he was immensely amusing. His conversation reminded me of his elder brother's.

I recall another round table, where the late Duke of Marlborough was the principal guest of the evening. It was a festive board, and every one present was considered to be somebody. The gathering was the precursor of the celebrated *Octaves* of Sir Henry Thompson—the perfection of pleasant hospitality. My immediate neighbour was James Payn, the novelist, an admirable *raconteur*, but the Duke led the conversation. All sorts of subjects came up, but he was able to speak wisely and wittily about them all. We others were out of it, although as journalists most of us were omniscient. I felt that Fleet Street had lost a most promising recruit in not having secured this Admirable Crichton. With his knowledge and flow of language what an excellent leader-writer he would have made, to be turned on a few minutes before the formes were sent down to the foundry. When the printer was leaving a space over and the compositors were hard at work on short takings and "making even" from one another's sticks, he would have been the ideal producer of copy. He spoke slowly and in perfect English. When his speech was taken down and printed, the proof —so far as the author was concerned—would have been a clean slip.

I have said that on the occasion to which I refer my neighbour was James Payn, the novelist. I had just read *By Proxy*, and congratulated him on the local colouring. I asked him how long he had stayed in China. "I have never been in China," he said, with a smile. "You can get plenty of local colouring by keeping your eyes open, and paying an occasional visit to the Reading Room of the British Museum." I expressed surprise—I was very young at the time—that such local details could be secured without a personal visit to the places described. " Not at all difficult to manage," said Payn. " Why, I knew a writer who had never been farther from London than the Isle of Thanet, and yet he was always writing thrilling tales of the other end of the earth. He made quite a little fortune out of a book called *The Wolf Boy of Japan*. He did indeed ! "

To return to the dinner at which I had the pleasure of meeting Lord Randolph Churchill. He was the life and soul of the party, although the company was of the very best. I have a particular purpose in recalling this ever-memorable occasion. I have often been asked what gave me the idea of the *John Bull* Dinner ? I reply : That pleasant gathering under the presidentship of that most genial and hospitable of hosts in Mayfair. Our good friend wished to bring into communication a troupe of trained writers and artists, with distinguished members of (what I may be permitted to term in this connexion) the outer world. Both of my neighbours on the occasion to which I refer were bearers of names of world-wide celebrity. We had the pleasantest evening imaginable. All that wealth, kindness, and good taste could suggest was at our disposal, and I could not help regretting—with a recollection of having assisted at a staff dinner, at which I presided, consisting of Sir John Tenniel and myself—that all this excellent material could not be turned to good account. When circumstances made it necessary for me to organize a *John Bull* Dinner for the consideration of the weekly cartoon of the paper I have the honour to edit, the delightful entertainment in Mayfair occurred to me. I have to thank my kind and honoured host of that ever-memorable occasion for giving me the suggestion which has fructified into what I venture to suggest, is accurately described as " the famous *John Bull* Dinner."

But the idea of Mr. Alfred de Rothschild had been partially anticipated. At his dinner, the staff of *Punch*, as I have said, met celebrated outsiders who were able to discuss the current topics of the hour, if it so pleased them. As a matter of fact, " business " of that kind, I fear, was neglected, and " shop " was rather the exception than the rule. In the *John Bull* Dinner to which I have referred, the guests come to the dinner to assist in the concoction of the cartoons, and so far it has worked admirably well. But to inaugurate the present Editor's appointment to the chief command, every one who had been connected with *Punch* that could be found was invited to a banquet. It was held at the *Albion*, and I really forget how many sat down to dinner. Quite fifty, if not more. The moment dinner was over, and after a little necessary speechification, the new editor announced that the cartoon had to be decided. The suggestion was taken quite seriously by several of those present. My friend, Mr. Clement Scott (who had done excellent service to *Punch* with his capital poems), had really a first-rate idea for a cartoon—at this distance of time I forget its exact nature—but his suggestion was received with roars of laughter. And then it leaked out that the regular staff were playing a practical joke upon their colleagues of outside Bouverie Street. Earlier in the day we had decided the large cut, and we only were there to thoroughly enjoy ourselves, with thanks to the proprietors and the new editor. But really, with my increased experience, I am not at all sure that the combined intelligence of all those present could not have been utilized to have schemed out the subject of a cartoon. Of course, the number present on the occasion to which I refer was unwieldy. The average number—in the season and not during holiday time—of the *Punch* Table is about ten or a dozen. This can be increased to eighteen—the average number of the *John Bull* dinner, counting staff and guests—without becoming unwieldy. Of course, fifty was too large a number, but if the experiment had been tried of obtaining the subject of a cut, I do not think it would have ended in disaster. But no doubt it was better as it was, as a punmaker might have felicitously observed: "There were many other cuts—from the joint. Not only cuts from the joints, but cuts of some of the *entrées*, as the *mênu* was an exceptionally long one."

But certainly, if the table staff was not materi-

THE à BECKETTS OF "PUNCH"

ally increased, the art of outside contributors was largely widened. In the days of my father, and when I joined the staff, to write for *Punch* was an exclusive privilege. It was confined to men of the standing of Thackeray, Jerrold, and (perhaps I may be permitted under the circumstances to add), à Beckett. But this widening had two disadvantages—if it were a disadvantage —of allowing Talbot, Howard, and Plantagenet to be able to boast of being Talbot, Howard, and Plantagenet of *Punch*. But this policy, I fancy, has recently been reduced to some extent. Nowadays, Talbot, Howard, and Plantagenet, if they become " of *Punch*," are recommended not to become Talbot, Howard, and Plantagenet of any rival paper. Still, it must be remembered that everything has a commencement, and the Talbot, Howard, and Plantagenet of yesterday may become the peers of the most celebrated writers tomorrow. Besides these lesser lights, a glance at Mr. Spielmann's list shows how stars of the past may be included in Mr. *Punch's* firmament. Sometimes those stars might have been mistaken for comets on account of their sudden appearance and disappearance.

The title selected for this volume of necessity causes me to talk a great deal about *Punch*. To me naturally it is an entrancing subject, but I trust that the enchantment of the name will not make me forget that there are other things in the world, and that the chief object of an author should be to prove entertaining to his readers

226

TWENTY-FIVE YEARS AT THE TABLE

Years ago there was a comic song in one of the burlesques that owed its popularity to its refrain that " such a thing was good—but only enough of such a thing, not too much of such a thing, but just enough of such a thing." So in writing this volume, I want to speak of *Punch*, but not too much of *Punch*, but just enough of *Punch*. So I may say briefly that during the performance of my duties of assistant editor for twenty-one years I did my best to fulfil the duties attaching to the office with diligence and propriety. That I succeeded I have reason to believe, from the very kind and gratifying communications I have received during that period from proprietors, editor, and other members of the staff. I have a large number of letters testifying to this pleasing appreciation, which will be, I hope, preserved as heirlooms by my sons and (if any) future generations. When the editor was absent I filled his place and presided over the deliberations of the Knights of the Round Table. But until he died I had the greatest assistance from my friend and colleague, the late E. J. Milliken, who was always ready to support me in the hour of difficulty. He has been very properly described by Mr. Spielmann as " a writer of all work and general utility in the best sense." I myself had had fair experience in the same field of labour, but when I was fagged out (as must happen in the records of the best regulated writers), he was always ready when possible—he was terribly handicapped by illhealth, poor fellow—to come to the rescue. I

227

have the last letter he wrote to me. It runs as follows. (In addition to my labours on *Punch*, I was editing the *Naval and Military Magazine*, which explains a reference.)

> " WOODCOTE,
>> " 83, LOUGHBORO' PARK, S.E.
>>> "*August* 4, 1897.

" MY DEAR ARTHUR,

" I am mending—but 'tis mighty slow work. I had hopes of being able to attend the Table to-night, but when the hour arrived I felt far too weak to venture ; still, I am on the mend. I have been out for my first totter. Next week I hope to turn up as usual. Meanwhile, if there should be anything special you wish done, either for *Punch* or your own magazine, *I can do it.*

" I presume that Frank is away and that you are *locum tenens.* I am sorry not to have been with you to-night. I hope you are well and flourishing.

> " Yours ever,
>> " E. J. MILLIKEN."

He was right : I was *locum tenens*, and presided at the dinner supported by my friends, Tenniel, Lucy and Guthrie, E. T. Reid, Phil May, and Bernard Partridge. The next entry in my diary is a sad one. " 11th August. Presided at the *Punch* Dinner. Present : Tenniel, Milliken, Reid, Lehmann, and Partridge. Last appearance of poor E. J. Milliken at the *Punch* Table. I had a very cheery chat with him—poor fellow."

I added these last words on hearing of his death. He died on August 26, just fifteen days later.

And this reference to the death of Milliken reminds me that, like him, my brother, Gilbert Arthur à Beckett, also died in *Punch's* harness. Literally, he wrote copy for Bouverie Street on his deathbed. When the *History of Punch* came to be written, I had to see Mr. Spielmann, who was staying at Malvern, about my father's connexion with *Punch*. It occurred to me that I might ask him how he had dealt with my brother. I had in my possession a paper that had been written by some one who did not know my brother's history, which stated that probably Mr. Spielmann would say that my brother had done very little work while he was staying at Dinan. I was to ask Mr. Spielmann to alter this passage, as I knew that my brother had worked very hard for *Punch* in Brittany, and, moreover that I might call attention to his gaining the prize for English verse open to all the School at Westminster at an unusually early age. When I reached Malvern I asked Mr. Spielmann if he would mind telling me what he had said about my brother ; or, at any rate, let me know if he had made any reference to his stay at Dinan. Mr. Spielmann said he had written that my brother did not do very much for *Punch* while he was sojourning in Brittany. Then I handed Mr. Spielmann the document I had received, and from this document Mr. Spielmann corrected the proof of the matter dealing with my brother's connexion with

THE à BECKETTS OF "PUNCH"

Punch. My brother was proud, like my father, of his connexion with *Punch*, and when I saw him during his last illness was most anxious to know if the editor was satisfied with his copy. Years before he had edited a most clever paper called *Junius*, to which I contributed, and I am pleased to think that every paper I ever edited had my brother as a contributor. To quote Mr. Spielmann : " When he died—on October 15, 1891—a chorus of unanimous regret arose in the Press, for he was one of those few men who count none but friends amongst their wide circle of acquaintance."

The date of the death of my friend, Mr. E. J. Milliken, in 1897, reminds me of an effort I made ten years earlier to celebrate, according to precedent, the Queen's Jubilee at Gray's Inn, of which my father—in common with myself—had been a member. It certainly was a delightful time, and none the less pleasant because Mr. Lawrence Bradbury, son of my dear friend, Mr. William Bradbury, and his cousin, Mr. Philip Agnew, were members of my company. It came about in this way. On account of the Jubilee one of our Benchers—His Royal Highness the Duke of Connaught—consented to act as treasurer, and it occurred to me that perhaps His Royal Highness and the other Hon. Masters of the Bench might like to do something in the shape of a Maske—once a most popular form of entertainment on state occasions. I approached the Bench on the subject, and, to my great delight, and, I confess, rather to my astonishment, the masters took a most favourable view of the project. I was appointed Master of the Revels, and Assessor to the Maske Committee, of which my old and valued friend, Mr. Hugh Shield, K.C., was chairman. Our Royal treasurer took a great interest in it, and when the performance was held acted as host, supported by Her Royal Highness the Duchess of Connaught. Amongst the other royalties present were the Duchess of Edinburgh, Princess Mary Duchess of Teck, and the Princess of Wales, then Princess May of Teck. I say I had a delightful time of it. I had been always fond of theatricals, and here was something quite new. I was able to secure an appropriate piece, the "Maske of Flowers," which had been performed at Whitehall before James I by the Members of Gray's Inn. It had to be edited, as I have said before, and I edited it. Then I had to get a scene painter, and I went to Mr. John O'Connor, who had painted the scenery for the A.D.C. at Cambridge, and who had reproduced some undergraduate rooms for the Haymarket when Tom Taylor's piece, "The Lesson for Life," was produced with "Lord Dundreary"—Sothern—in the principal character. Then the dresses were undertaken by my friend, Lewis Wingfield (brother of Lord Powerscourt), and all was in readiness. Then, to my sorrow, I found that, although Gray's Inn was greatly respected in the Royal Courts, it did not rank high from a dramatic and vocalistic point of view. We had one giant amongst us, Mr. Louis Coward, and he very kindly accepted the part of "Kawasha," but there was no other Gray's Inn man available. So I had to go to the Bar Musical Society for assistance, and ultimately got together a company (including ladies) of some fifty or sixty persons. We prided ourselves on being members of the Bar, or (so far as the ladies were concerned) with relatives belonging to the Bar. As a matter of fact, all our fair friends were either daughters or wives of barristers or judges, with one exception, Lady Cadogan, who, however, had forensic connexions. My friends, Mr. Philip Agnew (son of Sir William of that ilk), who was an accomplished musician—he had taken his musical degree at Oxford—kindly consented to learn the harpsichord for the occasion, and Mr. Lawrence Bradbury, a capital actor and a first rate vocalist, became a leading singer. Both my friends were members of the Inner Temple. Everything now progressed favourably. We held our rehearsals in the libraries of Gray's Inn, I hope to the satisfaction of the students. Mr. Prendergast, who was responsible for the music, looked after the singers. Mr. D'Auban, the ballet master from Drury Lane, trained the dancers, and I, as Master of the Revels, exercised a vague superintendence over everybody and everything. One day, when I expected certain members of the Press who were coming to draw the old Hall, two or three intellectual gentlemen put in an appearance.

TWENTY-FIVE YEARS AT THE TABLE

" You come from the *Graphic* and the *Illustrated ?* " I suggested.

" No, Master of the Revels "—with a nasty sneer upon the master—" we do not. We are not surprised, however, to find that you do not recognize us, as we are only members of Gray's Inn like yourself."

Now I took in the situation at a glance. I had obtained permission as Master of the Revels— everything was done as Master of the Revels— to screen a request that Gray's Inn men who were willing to take part in the " Maske of Flowers" should communicate with me without delay.

" I am delighted to meet you," I cried, " but I have very little time at my disposal. Can you sing ? "

" Think so."

" Then in you go," and I opened a door. " Mr. Prendergast is trying all our voices. He says I won't do because I can't take the upper C with sufficient clearness and pathos. I am sure I could if I tried. But seeing about fifty persons listening makes me so nervous. However, you may be more fortunate."

My brother of Gray's Inn hesitated and was lost.

" Can you dance ? " I asked Number Two.

" A little."

" A little I am afraid won't do. I can dance a little, but in the *pavanne* you ought to be able to walk on your toes. I have tried, but I can't manage it. It hurts. But D'Auban will see what you can do. He's in there attending to about forty first-rate fellows. He will stop them in a moment to try your toes," and I opened a second door.

But my second brother member of Gray's Inn hesitated and was lost. Ultimately I appeased them by constituting them a sort of guard of honour of beefeaters under the charge of an enthusiastic artist volunteer (Mr. Martin, the barrister), who was not only an excellent advocate, but also knew the pike drill. For weeks afterwards I used to come across my fellow members of Gray's Inn doing all sorts of wonderful gymnastics with their sticks and umbrellas, to the cry of "one, two," "one, two, three." "Try again." "One two," "one, two, three." "Try again." Later on, during the performance, they were of immense service in keeping the orchestra within bounds, and a gentleman with a double bass invading a gold chair reserved for one of our Royal Guests. To make a long story short, the Maske was a great success, thanks to the whole strength of the company (inclusive of Messrs. Philip Agnew and Lawrence Bradbury) working with a will that was simply delightful. I really believe the Maske made the Inn. It cost a good deal of money, but since that moment to this our numbers have been steadily increasing, and from being an Inn with an average of two or three barristers to be called a term we have before now headed the list of the four Inns in our numbers of those waiting to be called. The Press was unanimous in our praises. Mr. *Punch*, perhaps, was inclined to be a little chaffing about the harpsichords—he called them cracked pianos—and other details, but then Mr. *Punch* (as he should be) is always hypercritical about the productions of his own staff. However, in spite of Mr. *Punch's* genial banter, as I have said, the Maske did a great deal of good to the Inn, and I have always been proud of my title of the Master of Revels. Years ago it used to be held by worthy gentlemen who sometimes had to assume the authorship for others. Bacon himself is said to have had a pen in the composition of the "Maske of Flowers." He may have desired to preserve his incognito, as some of it was not quite palatable to the Court. My editing, however, put things to rights from that point of view. I may add that Her Majesty the late Queen Victoria was graciously pleased to accept a copy of my Maske, which now forms a part of the Royal Library at Windsor. It was shown to me the last time I was in that part of the Castle.

Amongst the many bonds of union that bound *Punch* men together perhaps there were no stronger than the ties of the Dramatic Authors Society. As Gilbert à Beckett was one of its founders it may not be amiss to devote a few pages to its history. It will have been seen from the date of the production of my father's farce "The King Incog," that he was one of its earliest members. The Society did not then boast a secretary, but only an agent. Later on, as I have shown, Sterling Coyne took up the position. In 1871 I was enrolled a member and remained one until the hour of its dissolution. Of the members of the staff of *Punch*, Mark Lemon, Douglas Jerrold, Henry Mayhew, Albert Smith, Shirley Brooks, Tom Taylor, F. C. Burnand and my brother Gilbert were members. The original idea was to guard against piracy, and no doubt Charles Dickens had something to do with the proposal. I have referred in another page to the dislike that Dickens had for a premature disclosure of his plots, and the pains he took to circumvent the schemes of the buccaneer dramatist. The circuit system of Mr. Crummles was the order of the day when the Dramatic Authors Society was organized. Every theatre in the country belonged to it and was assisted according to its means of payment. It was the duty of each subscriber to pay so much a night and then send up the bill of the evening's performance to the Secretary of the Dramatic Authors Society, who entered in the amount to the credit of the Member. Thus, say Smith had written a one-act farce, Snooks a two-act comedy, and Larkins a one-act burlesque, the amount would be divided into fourths, of which Snooks would take one half to the quarters apportioned to Smith and Larkins. Say the assessment for the night was four pounds, then Smith and Larkins would get a pound apiece and Snooks two pounds.

This system worked very well while the remuneration of the dramatist remained at one hundred pounds an Act, which was the regulation sum in the mid-Victorian era. But all this was changed when Dion Boucicault introduced the system of percentages. The moment that a dramatist's remuneration depended upon the takings of the house his fortune was made. It was very much the royalty system applied to plays instead of to books. There was an immediate revolution. Tom Robertson, W. S. Gilbert and the present editor of *Punch* naturally wished to get something better than a few shillings a night for their newest plays in the provinces, and a resolution was passed giving them the necessary powers of reservation. The provincial managers complained that all the newest London pieces were out of the provincial market and asked what was the use of being assessed for old and unattractive plays. So by degrees the Society disappeared, having for an agent, I believe, Mr. Douglas Cox, who had once been the assistant of Mr. Palgrave Simpson. I have a very vague recollection of how it all ended, but I am under the impression that we knew that somehow we had been using a Provident Fund, or something of that kind, to defray the expenses of an annual dinner at the *Star and Garter* at Richmond. All this happened many years ago, so that the blessing of the Statute of Limitations may be considered to have buried the past in the past. The effect, however, of the collapse of the assessment system for years threw the provincial theatres out of gear. There was no one to look after them, so the pirates became reckless and played what they listed. I remember seeing "Our Boys" on one occasion

THE à BECKETTS OF "PUNCH"

labelled "Children," and on another "The Two
Roses" appearing as "A Couple of Flowers." And
the reference to "Our Boys" recalls to mind the
adventures of a piece of my own that I wrote over
thirty years ago and which still cumbers my book
shelves. As its history is instructive to aspiring dramatists I give briefly an account of its adventures.

I had written a play in 1870, or thereabouts, for
Miss Litton at the Royal Court Theatre, called
"About Town," which had a very good success—ran
for 150 nights or so, which in those days was a very
long career. Miss Litton was so pleased with it
that she commissioned me to write another piece.
I was to work for the same company. I had a
leading man in Mr. George Rignold (who, I believe,
is now known at the Antipodes as "the Henry
Irving of Australia"), Miss Kate Bishop (still a
delightful actress), Mr. Edgar Bruce, Mr. Edward
Righton, Mr. H. J. Hill, Mrs. Stephens and herself.
I am sorry to say that out of the seven characters
only two survive. I set to work and made Mr.
Edgar Bruce a young swain, the protégé of a
middle-aged doctor, Mr. George Rignold, in love
with the charming daughter of a self-made millionaire of an offensive type. The daughter was to
have been Miss Kate Bishop, and the millionaire
Mr. Righton. Then there was a charming ingénue
intended for Miss Litton, and a cynical swell
sketched for Mr. H. J. Hill, if he would consent to
accept the character. I forget what it was all
about, but I know that there was one situation

238

with which I was very pleased. Harold (the young protégé of the middle-aged doctor) was in love with " Violet " (I think I was going to call Miss Kate Bishop " Violet)" ; so was the doctor. But Harold, being a noble sort of fellow, suppressed his affection not to interfere with the happiness of his guardian and benefactor. Violet, who had been wearied to death because she loved Harold better than the doctor, was reposing, in fact, fast asleep. The two men regard her, when she begins murmuring. " Hush ! " cries the doctor in a stage whisper," she is talking in her sleep." " Come away," suggests Harold. " No ! " cries the doctor, suddenly becoming suspicious, " I will know the truth ! " " Harold," says Violet, in a voice which though low and sweet should have reached the back of the gallery. " Harold ! I love you ! " " Ah ! " exclaims the doctor, " you have deceived me ! " He buries his head in his hands and curtain. I forget much about the rest, but it ended happily, of course, somehow.

Well, I wrote as hurriedly as possible, sitting up all night to complete the acts, and carried it to the Court. But alas ! Miss Litton had determined to give up management and the company were to be scattered. I did not much care. I saw Mr. George Rignold as the doctor, and Miss Kate Bishop would have been charming as Violet. But it really did not much matter. I knew everybody more or less behind the scenes and would soon get rid of it. By the way I had christened it " The Old Love "—struck me as pretty and not used—"The Old Love." Violet had been in love with Harold before she met the doctor. Hence "The Old Love"—very pretty and appropriate. I looked through the papers and it struck me that it was just the piece for James and Thorne. Lucky omen, they were at the Vaudeville, built on the site of the newspaper office of my old journal the *Glowworm*. I obtained an appointment with James and Thorne and read them my piece. They were both delighted with it. James would like to play the self-made man, but he must be written up a bit—but I could easily do that. I acquiesced. Thorne thought he would make something out of the doctor—but he would have to be written up, but I could easily do that? I acquiesced. The other people did not much matter, but if there had to be any writing I could easily manage that? I acquiesced. They consulted. Then they turned to me. They thought my piece very good indeed—emphatically, they liked it. But there was this difficulty—H. J. Byron had promised them a piece which ought to have been in the theatre long ago. Now if Byron didn't send in his play by Monday they would put up my piece on rehearsal at once. What was it called? "The Old Love." Ah, first rate title, but wasn't there an "Old Love" at the Surrey some twenty years ago? I didn't think so, but if there were I had a second title, "Autumn Leaves." H'm, they didn't like "Autumn Leaves" so much as "The Old Love"—no more did I. But they would settle all that when we knew what Byron was about. We parted. Byron's piece was finished, and turned out to be "Our Boys," and ran, I think, for fourteen hundred nights !

But it did not matter much. I would soon get rid of my piece. It was encouraging that both James and Thorne were pleased with it. Now it so happened that in the composition of this volume I have had to consult a number of my diaries, and so I have been able to follow "The Old Love" from time to time. For the last thirty years I have been a fairly busy man, as besides my *Punch* work, which unavoidably was really hard—owing to *force majeure* I was frequently *locum tenens*— I have often had other editorial duties—now a weekly paper, now a monthly magazine, and so on. But leaving this continuous work out of the question, I made up my mind I would not think of commencing another three act piece until I had got rid of "The Old Love." I was quite prepared to alter it, but not to write anything new. Stay, I forgot. I wrote a play called "Long Ago" in one act, and then somebody wanted me to write three acts in front of it. I did the work, as Mr. Sydney Grundy did his when he extended his "Affair of Honour" into three or four acts. But I was firm about "The Old Love." Looking through my diaries, in the course of years I found "The Old Love" changed its title to "Autumn Leaves." Mr. William Terris liked it but wanted it in two acts. Apparently it was changed into two and rechristened "The Old Love." Then somebody produced a play called "The Old Love and the New." It had by this time got into the hands of Mdlle. Beatrice, who had absolutely put it in rehearsal and announced it for production somewhere in the provinces as " Far Above Rubies." I recollect that I wrote up Violet and gave her an education in a French convent to account for Mdlle. Beatrice's accent. Then I got it back again—I don't know why—and took it to Mr. Herman Vezin, who wanted to play in it. Then my old friend Arthur Cecil, otherwise Arthur Blunt, listened to me while I read it and said he saw himself as the doctor. Then by this time the popularity of " Our Boys " being on the wane, it went back to James and Thorne. But Thorne saw himself more in the millionaire and James wanted the doctor. But of course both had to be written up a bit. Then Sir Augustus Harris had a look at it to see whether he could place it at Newcastle, where he had a theatre. But apparently he could not, because I found it turning up in my diaries, now called " The Better Man." But one thing I remember about it is that every time I read it I made my middle-aged doctor older. Originally he was in the prime of life, just five and thirty. Next he was still in the prime of life, but was now between forty and fifty. Once more, still in the prime of life, had just turned sixty. But other work kept me from haunting the theatres, and I gradually forgot all about " The Better Man," or " Autumn Leaves," or whatever the blessed thing was called.

Not very long ago a son of mine, who wanted a play for amateur theatricals, began reading some brown-papered play books. " Hallo," he cried, " this isn't so very bad, but it seems a bit old-fashioned. " He read a dozen lines or so. I listened lazily and fancied I had heard something like it, somewhere. After a while I gave my candid opinion anent its value. " What rot ! " I exclaimed, " Who is it by and what is it called ? "

" I don't know who it's by—there is no name to the authorship. But it is called " The Old Love!" Oh dear, and I used to think that play of mine excellent—thirty years ago !

There is a fashion in plays as there is a fashion in everything else. What is popular one season fails to please the next. " The Old Love" was and is distinctly out of date. And this consideration conjures up a memory.

A round table at Evans'. A glee being sung in the far distance. The habitués never think of entering the hall, which was built by the proprietors when the café became highly successful. A steak or a chop, with magnificent potatoes in their jackets. Paddy Green going from group to group, offering his snuff-box, and asking after all " who sit round the hearth at home." There have been special tables for certain comic papers. To one of them came Thackeray, to another the earliest staff of that once popular periodical, *Fun*. But the little table I have in my mind has three occupants—Lord Henry Lennox, Sergeant Ballantyne, and Lionel Lawson. The last specially attracts me, as the uncle of the Right Hon. Baron Bernham (past president of the Institute of Journalists, the most popular recipient of this year's Birthday peerages), and the originator of the old— as it now will be called—Gaiety Theatre. The three held their own—Ballantyne intensely witty, Henry Lennox, in spite of his die-away manner, shrewd, and a good listener, and Lionel Lawson, the best of friends to his friends, and the bravest of enemies to his enemies. Not that he had many of the latter, as he was good-natured, *débonnaire*, the best type of the now old-fashioned man about town. I see that Mr. John—" Practical John " —Hollingshead has written a book about the Gaiety Theatre. I have not yet had the advantage of reading it, but no doubt the author has done justice to the level-headedness of Lionel Lawson at a time when the fortunes of the theatre were still undecided. In the days when the directors were inclined to patronize Tom Robertson and H. J. Byron as sensational dramatists, and had neglected to light " the sacred lamp of burlesque " —that " sacred lamp " that Alfred Thompson did so much to popularize by his shades of blue and green silks—then a revelation.

As the Gaiety vanishes, to appear phœnix-like within a hundred yards of its old site, it may not be out of place to consider the secret of a play-house's success. It certainly appears to have been discovered by Messrs. John Hollingshead and George Edwardes. In their case their golden rule has been to keep the same class of entertainment for more than thirty years. Fortunately the character of the neighbourhood did not change.

" See to your pit and gallery, and the stalls, private boxes and circles will look after themselves. Drury Lane fed the galleries of the Gaiety, Drury Lane and the Lyceum. The Adelphi and the Vaudeville used to rely for a part of their audience upon the lodging-houses in the streets running at right angles with the Strand. If you look into the history of any London play-house you will find that to change the species of entertainment was to change the luck. Mr. J. L. Toole used to say, " Keep your eye upon your father and he will pull you through." By altering the word " father " to " programme," with the caution added : " and do not let it be changed," and the same sentence would become applicable to a play-house : " Keep your eye upon the programme, and do not let it be altered, and it will pull you through."

Take, for instance, the Princess's, now closed, and, so far as I know, not likely to re-open for some time. It made its reputation as a Shakespearian and melodramatic house in the days of Charles Kean and Dion Boucicault half a century ago. In 1859 Mr. Augustus Harris—father of the Knight of that ilk—became lessee. The new manager, fresh from the control of the opera at Covent Garden, tried to make his new theatre a kind of Opera Comique of the Parisian type. He got Planché to write a delightful play, called " Love's Telegraph," with charming music. But it would not do. Then he brought over some French Zouaves who had started the Théatre d'Inkerman in the Crimea. They played a piece of a musical character during the war which was supposed to be raging, in Oxford Street. Then when the last scene was reached they were called to their rifles by a night attack of the Russians. There was a good deal of firing, and the curtain fell upon a final tableau of the chief of the company waving the Tricolor to the strains of " Partant pour la Syrie," the French National Anthem of the period. But it was not successful, so Augustus Harris the First reverted to romantic drama and Shakespeare. He engaged Mr. Fechter, and produced " Ruy Blas," and later on " Hamlet," and all went well. I venture to say that if Sir Henry Irving were to open the old Princess's with any of his repertoire the fortunes of the house would revive immediately. Sir Henry suggested at the Boz Club in the present summer that he would like to play " Pecksniff." Why not try it at the Princess's ? The house has one Dickens tradition. In it was produced a version of "Barnaby Rudge," with a cast inclusive of Mrs. John Wood. But the good knight would do even better were he to play " Hamlet " or " Macbeth." Fechter was excellent in the first, and Charles Kean introduced modern attention to detail in the second. The Royal Princess's Theatre is still to be rejuvenated by Sir Henry Irving.

Strange to say, all the legitimate theatres—as they used to be called—had a trump card at Christmas in the pantomime. Only one has followed the tradition—Drury Lane. At the

Princess's the pantomime was a gorgeous affair. As a very small boy I remember seeing danced by a number of good-looking ballet girls (Covent Garden and the Princess's were famous for their ballet troupes), a rifle dance in celebration of the Volunteer movement. I came across a faded photo of three of these agile females only the other day. After a forty years' absence from the boards of the old Princess's, I wonder what they are doing. Augustus (the First) Harris gave up the Princess's, and took his pantomime to Covent Garden. A story is told of a young dramatist taking a scenario to Harris for his opinion anent its merits. "Not bad," he said. "Well, if I were you, I would turn it into a blank verse play, and try it at the Lyceum." "I have," replied the author, "but they won't take it." "No?" returned Harris. "Then why not make it into a five-act comedy, and carry it to the Haymarket?" "I have, but they say they don't want it." "Well then," continued Harris cheerily, "just you follow the lead of H. J. Byron, knock it into a burlesque and show it at the Strand." "I have," replied the author mournfully, "but they say they can do nothing for me." "Well, my dear fellow," said Augustus the First, clapping his visitor on the shoulder, "you cut the burlesque down a bit and I will see if I can't bring out your piece as a pantomime." I am afraid the scheme did not come off, as H. J. Byron was the stock author at the Princess's, and the story is not told of him.

The reference to Sir Henry Irving reminds me that at a dinner of the members of the Boz Club, Mr. Oscar Browning referred to the chairman of the evening (Sir Henry himself) as once having been connected with some theatre near the Tottenham Court Road. He had been introduced to Sir Henry Irving there.

My thoughts flew to the Dust Hole, as the old Queen's Theatre used to be called a quarter of a century before the Bancrofts acquired a lease and turned, so to speak, a coal cellar into a boudoir. But I soon found I was on the wrong tack. " I was introduced," said the speaker, " to Sir Henry by my old friend John Clayton. He and our chairman were playing in a Dickens drama." " Yes," promptly replied our chairman, " it was 'Oliver Twist.' " Then it occurred to me that the genial Cambridge don was referring to that very respectable and commodious temple of the drama the Queen's Theatre, Long Acre, which at an earlier period had been known as St. Martin's Hall. The proprietor in the days of Sir Henry Irving's engagement was Mr. Henry Labouchere.

I was put on the right road by the reference to " John Clayton." He was one of the first of that class, which certainly cannot be accurately described as " rogues and vagabonds," to give up a career in another direction to " go upon the stage." How things have changed since that date! The Queen's of Long Acre flourished in the sixties. " Jack Clayton " (his real name was Calthorpe, and he was the brother of an eminent artist, and the son of a physician) told me that his life was made miserable by the half-concealed animosity of his green-room companions. He did not belong to " the profession," and was regarded as " an amateur." He was " taking the bread out of the mouths " of a deserving class of the community. And this being so they jeered at his friends, and even objected to his costume. " I give you my word," he said to me, " I am perfectly afraid to put on my evening clothes after the performance is over, when I have to go on anywhere, because they all sneer. It isn't the clean shirt they object to, but my giving myself the airs of a swell." His companions were not snobs, but they loved the liberty of Bohemia. Nowadays, the men who have taken to the theatre without being brought up at the wings can be counted by the score. Other times other manners. And as the status of the actor has given rise to many angry discussions I will steer clear of the subject. I will merely say that the actors of yesterday—say half a century ago—were very different from the actors of to-day.

If the hon. member for Northampton were in an anecdotal humour I believe he could tell many a good story about his tenancy of the Queen's. He had a most excellent company, and amongst the last a gentleman of the name of John (otherwise Jack) Ryder. This gentleman belonged to the old school, and had such a way with him that he could give vent to the most questionable sentiments, and yet receive the heartiest applause from the gallery. On one occasion when he was playing in one of the earlier pieces of the late Sir Augustus Harris, he—as an old country vicar—had to remonstrate with his son for getting into an " entanglement " of a mercenary and embarrassing character. " When I was a curate, my boy," he said, or words to the same effect, " I got into a similar entanglement myself, but when I found that she stood in the way of my professional advancement, I cast her off for ever ! " This announcement was always received with thunders of applause. Jack Ryder was stage manager at the Queen's Theatre, Long Acre, and was attending a rehearsal of a thunderstorm. " That won't do," he shouted, as there was a rather feebler roll than usual. " Please, sir," said the official in charge, " that's not my thunder, it's real thunder. There's an awful storm going on outside." " Well, real thunder isn't good enough for Jack Ryder. Now let's try something better ! " He was quite right ; things must be written large on the stage. The cheek requires a tinge of rouge, and the storm ultra-bright lightning and ultra-loud thunder.

At the Boz Club banquet Sir Henry suggested that in spite of Crummles, the " real pump and two splendid tubs," Charles Dickens dedicated *Nicholas Nickleby* to Macready. This reminds me that there was a point of resemblance between the author and the actor. When Dickens was playing in an amateur performance before Queen Victoria and the Prince Consort, a request came to the great novelist that he should present himself as he was in the Royal Box. Charles Dickens waited until he had divested himself of his stage costume, and was ready to appear in evening dress. Macready would never allow his son (who was at Westminster) to see him act. He made one exception to the rule : he allowed the boy to be present at his farewell performance. Both actor and novelist believed in keeping the stage life distinct from the *vie intime*.

Chapter VIII

MY FATHER'S FRIENDS

ONE of the best cartoons ever drawn by my
friend, Mr. Linley Sambourne, was one de-
picting " The Mahogany Tree," on the occasion of
Mr. *Punch's* jubilee. It was published as a supple-
ment, and my friend, Mr. Spielmann, says of it
that the temple in which the banquet was held was
as unlike the real room as possible. Well, I suppose
he was right. The portraits of the staff were good
enough. I remember what trouble Mr. Sambourne took to get us all right. One by one we
sat at a table with an imaginary banquet before
us, holding up a glass in the pose devised for us
by the eminent artist, who " snap-photoed " us
to his heart's content. The photo he took of my
brother Gilbert is far away the best portrait of
him that we have in the family. It was cleverly
arranged, and the men were placed at Mr. *Punch's*
hospitable board in the order in which they
actually sat every Wednesday at the Bouverie
Street table. And there was an air of *bon
camaraderie* quite characteristic of the staff as it
existed in 1891. The present editor was presid-

ing, supported by the pens and pencils of his
staff, and pledged by the two principal proprietors, William Bradbury and William Agnew.
Then, round the room were memorials of the
departed. Charles Keene had only recently died,
and we still had with us George du Maurier. Then
there were portraits of the past editors, and
statues of Thackeray and Leech. Very unlike
the real room, and yet very like it. Now and
again, when I was an every Wednesday guest at
the *Punch* table, I used to be left alone in that
room writing perhaps a note to Mr. Swain, the
engraver, or to the official who kindly undertook
the production of the photographs required by
the artists for their cartoons. And on more than
one occasion I fell into a reverie and conjured
up, " in my mind's eye, Horatio," some of those
who had been our predecessors. First there was
my father. I saw him as I knew him seated, with
his head resting on his right hand in the old
familiar fashion. He was silently taking note
of everything, and smiling as he made some
humorous sally that set the table in a roar—
generally at the expense of Douglas Jerrold, that
great energetic little man, with the mane of a lion
and the clear blue eyes, frank, free, and clear as
the eyes of a British sailor. Smiling approval
was Thackeray, in whose defence the thrust
was delivered. Thackeray—maybe to restore
peace—would ask my father about some police
court case that had found its way into the evening
papers. " I think it will do for Policeman X,"

Thackeray would say. " Got one in hand,"
Lemon would observe, " and not often the case.
You are terribly behindhand with your copy
sometimes, and do not fear the power of the
brigand chief." Thackeray would smile at his
editor's assumption of melodramatic dignity—
he was accustomed to it. Next Ponny Mayhew
would hand my father a book : it was intended
for his godson, my younger brother. " Hope he
will turn out as a good, amiable, ruffianly, benevolent tyrant, like his father before him." My
father would smile and say, " They have sent me
a bust of you, Ponny, labelled Horace. You
look very classical, as if you had just been publishing the Odes." " Of Poland, of course,"
would put in the Professor; " but we won't hear
it on this occasion." " No, and spare us your
recitations from Shakespeare," would put in
Shirley Brooks, the man with the best memory
for quotations in the assembly. " Anything for
me ? " Leech would ask, and Lemon would say
that there were still a number of initials in the
cut book, but he would get some proofs posted
to him for his inspiration. Then the vision
would fade away, and I would be still in front of
the letter I was writing to Mr. Swain or the
gentleman who kindly saw to the photographs
needed by the cartoonist. But even then I saw
Lemon bidding all his " merry men "—" Mark's
merry men "—good-night, and telling some of
them that he would call upon them in the morning.
It was the custom of the best of editors to visit

his artists on the day following the creation of the cartoon, to see " that everything was ship-shape."

How many men have sat at the famous table with its oblong boards, with the initials of the diners cut deep therein! Charles Dickens has been there—he who sent one witticism to *Punch*, which was rejected by Mark Lemon! Well, Dickens shared the same fate as the Rt. Hon. Joseph Chamberlain, who told me that he too had had a witticism rejected by the powers that were in Bouverie Street. Then there was another eminent outsider in the person of Joseph Paxton. He was the head gardener at Chatsworth, the seat of the Duke of Devonshire. He was a friend of Dr. Mark, and on one occasion " the merry men " paid a visit to the ducal conservatories. Paxton designed the Exhibition of 1851, which came to be called the Crystal Palace. It was on the lines of a huge conservatory. I can just remember as a child in arms the opening of the Exhibition of 1851. I have in my possession the season ticket that was owned by my father, with his signature thereon inscribed. I can recollect a model frigate in the Serpentine, and that it cost my mother half a crown to get from one side of the road to the other opposite Sloane Street—that was the regulation charge of the cabmen. I remember my father's return, and hearing him talking about a lady cousin of his (the widow of a captain in the Royal Navy) hanging on to my father's arm and passing the *cordon* of police

THE à BECKETTS OF " PUNCH "

("who made way for the magistrate "), to his great indignation.

" You know, we don't see the woman from year's end to year's end, and yet when it serves her purpose she clutches hold of one's arm as if she were one's wife."

" My cousin Fanny always knew how to take care of herself, dear," puts in my mother; " but we got rid of her when we entered the building."

Then Cox announces that dinner is ready, and I am sent to bed, for it is only when company are present that I am allowed to come down to dessert. I retire to rest, and am alarmed by the portrait of an old lady said to be by Holbein, and reputed an ancestress. If she were she was a very stern à Beckett—for the women of the family have the tradition of better profiles than the men. Later at night my father (who had written a leader for the *Times*) himself went to bed.

Another of my father's friends—Albert Smith. I cannot help thinking that he has been rather roughly handled by some of those who pretend to know a great deal about the secrets of the Round Table. I have seen it suggested that he quarrelled with *Punch*, or, rather, *Punch* quarrelled with him, because he reproduced in the *London Charivari* some translations from the French comic papers. The writer of the articles to which I have more than once referred, which appeared in the *Pall Mall Magazine*, makes the suggestion. I know there was some sort of a tradition to the same effect in Bouverie Street. But, on consideration, it appears a little absurd. First, it was not considered a very great crime this translating from the French in the early days of the nineteenth century. It will be remembered that Crummles regretted that every actor and actress could not speak French. If they had been linguists to the necessary extent, the stock authors would have been superfluous; the ladies and gentlemen of the company could have translated the French play as they ran through it at rehearsal. I remember as a boy that every dramatic author went to Paris for inspiration, and never thought of making the slightest reference to the colleague on the other side of the Channel. The fact of thinking in English thoughts that had already been thought in French gave to English authors a distinct right to originality. So, if Albert Smith had "annexed" a few ideas from the Boulevards, I do not think it would have been considered such a serious crime by Mr. Mark Lemon. Next, to the last Albert Smith was on the best of terms with the *Punch* people. At the opening of his entertainment of "Mont Blanc," if I am not much mistaken, Ponny Mayhew appeared dressed as a French gendarme, and insisted upon seeing the passports of the invited guests. The passport was the card of invitation, and a copy was, and probably is, hanging up in Mr. *Punch's* dining-room. Then one of the prettiest of Leech's drawings represents the great St. Bernard dog who used to parade in front of the proscenium between part one and part two. I remember the dog well and the attention he used to receive at the hands of the beautiful young ladies who used to occupy the front row of the stalls. Then there was the burlesque in which Albert (he used to be called Albert by my father) took part, in conjunction with a number of other *Punch* men. If the author of *Ledbury* had been turned from Mr. *Punch's* door in disgrace, it was scarcely likely that all these memorials of him would have been allowed to appear in *Punch's* pages and on *Punch's* walls in Bouverie Street. When there is a desertion, the paper is not always in the right —there may be many other reasons undiscovered. Probably Albert Smith found Douglas Jerrold uncongenial company, and, being able to keep his head above water without the assistance of Bouverie Street, trusted to his own resources, and, as it happens, with the luckiest results. " Mont Blanc " at the Egyptian Hall was one of the best and cheapest of entertainments. It was —to use the phrase of the picture galleries—a one man show. I use the phrase to explain that it was worked by a solitary individual, Albert Smith, a man to work the scenery and a proscenium. Albert was a very good musician, and used to play his own accompaniments. I remember the entertainment now perfectly as if I had been there but yesterday. The proscenium represented a Swiss châlet. In the foreground was a trench containing real water and waterlilies. In front of the châlet was the small piano upon which were placed Albert Smith's properties —a model of a *diligence*, a wooden pipe with a bowl filled with water, and a copy of *Galignani's Messenger*. Mr. Smith used to enter from a door in the châlet and then introduce his entertainment. He used to describe the journey to Chamounix—here the model of the *diligence* was useful—and his remarks were illustrated by views shown in the châlet, which turned out to be a built-up curtain. The end of part one was a long yarn by the engineer on board the Austrian Lloyds steamer. "He told me the stupidest story I heard in my life," said Albert Smith. "Now, ladies and gentlemen, with your kind permission, I will attempt to tell it to you." Then Albert Smith used to sit down with his hookah and repeat a long rambling tale about nothing in particular, emphasizing the points with gurgles from his pipe. End of Part I., and appearance of the dog with boxes of chocolates for the children of the entertainer's friends. I was one of those children, and can declare that the chocolate was excellent. By the way, the presentation of bonbons was subsequently imitated by Mr. J. L. Toole, who, as it happened, was another friend of my father. "Johnnie" told me how once my father took the chair at a meeting where "Trying a Magistrate" was to be recited. My father, according to my friend Mr. Toole's account, was selected for the pleasure and honour because he happened to be the magistrate of the district. In the course of the entertainment " Johnnie " mentioned a name. Immediately some one in the audience got up and said that the name was his own, and that Toole intended to insult him. There was a row, and my father, as a magistrate, had to use his authority to keep the peace.

To return to Albert Smith. The second part showed the actual ascent of Mont Blanc, with a comic picture of the descent. The panorama was rather on a small scale, but I perfectly well recollect *Les grands Moulets* with realistic effects. The last feature was a topical comic song written up to date from entertainment to entertainment. It turned upon *Galignani's Messenger* as a paper being " the best of them all." Albert Smith used to accompany himself on the piano, and sing or almost talk his song with great effect. A very pleasant entertainment, to which all London flocked. I am quite sure there was no ill feeling between Mr. Albert Smith and the *Punch* staff. The Egyptian Hall was associated with the entertainments of Albert Smith for several years. When " Mont Blanc " became antiquated, I remember it was replaced by a show about " China." And in this last production Albert Smith gave great offence to some of his warmest supporters. Although Albert Smith could always count upon a certain number of people moving in society, the bulk of his audience belonged to that class of persons who hated the theatre and patronized the productions of Mr. and Mrs. German Reed. Talking of Christian

MY FATHER'S FRIENDS

Missions in China, Albert Smith said that the show convert was a not too respectable billiard marker. Immediately there were "*reclamations.*" I forget how the matter ended. I fancy that Albert Smith died about this time. He was very good looking. Long before the "beard movement," as it was called, he used to wear a bushy hirsute adornment that might have caused the envy of a Crimean veteran. Poor Albert Smith! my recollections of him were of a kindly, amusing gentleman, fond of his friends and with very few enemies. I do not think he was likely to get on with Douglas Jerrold. The latter was a democrat of democrats, and the former had no objection to a title. Not that Albert Smith was a snob; but his lines lay among those whom Thackeray used to call the "upper suckles," and Douglas Jerrold resented the undoubted fact.

I have already said that I met my friend John Tenniel at the Egyptian Hall. It was when he was accompanied by George Rose, the narrator of "Mrs. Brown." I was present at the opening of Mrs. Brown's entertainment. Arthur Sketchley, no doubt recollecting "Mont Blanc," had devised an entertainment called "Paris." Not to clash with the earlier show, the route chosen was via Newhaven and Dieppe. I was present in the dual capacity of critic and friend. George Rose had become possessed of a mechanical piano—then a novelty—and he proposed trying it on the occasion. Somehow or other the stops had got out of order, and it did not matter what tunes were set, the piano, after a few bars, always ground out the National Anthem. The result was, that whenever the piano was set playing, there came in a few minutes the musical signal for departure. Then in this same Egyptian Hall I was present at the début of Artemus Ward, who had become a great friend of George Rose, and probably secured the room at his suggestion. The reception the lecturer obtained on his appearance was very cold. A British audience had to understand him. Artemus Ward was sad to a degree, and said the absurdest things in a voice suitable to a funeral. But when the audience discovered the pleasantry, they simply roared. I had met Artemus Ward at George Rose's, and went round to see him. "I was just scared," said he, "when I saw them just looking like a row of ghosts. I never heard, sir, anything more welcome in my life than that laugh!" At that time I was editing the *Glowworm*, and was very anxious to have Artemus Ward as a contributor. But his terms, with our limited capital, were prohibitive. However, he was secured by Mark Lemon for *Punch*, and appeared for a number of weeks in the *London Charivari*. His articles were not a great success. They had not the freshness and spontaneity of his customary copy. I fancy he was as nervous with his British readers as he had been with his British audience, and did not let himself go. His lecture in *Punch* reminded me of "Mrs. Brown at the Play," with half the humour left out. He seemed to have formed his style for British readers on that of his friend George Rose. He was in ill health when he came to England, and died, poor fellow, in this country. I went to his funeral. He dined with me once at the Civil Service Club— a building to which I have already referred—and introduced the son of the American Minister. He was the best of good company, but always kept that grave face. He would laugh, however, on occasions, and when he did he laughed long and heartily.

The Egyptian Hall was a Home of Mystery on the night of Artemus Ward's first lecture, as it has become again now that it is in the hands of the accomplished Mr. Maskelyne, who represents Maskelyne and Cook. Very many years ago I was invited by my brother Gilbert to see the entertainment with a view to joining him in writing an entertainment for the firm. But some extremely clever manipulation of plates did not inspire me. Since then the "Sketches" have become quite excellent and amusing, and I regret that I lost on behalf of my brother and myself the chance of becoming a stock author. The Egyptian Hall, too, was the scene of an entertainment given by Edmund Yates and Harold Power. The latter was a great friend of the *Punch* men, and accompanied them on their visit to Manchester when the staff of *Punch* went to the rescue of the family of their colleague Bennett. I knew Harold Power very well, and

he was a kind, good fellow, with an audacity
that was perfectly amazing. It is a tradition
that when he went to Manchester he returned
thanks for every health on the toast list. In
every case he was up before the speaker told off for
the reply, and literally took the words out of his
mouth. So goes the story. I was not present on
the occasion, so can only rely on the report of others.

Round and about the Egyptian Hall great
changes are taking place. Piccadilly is to be
further widened, and the coaches that used to
start from the *White Horse Cellar*, I fancy, have
found other points of assembly. The reference
to the *White Horse Cellar* recalls to me a memory.

I had seen the Derby won from the top of a
coach on the Hill, and, according to the custom
of the day, was talking over matters with those
" who had come on " at a small table in Cremorne
Gardens. A month ago, looking over some papers,
I came across my season ticket for the year. It
is signed by Mr. Baum, a gentleman who also ran
the Alhambra after that place of entertainment
had changed from a rival to the Royal Polytechnic
Institution (under the title of " The Panopticon ")
into a competitor with the Oxford and Canterbury
Music Halls. Cremorne Gardens was on the wane
in 1870, and usually a very dreary place. It
woke up a little on Derby night. There was
some dancing going on at the central platform,
and there was a parade of men about Town,
round and round, round and round, round and
round the dancers. No one ever thought of

dancing save, perhaps, on Derby night, and then the dancer would be restrained by his friends under the friendly superintendence of the uniformed " chucker-out." But people were " a bit off colour " in 1870, and in no mood for skylarking, for war was in the air. A quarrel was brewing between King William of Prussia and the Emperor Napoleon of France. The King was being forced into a war by Bismarck, and the Emperor, dissatisfied with the recent *plébiscite*, was preparing to stake his own existence as a monarch on the hazard of the sword. Still, all Englishmen took the deepest interest in the finish of the Derby. It was run at Epsom at 3.29 p.m., and the result was known in Bombay at 5.57, and in Calcutta at 6.25. So related the newspapers of June 2.

Many of my companions were journalists, the guests of a very popular peer, who prided himself upon his Derby gatherings. We were talking of the chances of war, and where those chances might take us. I myself had no idea that I should be off to France and Germany, but before the year was out I was destined to act as a " special " for the *Standard* and *Globe* in both countries. Every one knew that Dr. William Howard Russell would be sure to represent the *Times* ; the other appointments were less certain. Of one thing no one dreamed—that by Christmas the Emperor would be a dethroned prisoner, the Empress and Prince Imperial exiles in England, and Paris cut off from London save by balloon post.

THE à BECKETTS OF " PUNCH "

A propos of the siege of Paris. After this pause of more than thirty years, there are still two special correspondents left amongst us who acted for newspapers in the surrounded city. They are both members of the House of Commons. The first is Mr. Thomas Gibson Bowles, who represented the *Morning Post*, and the second Mr. Henry Labouchere, who, as " a besieged resident," wrote a most delightful description of Paris day by day for either the *Daily News* or the *Star*. At the time the authorship of these letters was a secret, and it is just possible that they may have appeared in the *Standard*. I cannot remember, but they were most amusing. I was in sympathy with the author, as my duty was to supply, as " a Roving Commissioner," light copy to the *Globe* (then edited by Mr. Marwood Tucker, and managed by Mr. Madge), and " heavy work " to the *Standard*, under the control of the late Captain Hamber. It was not altogether a novel experience to have to deal with the same subject from two points of view—comic and sedate. I had done the same sort of thing before as the editor of a serious daily and a humorous weekly.

I did my best, but I cannot claim to have rivalled the feats of a friend of mine, a brother journalist of those distant days, who managed to mingle the tragic with the comic in a most effective fashion. He described the last moments of a dying Englishman who had joined the French Army. The poor sufferer noticed a dog and two men with a kind of theatre on the field of battle. They were camp followers and also street performers. To cut an admirably recounted story short, the dying Englishman's last moments were soothed by a performance of " Punch and Judy." The tale ended somewhat after this fashion : " The sun sank on the horizon, leaving the cannon in silhouette ! The warrior smiled at the hero of the drama knocking down the ghost ! The curtain fell, hiding from view the sorrowful face of dog Toby ! All was silent ! The Englishman in the French uniform was at rest ! "

To be up to date. At this time when, thanks to the patriotic action of King Edward, our good neighbours the French are becoming better and better neighbours, it is well to remind them of our action more than thirty years ago—not to boast, but as a guarantee of goodwill. The moment Paris was thrown open we rushed in food, the outcome of a public subscription, to the aid of the starving inhabitants. During the war our sympathy was entirely with our neighbours. I myself, acting for the *Standard*, had something to do with getting up a fund to help the French prisoners on the Rhine. And this was only one of many benefactions of a similar character. Lastly, when the rival songs of France and Germany were sung at the Alhambra, the British public cheered to the echo the first, and hooted the last. How we loved the French in those days of disaster to the French nation ! " We shall be avenged by our children," said Hervé, the composer, to me on the stage of Covent Garden. And I did not smile. It occurred to me afterwards that the children of Hervé must have been in arms—not altogether a bad example to their fathers. But let that pass. It is pleasant to remember that nowadays, when France is strong and prosperous and our good friend, that she was equally our good friend, so far as we were concerned, in the days of the Terrible Year 1870–71.

A propos of Paris.

I am dining once more at a round table. This time it is in the Hôtel du Helder, Rue du Helder. The dinner has been foretold by a friend at the British Embassy at the Rue Faubourg St. Honoré as the probable climax to a projected duel. A brother journalist—thirty years my senior—has called me out. Unfortunately, during my visit to Paris, a paper of which I had been the titular editor had contained a rather savage attack upon my host. Unconscious of the article, I had visited the great *littérateur*, and asked him to write for us. He had received—as press censor for the Emperor —an early copy of my paper. He was indignant. I was the editor: who wrote the article ? Very sorry—against journalistic etiquette to give up the name of the contributor. I had not seen the article, but I would accept responsibility. He would commence an action for libel. A bow. Had the article appeared on the French side of the Channel, the Aggrieved One would have settled it as gentlemen wearing swords were wont to settle affairs in the last century. Saw a gleam of light. Anything better than an action for libel. In a nervous voice, " Very pleased to give him the satisfaction of a gentleman, but might I please choose swords ? " N.B.—Had learned single-stick as a boy under the supervision of Dominie Birch, and had noticed that, in the French duels, the combat terminated after the first scratch. All I would have to do would be to avoid running on my adversary's sword. The Aggrieved One was rather startled at my suggestion—I was not two-and-twenty—but he ultimately consented. Rushed to my diplomatic friend at the Embassy. " You will not fight," said he ; " he will forgive you on account of your youth, and ask you to dine with him at the Hôtel du Helder. In the meanwhile, Major Byng Hall can represent you." The prophecy was fulfilled. My subsequently good friend Whitehurst, of the *Daily Telegraph*, did forgive me on account of my youth, and asked me to dine at the little round table in the Hôtel du Helder. A much pleasanter function than weapons for two, and coffee for one.

I am seated at another round table. This time I am enjoying breakfast with M. de Blowitz, the great correspondent of the *Times*, who took the lead once enjoyed by Whitehurst. I have been introduced by my friend the late Sir Augustus Harris. The great correspondent is a little out of temper because I have experienced a difficulty in finding his flat, and consequently have arrived

rather late. He takes his revenge by calling
me by the name of a paper my father helped to
found. The paper for more than half a century
has been renowned for its wit and wisdom. So
when I accept or refuse a dish, or ask some one to
pass the salt, M. de Blowitz cries out, " Excellent !
There spoke *Punch.*" Notwithstanding this, I
am very much impressed with M. de Blowitz.
He is an excellent fellow. Before I leave he
presents me with a book describing his adventures in a train with a restaurant car, on his road
to Constantinople. In spite of his admirable
contributions to " the leading journal," he seems
prouder of this guide-book than all his journalistic
work put together.

How many times I have visited Paris ! All my
life. I knew the Gay City in the days of the third
Empire, when Offenbach and Hortense Schneider
reigned supreme at the Varieties. I was at the
first night of " La Grande Duchesse de Gerol-
stein," and saw it reproduced at the St. James's
Theatre, when their present Majesties were in the
Royal Box, and our dear Queen, who was then
our dear Princess, was delighted with the drolleries
of the rise and fall of ex-Commander-in-chief
Private Fritz. I was in Paris just before the
march *à Berlin.* I was there after the Commune,
when the ruins of the destroyed city were still
smouldering. I have dined later on with Edmund
Yates at the Café Anglais, when we enjoyed the
best possible Bisque soup. I have seen all the
Exhibitions from the first in 1855 to the last of a

year or so ago. To the last but one I went in the company of a number of life-long friends, representing the staff of a paper to which I contributed every week for a quarter of a century or thereabouts.

Chapter IX

MEMORIES OF BOUVERIE STREET AND ELSEWHERE

IN days gone by it was the tradition to keep everything connected with *Punch* a secret. Those who were summoned to the Bouverie Street Board were " tiled." But with the publication of the *History of Punch*, with the sanction and assistance of the proprietors and the hearty aid of the staff, a new régime commenced. Since that day the secrets of the prison-house, or rather the stories of the delightful banqueting-hall, have been revealed with the greatest frankness. Certainly nowadays the public take a deep interest in the doings of our papers, especially in that paper which has "the comic" added to its name. For twenty years it was my duty to see the correspondence of *Punch*, and I can testify to the great interest taken by outsiders in the conduct of the paper. If by an oversight a joke got into its columns which had appeared earlier elsewhere, there were always two or three correspondents to point out the error. If some clergyman—the clergy were generally the culprits—had sent in some remotely biblical quip or crank, there was always a censor ready to denounce any frivolous reference to sacred things.

Only those who have been in the inner circle of Mr. *Punch's* offices can fully appreciate the immense importance the long-established comic paper has in the eyes of scores, nay, hundreds of its readers. If there is a variation in the policy, an almanac, say for instance, produced almost entirely without letterpress, some rearrangement in the pages of the advertisements, or the adoption of short stories in competition with the monthly magazines, enthusiastic connoisseurs are ready with criticism. It is a saying in newspaper land that " change in a paper is a tacit admission of failure," but such an assertion is of course confined to the older generations. The more modern method is to try everything, in the hope that something will " catch on " and please the British public.

Punch has not been behind the spirit of the age. Comparing the current issue with the numbers of the past, the progress is easily discernible. The larger size, the more serious turn of thought, the absence of that objectionable jollity which was wont to pain the judicious, are latter day features which no doubt have decided attractions for the general reader. And the staff themselves, consisting of men who, although well over forty or thereabouts, have not reached the extreme old age (from the present century standpoint) of five and fifty, are quite able to hold their own and more. Speaking ' personally, my twenty-seven years spent with *Punch* had many compensations. In Bouverie Street I made many friendships. I shall never forget the names of Leigh, Tenniel, Taylor, Du

Maurier, Keene, Milliken, and Bradbury in the past ; all of the bearers of these names were kind, genial, considerate gentlemen. It might perhaps be invidious to speak of those who still sit round the mahogany tree that Thackeray immortalized, and yet I cannot forget the delightful days I have spent with Sambourne, Guthrie, Lehmann, nay, all my old comrades with scarcely an exception. As personal confessions are nowadays popular, I may say that I have every reason to believe—I have my doctor's opinion in support—that I am not worn out, although forced to admit to have reached and passed the age of twoscore and ten. Certainly the work of an assistant editor is not without its anxiety, and may have the effect of ageing too readily. It will be gathered that my own experience has shown that a journalist can do quite well without a holiday. But as a journalist speaking to brother journalists—and nowadays the entire British public, so far as I have been able to judge, writes for the papers—I would advise moderation in work. Certainly two weeks in the fifty-two should be devoted to unadulterated recreation. That I have not followed my own teaching has nothing to do with it. A doctor is never expected to take his own physic, and the man who is guided by his own law is said by experts to have a fool for a client. But again, speaking for the benefit of my brother journalists, taking stock of myself, I cannot say that I am much the worse for wear. As an instance of this I may note that, although I had many other things to do, I knocked off the present volume within the space of little more than a fortnight. I had seen indications that a certain part of the life of my father—Gilbert Abbott à Beckett, friend of Thackeray and Dickens, Metropolitan Police Magistrate, and man of letters, who died half a century ago—was to be r viewed, and I thought it advisable to appear as his champion. Not that the man who died amidst the respect and the regret of his fellow-countrymen on both sides of the world—for his name and fame had reached the antipodes—needed a champion even in the person of his own son. But his portrait as a devil with the pleasing likeness of his two friends Douglas Jerrold as a serpent and Mark Lemon as a potboy had been unearthed from a scurrilous *brochure* and had been given to the world (see the *Pall Mall Magazine* of the first quarter of 1903), and I thought it time to say my say on the chance that the same line of reminiscences might perchance be continued. My father had been proud of his title, à Beckett of *Punch*, and I have done my best to show that even when a schoolboy he was a good journalist, and if in speaking of my father I have incidentally shown that I have not been altogether an absolutely unworthy son of such a sire, so much the better.

But having said this, I hasten to add that I have done my utmost to avoid wearying my readers by becoming a bore. An author with a purpose or a man with a grievance is usually a nuisance, so I have tried to be as entertaining as I can by telling

275

stories, old and new. I hear it said on all sides that the public taste points at present in the direction of anecdotage. My excellent friend Mr. T. P. O'Connor has certainly made a great success with his papers, which depend to a large extent for their popularity on reminiscences. Again, I have recently found that in a paper it has been necessary for me to create—in spite of evidence to the contrary, one must live—short stories in paragraphs are immensely popular. So I have tried in this volume to combine the purpose with the paragraph. Years ago I published a series in a paper called " How Things are Done," and this is how this thing has been done. In the same periodical, by the way, I wrote a second series called " Written on the Spot," which consisted of papers that never were written on the spot. How can one write on the spot during a shipwreck or in a battle charge, for instance ? An artist can draw on the spot, one knows from the pictures that appear in the illustrated papers. Was it not Keene who had that delightful cut in dear old *Punch* showing an artist, kept from sinking by a lifebelt asking for a piece of india-rubber as he wanted to alter a sketch he was making of a sinking vessel ? So I return to my muttons—let us hope no one will write "chestnuts."

The task at the *Punch* Table, the way *Punch* cartoons are settled, and the art of it, in my humble opinion have been done to the death. Then there have been lectures on *Punch*. I myself gave one —by consent of the proprietors—a few years ago in aid of a hospital fund. I was naturally a little nervous, as I had never appeared on a lecture platform before. My friends the proprietors of *Punch* had kindly allowed me to use any illustrations I pleased, and I had collected about a hundred. But I had been warned that when once I got into the dark with only the disc I should have to trust to my memory. So I carefully prepared the lecture, and bought a small lantern to test the slides. I thought it well to have a rehearsal, so I got my younger son to see to the views while I spoke. There was one other member of my audience, my wife. I began my lecture. The gentleman with the lantern murmured. "What's the matter ? " I asked. " I think that is an old joke," replied my son. " Oh, is it ? " and went on with the lecture. Another sign of dissatisfaction. This time from the lady of the trio. " What's the matter ? " " I don't think I would say that, dear." " Oh, wouldn't you ? " and I went on with my lecture. But these interruptions annoyed me, and I got very angry, raising and raising my voice, and by the next morning was so hoarse that I could scarcely speak, and the next day was that fixed for the lecture. I faced the audience, and then another *contretemps* happened. I had to put my handkerchief to my nose. I stopped my lecture, fortunately seeing the secretary of the association near at hand. " Ladies and gentlemen," I said, " I must now pause for a few minutes, as your secretary wishes to make an announcement of much importance." And I quitted the platform. " What did you say about me ? " asked the secretary. " I have no announcement to make." " You must," I replied. " Don't you see that I have haemorrhage at the nose ? " So on went the secretary, while I applied the customary remedies, a cold key down the back and so on. The haemorrhage fortunately soon yielded to treatment and I was able to resume my place on the platform. Subsequently I asked what statement the secretary had made. " I don't know," was the sad reply, " I talked for three or four minutes against time, but I can't remember what it was all about, and I hope my forgetfulness will be shared by the audience." I got through my lecture successfully, but fancy those present were better pleased with the pictures of Tenniel, Keene, Du Maurier, Phil May, Partridge, Leech, and Raven Hill than my yarns about how the cover came to be changed four or five times. Stay, it is only right to add that when the lecture was over my old friend Sir Henry Thompson was kind enough to say that he had never been more interested in a lecture in his life.

But in spite of this commendation by an expert in good stories—for has not all the intellectual world dined at the *Octaves* in Wimpole Street ?— I will not give the chat of the banqueting-room year by year, much less week by week. I have a collection of autograph letters, and as I run through them they may inspire me with suggestions. Their faded ink may call to recollection under what circumstances they came to be written. Here is one from the late Sir John Holker—

MEMORIES OF BOUVERIE STREET

"*May* 7, 1881.

" MY DEAR à BECKETT,—

" I have been to the Carlton Club and everybody says that Salisbury is the man. *Vide* also *St. James's Gazette* of this evening.

"Yours very truly,

"JOHN HOLKER."

The occasion I recollect was concerning the leadership of the Conservative party in the House of Lords. The subject chosen was the " Judgment of Paris." Who was to be Venus ? And here we have a proof of the difficulty of prophesying unless you know. The cartoons of a comic paper have to be settled, drawn and engraved or processed seven days before they are published. So on every Wednesday the seers of Bouverie Street and 5, Henrietta Street look into the middle of next week. I remember hurrying to my friend Jack Holker, and getting him to promise to get me the necessary information if he could, and in the week he was able to send me the above letter.

Here is another letter of a different kind written to me by a very old friend of mine, Mr. T. H. S. Escott, who succeeded me as editor of the *Glow-worm*, and wrote admirable articles (which would bear republication) in my first magazine, the *Britannia*.

" 38, BROMPTON CRESCENT, S.W.

" *March* 29, 1883.

" MY DEAR à BECKETT,—

" Will you kindly write a par. for the *World*,

279

about Mrs. Forbes Winslow and Lady Barrington?
" Yours,
" T. H. Escott."

This is a peep behind the scenes, showing the work of a newspaper office. As a rule every celebrity of the smallest importance has an obituary notice set up and ready to be used at a moment's notice. Most of them commence, " We regret to announce the death of so and so, which took place "—and here comes a blank. During the jubilee of *Punch* I was asked by the editor of a well-known illustrated paper to write the obituary notice of one of my best loved Bouverie Street colleagues. I objected : it was too grim an idea. " What nonsense ! " said the editor, " your notice won't kill him. He will never read it ! " But I could not get over my scruples to " join their funeral party," as the editor pleasantly put it, so I suppose my friend's obituary notice has been written by some other pen. On the occasion referred to by Mr. Escott the courtesy of Edmund Yates was particularly shown. He knew that Mrs. Forbes Winslow, who had died early in March, was a lady I held in the highest esteem, not only as the widow of my father's greatest friend, the late Forbes B. Winslow, M.D., D.C.L. (Hon.) Oxon., but as the mother of my wife. Lady Barrington was her neighbour in Cavendish Square. Of course I promptly obeyed orders.

Here is another letter. It is written by the late Lord Leighton.

MEMORIES OF BOUVERIE STREET

"2, HOLLAND PARK ROAD,
"KENSINGTON.
"DEAR MR. à BECKETT,—
"I shall be very happy to show you my picture on Sunday next—after three.
"Yours sincerely,
"FRED. LEIGHTON."

I recollect this was in anticipation of Show Sunday. I wanted to see Sir Frederick too about the Royal Academy banquet. I was editing the *Sunday Times*, and, do all we would, the Burlington House authorities would only open their doors to the *Times* representative. I have referred to this matter in another place. I remember I had a long chat with Sir Frederick, and that he was most sympathetic. He said he was entirely in favour of inviting reporters to be present as at any other public function. But I subsequently heard that in spite of his advice the powers that were refused to alter their attitude. To this day only the *Times* representative is permitted to be present on behalf of the Press. However, nowadays amongst the general company appear the names of the editors of the principal papers. It is a kind of concession, but not a very valuable one so far as the Press is concerned. The editors are there as distinguished individuals in their personal capacity—not as representatives of the papers of which they are the editors.

Here is another recalling the memory of a most charming lady whose portrait appeared in *Figaro in London* as " Ariel," but who, when I knew her, was a grandmother—

> " 26, MORTIMER STREET,
> " *March* 18, 1876.

" MY DEAR MR. à BECKETT,—

" Will any day after next Wednesday suit you as well for our chat ?   Mr. Reed has just lost a brother, and of course that unsettles us till after the funeral, which takes place next Wednesday; Friday, if convenient to you, any time before three, would suit us, or even Thursday before one o'clock. Perhaps you will let me know ?

> " Sincerely yours,
> " PRISCILLA REED."

This was from Miss Horton, who had married Mr. German Reed and produced the once celebrated Mr. and Mrs. German Reed's Entertainments.   I was one of the stock authors, and a new piece was needed—not that it ever was called a piece, that would have been too much for the audience, who prided themselves (most of them) upon never entering a theatre. The respected lady to whom Mr. Escott referred, for instance, had a rooted objection to visiting a theatre, even the opera, and yet was quite ready to go to the St. George's Hall. The plays were called " First parts " or " Second parts," and the " books of the words " gave a *précis* of the stories, with every character introduced as " Illustration."   The company was a very small one, Mrs. German Reed (a hostess in herself), her husband (who was an admirable musician and a fairly good actor), first John Parry, and then R. Corney Grain, and then a tenor and a young lady. Miss Fanny Holland was for many years the leading singer. Then came Arthur Cecil Blunt, who was for a long while a member of the tiny company. Sometimes actor-managers are a little thoughtless. The German Reeds were a pattern of kindness and courtesy. The above letter speaks for itself.

Here is another letter which has a particular interest to me—

        "ARCHBISHOP'S HOUSE,
           " WESTMINSTER, S.W.
                " *Feb.* 17, 1887.

" MY DEAR MR. à BECKETT,—

" I shall be most happy to see you this afternoon before 5 o'clock, or to-morrow morning before 1. To make sure I will say 10-$\frac{1}{2}$.

              " Believe me,
           " Always faithfully yours,
        " HENRY E., Cardinal Archbishop."

This was from Cardinal Manning. I wanted to see him upon a matter which I had very near at heart. In common with all her subjects, I had the deepest veneration for Her Majesty the late Queen Victoria. It was in Her Majesty's honour that I got up the " Masque of Flowers " at Gray's Inn, and it was in her honour that I organized (being subsequently assisted by the late Sir Walter

THE à BECKETTS OF "PUNCH"

Besant and his friends, Sir William Robinson and Sir Arthur Trendell) the Queen's Eightieth Birthday Celebration Committee, of which I was hon. secretary. Like all her subjects, I wanted to do Her Majesty honour, and it occurred to me that if the Church to which I belonged would join in the chorus of praise, it would be a good thing. So I sought an interview with Cardinal Manning, and met, as usual, with a prompt response. I was ushered in, and found my dear friend looking far from well. He met me with his customary smile, and, referring to the interview we had had some twenty years ago, said—

" Well, Mr. à Beckett, have you come to offer me another sporting paper ? "

" No, your Eminence," I replied, " I have not. But I have a scheme to lay before you that I hope will be more practicable."

" I hope so too."

But, alas ! it was not. My idea was that no crowned head had ever deserved " the Golden Rose " so thoroughly as Her Majesty Queen Victoria. I suggested that it would be a grand thing, both for our Church and our Sovereign if " the Golden Rose " could be bestowed upon Queen Victoria. Cardinal Manning was very sympathetic. He took a deep interest in the matter. Could it be done ? As to the personal claim there was no doubt. Never had a better woman lived. As Queen, wife, and mother, she had merited universal respect. And now, at the close of her long blameless and honoured life, the peoples of the world—yes, outside, but including her own subjects—were willing to honour her, full of affection and veneration. Would not the Church of Rome, which had conferred upon her ancestor her proudest title, "Defender of the Faith," do something to associate itself with the universal acclamation ?

" ' The Golden Rose ' ! " said the Cardinal. " It would be a grand thing if the Holy Father would bestow upon Her Majesty ' the Golden Rose.' "

We discussed it. The Cardinal told me that the late Pope Leo XIII had a deep personal friendship for the late Queen. They had met at Brussels, where the Holy Father had been Papal Nuncio, and the future Pope used to sit next Her Majesty at dinner. There was this difficulty. "The Golden Rose had never been bestowed upon a sovereign outside the pale of the Church. But, I argued, there had been no active attack upon the Church. The Queen had been brought up in the faith of her forefathers for some generations. Would that get over the difficulty ? The Cardinal said he would think it over and see what could be done. Then there were the pains and penalties of premunire. Could the Queen safely accept " the Golden Rose " from the " Bishop of Rome ? "

" I should like to see any one object ! " I exclaimed. " I can speak for the Press : why, there would be a shout of execration from Fleet Street to—to everywhere ! "

" Ah ! there spoke the journalist, Mr. à Beckett," commented the Cardinal ; " you are not leading up to repeating your offer about the *Glowworm* ? "

When I left him the Cardinal Archbishop said that he would see what could be done. The idea was quite good, and he was sure that the Holy Father, if he could, would adopt it. To a reception given by Cardinal Manning to Monsignor Persico, the Papal Legate, I was invited. The monsignor had brought with him a magnificent mosaic, the gift of the Pope to the Queen. Cardinal Manning said a few words to each of his guests as they greeted him. After I had kissed his ring he murmured with a smile—

" The dear lady has received a very beautiful mosaic from Rome. It would have been ' the Golden Rose' had it been possible."

Here is another letter from my friend Sir Frank Lockwood—

"26, Lennox Gardens,
"Pont Street, S.W.
" *July* 19, '89.

"My dear à Beckett,—

"Very many thanks for your book, which I prize very much. I *am* glad to be out of the Commission.

"Yours ever,
"Frank Lockwood."

The book to which my friend referred was a reprint from *Punch* of my Briefless articles, under the title of *Papers from Pump-Handle Court*.

The Commission was the Parnell Commission, which had a fascination for me. *Punch* had claimed a seat at the reporters' desk, which had been granted, and the present editor had commissioned me to report thereon. During the course of the inquiry I was in constant touch with Frank Lockwood, who was continually sending me up admirable caricatures of the principal personages in the proceedings. I urged him to send them to the editor of *Punch*, but he was very modest and most reluctant. Some time after the end of the Commission we had a chat about his drawings. He wrote me as follows—

> "2, PAPER BUILDINGS,
> "TEMPLE.
> "*July* 7, '90.

"MY DEAR à BECKETT,—

"I enclose some very rough ideas of that I mentioned to you the other day. If you think Mr. Reed can make anything out of them I should be very glad, and could supply him with more. I have neither the time nor the talent to do anything fit to be seen myself.

> "Yours ever,
> "FRANK LOCKWOOD."

But subsequently I think he did pluck up courage, and some of his ideas went into *Punch* from the originals. He was accustomed to send his friends every year a Christmas card, and all the designs were delightful. While I was in the Com-

287

mission Court I heard the cross-examination of Pigott—a very painful experience. The man, when he was cornered by Sir Charles Russell —subsequently Lord Russell of Killowen—tried at first to laugh off the terribly crushing effect of the questions put to him. He attempted to join in the merriment of the Court, and then paused. " Are you not ashamed of yourself ? " asked Sir Charles. Then the manhood of the witness who had just given proofs of his perjury made a feeble effort to assert it, and he expressed indignation in a trembling voice. It was pitiable. Later on I was amused to find a very excellent portrait of myself seated in the background listening to Pigott, who, to quote a favourite phrase of Sir Augustus Harris, was the " central figure." It came about in this way. There was a dispute about seats, and as Mr. *Punch* had a place reserved for his representative, I retained it, much to the chagrin of a well-known artist, who coveted my coign of vantage. As a joke he put me in the same composition with Pigott. I hope I served as a contrast. I have heard two pieces of the grandest oratory in my life. And, strange to say, they both were connected with what may be called the Irish Question. The first was the address that Barrett, the Fenian convict of the Clerkenwell explosion, made to the judge when he was called upon to show cause why he should not be executed. It was really deeply impressive, and caused the judge to express genuine regret that so gifted an orator should have to be condemned to death.

There was not a scrap of bombast in it, and was the speech of a patriot who had never counted the cost of his action—had never intended to be a murderer. The second magnificent burst of oratory was the peroration of Lord Russell of Killowen at the end of the Parnell Commission. When it was over my old chief, the President of the Probate, Divorce, and Admiralty Division (it was and still is my division at the Bar), who was also the President of the Commission, sent a line to Sir Charles congratulating him upon his speech. By the way, it was notable that from first to last Sir John Day never uttered a word during the whole of the Parnell Commission. For his reticence his Lordship was called to account by some of the Press. It must have been difficult for him to keep silence, because Sir John off the bench was one of the wits of the day, and there was plenty of opportunity for a sally during the weary length of the Commission's sitting. But Sir John from the first made up his mind not to utter a word, and he kept to his determination.

Then I come to a letter that leads me to another train of thought. Here it is—

"6, ALFRED PLACE WEST.
        "*Friday.*

"DEAR MR. à BECKETT,—
    "We produce your comedy 'About Town' on the withdrawal of 'Marriage Lines.' Will it be convenient for you to read on Monday at 1 o'clock ?

THE à BECKETTS OF "PUNCH"

If you can look in here on Sunday, I should like to see you.

> "Very sincerely,
> "M. LITTON."

This referred to the play I had written which led to my second piece that was called "The Old Love" and a number of other titles. I remember perfectly well going to the Royal Court Theatre and meeting the company face to face. I had received a tip from Dion Boucicault, who I knew intimately—he had written a *feuilleton* for the *Glowworm*—which let me into the secret of securing the attention of the *dramatis personae*.

"Look here," said Dion Boucicault, "when you have to read a piece, take your time. Ask for a tumbler and a glass of water, putting the script on the table. Take out your watch and chain and a notebook, and before you begin look at your watch. Then make a note of the time in the notebook, and then you can begin."

I followed the directions of my distinguished friend with the happiest result. Messrs. Rignold, Edgar Bruce, Edward Righton, and H. J. Hill were all attention. So were Miss Litton—who had heard the piece before—Mrs. Stephens, and Miss Kate Bishop. I was immensely amused to notice the demeanour of my company. At first every one was attentive, waiting to learn what part was destined for himself. I put the word in the masculine, because all the ladies listened most kindly to the end with gratifying interest. Then, as the question of personal identification was answered, the actors allowed their attention to wander when they were not on the scene. It was like conducting an orchestra. The moment my bâton-like voice pointed to the serious lead, then the serious lead became very attentive, and the rest of the company looked about them. Then, when the bâton pointed to the junior lead, the serious lead went off duty, and so on. However, I got through the reading very pleasantly, acting the parts according to the best of my ability. I am glad to say that when the comedy was duly rehearsed the acting was a considerable improvement on my original. This was as it should be, for as a young man I was exceedingly fond of amateur theatricals, and for a long while enjoyed the reputation of the worst amateur actor in London, according to the valuation of my colleagues. I confess I had some difficulty in learning my lines, but always attempted to get my " cues " all right. When I had to take a leading part (by order of the Master of the Revels) in the " Maske of Flowers" at Gray's Inn, I partly overcame this difficulty. As I had the editing of the play, I so altered it that Invierno —irreverently termed " Old Father Christmas " by Mr. *Punch*—had a scroll brought to him, supposed to contain a message from the Sun. But I added to this message my own part, carefully written out. After I got my scroll I was wonderfully " easy " with my words. But before the scroll arrived "Old Father Christmas" was nervous and unhappy. I am glad to say, or rather repeat, that "About Town" was quite a success, and ran for 150 nights—quite a record career in the early seventies.

And here I must stop. One recollection conjures up another, and if I exhausted my stock I might at the same time exhaust the patience of my readers. In looking over my correspondence, I have dealt—with a couple of exceptions—with the notes of those of my friends who are dead. I have hundreds from those whose friendship I still enjoy in the land of the living. They all by their kindly terms remind me that I have spent the best years of my life to the satisfaction of proprietors, editors and staff. Should occasion arise I may have the pleasure in the future of drawing on my greatly valued store for a companion volume to the one just completed.

I have called this book *The à Becketts of "Punch."* My father was the first à Beckett of *Punch*. After his death my brother came into the title, and after his death I have had the same title bestowed upon so unworthy a representative of the à Beckett intellect as myself. But this I can say, that whenever the honour has been conferred upon a member of my family the recipient has been proud of it, and has done his best to make the title from the date of its receipt more and more valuable, until the day has been reached for its necessary surrender. And I say this on behalf of my father, my brother, and myself.

Chapter X

ADVICE GRATIS

A FEW WORDS ON PARTING

IT will be seen from what I have written that I have been a journalist nearly all my life. And this being the case, it may not be out of place to give an opinion anent the Press as a profession. To speak by the card, I suppose writing for newspapers can scarcely be classed as following a profession. Purists would insist it was merely plying a calling. Purists would be right, as the only recognized professions are arms, law, divinity, medicine, and music. Still the Press in a free country like our own ought to be given a high place in the public esteem. The journalist can do great good or much evil. Would it not be as well—in these days of technical training—to carry the education of journalists a step further, and found a chair in one of the Universities with the view to making the training of writers for the Press much better? That admirable body, the Institute of Journalists, have taken a step in this direction. It is now their plan to invite intending members to undergo a preliminary examination. But alas! the submitting to the test is to be voluntary. Those who pass will get certificates which may be and should be of value to them in their coming careers. But membership of the Institute will still be open on the existing terms—he must prove his claim to the title of Pressman.

I have been led into making this suggeston by the burning question at this moment agitating "newspaper land"—the relationship existing between employer and employed. Could there not be classes for proprietors, editors, and staffs ? I had very strong opinions upon the subject when I had the honour of addressing my fellow-members of the Institute as their president some years ago. One of the finest passages in my speech—in my opinion; I do not know how far it was shared by others—was an eloquent defence of the pressman *qua* proprietor. I instanced the relations that had existed in my own case between myself and the proprietors of *Punch*. I spoke of the friendship that had existed between the employers and the employed for a couple of generations. I was moved almost to tears by the touching picture of two families living side by side, working side by side. My friend Spielmann seems to have felt something of the sort when with characteristic care he drew in his grand work, *The History of "Punch,"* a family tree of the contributors to the celebrated periodical. In this pleasant production the intermarriages between the members of the staff were fully recorded. The general impression left upon the intelligent reader was that Bouverie Street not only contained a banqueting hall—but also could claim to possess a veritable temple of Hymen.

ADVICE GRATIS

It is true that I could not trace one union between the families of the proprietors and the families of the staff, but that was a detail. In my speech to my fellow-members I pointed out what excellent people proprietors always were. And I still hope they ever will be. And yet I cannot help feeling that a special class might be organized, say under the joint auspices of the Newspaper Society and the Institute of Journalists, to teach proprietors the duties they owe to those who serve them so long, earnestly, and faithfully. There has been much complaint of late that men who have devoted the best years of their lives to journalism have found themselves cast adrift at middle age—when they have reached fifty—on the score that younger fellows are required to perform their duties. I have in my mind the case of one of the best practical journalists I have ever met being told to go for no other reason than that he had reached half a century of years. As this case of dismissal was contrary to the traditions of the calling, my friend had to submit to considerable derangements of his domestic *ménage*. In the days of old long and faithful service was a recommendation to continuance in office, and in some cases led even to a not unmerited retiring annuity. But the modern view is opposed to this praiseworthy generosity, and now I fear most should look to Mr. Chamberlain to include pressmen in his scheme for Old Age Pensions. No one knows what the dim and distant future may have in store for him. Other manners, other proprietors. A life may have been spent in the service of a journal, and one fine day a coming man may

actually arrive, and the liver of the life may be asked
to go—with perfect politeness and gratifying expres-
sions of regret—on the score that having turned fifty
he is too old for a journalist, and his place is required
for men with newer ideas.   Now, I am not sure there
should not be a class to study this question, to which
proprietors should be admitted for their own sake as
well as for the sake of those they employ.   The journalist of the old school never gave a thought of asking for an agreement.   Like the actor and the playwright of half a century ago he trusted the manager,
whose word he considered as valuable as his bond.
Taking my own case, I until quite recently have
never had an agreement in my life.   I have edited
a daily paper, several weekly papers, a couple of
magazines, and have never had—until quite recently
—a written agreement concerning the question of
notice, etc., with any of the proprietors.   So I know
from my own personal experience there can be unbusinesslike journalists.   I once was describing the
matter to my friend, the late Sir Walter Besant,
and told him that I had never had an agreement in
my life.

"What!" he exclaimed.   "Do you mean to tell
me that you have never taken the ordinary businesslike precaution of providing for the future?   What
would you do, if by some combination of circumstances you found yourself without a billet?"

"But I never should find myself without a billet,"
I replied.   "As long as I am equal to my work I
shall never lack employment, and if my brain fails
me my friends will look after me.   If I attain

296

extreme old age, no doubt my friends the proprietors will consider my long and faithful services and give me a pension if I required one."

" And you are really happy in that belief ? " asked Sir Walter.

" Absolutely and entirely happy in that belief."

" Then Heaven keep you."

" Amen," I replied, and laughed heartily. Sir Walter looked at me and said—

" You seem to have a great deal of faith in proprietors."

" Yes," I replied, " I have. You see, I have been fortunate enough to find my lines in pleasant places. My father was one of the founders of *Punch*, my brother was also on the staff of *Punch*. I have worked for *Punch* for more than a quarter of a century—for over twenty years as senior of the literary staff after the editor and his *locum tenens* in his absence—and I am sure of my position. I have any number of letters from all concerned proving this to me."

" I see, I see," said Sir Walter ; " but supposing *Punch* were to stop."

" You are supposing an impossibility."

" I know I am. But for the sake of argument, supposing it did. What would you do then ? "

" If it pleased God to give me health and strength I would begin my life again."

But Sir Walter was obstinate. He was a dear, kind, but extremely opinionated person. He still insisted that every journalist should have an agreement. And in the light of certain cases that have

come before me—especially in connexion with my
position in the Institute—I am inclined to agree
with him. Yes, perhaps it is as well that every
journalist should have an agreement. It can do no
possible harm and it may do an immensity of
good.

And then in the proposed Press University there
should be lectures for editors. Speaking for myself,
I have done my best when an editor " to behave as
sich."   On one occasion a would-be contributor
called upon me and asked me for work. He was a
complete stranger to me. I explained that we really
could not afford to employ him. I told him that
the paper for the sake of economy was practically
written in the office. I never saw any one so surprised and so pleased.

" Well," said he, clasping my hand, " I cannot
sufficiently thank you for your frank and cordial
explanation. I assure you that some editors have
almost insulted me. They have sent back my copy
sprawled over with blue pencil impertinence. I
have had to have it rewritten because it had become
useless, thanks to the disfigurement. I cannot thank
you sufficiently."

" For what ? "

" For treating me like a gentleman."

" What rot ! " I replied, I fear not too elegantly.
" My dear fellow, if we can't give you coin we can at
least offer you courtesy."

Then there is another question that might be
dealt with in the proposed lecture to editors—the
return of unsolicited contributions. While I held

the assistant editorship of *Punch* (" in the days of my youth," as my friend Mr. T. P. O'Connor might add) it was part of my duties to examine the numerous letters that were sent to the office containing suggestions, reproaches, and contributions. I made it a rule to return articles absolutely useless at once if they were accompanied by a stamped and addressed envelope. If they were good enough I submitted them to the editor, or if I were acting as his *locum tenens* dealt with them myself. There was as little delay as possible considering the letters averaged, I should judge, about fifty envelopes a day. But some of the absolutely hopeless amateurs were rather trying. If they did not get a reply almost by return post they bombarded "us" with remonstrances, and sometimes threatened " us " with legal proceedings. I know that in some newspaper offices a long time is taken before the editor answers the would-be contributor, perhaps too long a time. I qualify the stricture with a " perhaps " because I know how soon the baskets devoted to "Answers to Correspondents " become congested.

Then, of course, the editor should be kind and considerate with his staff. The great man (how often I have been " a great man " myself !) should remember that those who call him their " chief " have domestic arrangements on the same lines as himself. It is unreasonable to be yourself selfish, and in my opinion you are scarcely fair to your proprietor if you overwork your subordinates. A man if he does not get a fortnight's—nay,I will go so far as to say three whole weeks'—leave once a year stands a chance of becoming stale, and consequently unprofitable. And really it is to the editor's personal convenience to think of his sub. as himself. Besides the claims of the paper, which are and should be paramount in the minds of every one, personal friendships, readiness to evince kindnesses between colleagues, are of the greatest possible value in the wellbeing of an important journalistic venture. Speaking for myself as an editor past and present, my relations with all my staff have been invariably of the most delightful character. And in that staff I include as a practical working journalist those most important personages the Printer and the Reader. If you are on good terms with your printer —you should be, for they are one and all the best of fellows—he will do his best to help you. And the oldest journalist should not be too old to consider suggestions from his printer. The man who actually makes up the paper can give you many a valuable hint of " how it will look " when you are putting the pages together. I remember I was once the editor of a paper—it was many years ago—when we used to go down to press at 1.30 p.m. On one memorable occasion there was a smash of the formes before they had reached the foundry. But, thanks to my clever printer and the capital Chapel of Compositors at his back, we were only half an hour late. Oh, how we worked ! The galleys were ransacked for anything that would do. We got together the correspondence that had been " standing over " for twelve months. The compositors set up at express train speed, and down we went only thirty minutes late. I was immensely pleased, and so were my good friends the printer and the compositors.

When I left the paper I was succeeded by an excellent man, who later on matured into a most admirable journalist. But at the time of which I am speaking he was in his " salade days "—he was not quite in touch with the composing-room. He scarcely knew the printer by sight. All communications with the compositors must come from the sub-editor ; the editor would see the sub-editor and give the necessary directions, and the rest of it. I happened to meet the printer of the paper a few days after my friend had assumed supreme command.

" Well, Mr. Printer," I said, " and how did the paper get on the day after I left ? "

" Well, sir, not quite so well as I could have wished. You see, we had some difficulty in finding out what was wanted in the editor's room, and somehow or other we went to press two hours late."

My friend spoke quite gravely, but there was " a wicked twinkle in his eye " (to quote an old comic song) which was not without its meaning.

Then there is the reader. If he is a good reader—and they are all or nearly all good readers —what a comfort he is to the editor pressed for time. I once had the honour of returning thanks for something or other at a banquet given by Correctors of the Press. I made a score by talking of the reader " as the good little cherub that sat up aloft and watched over the fortunes of poor

hacks." I also gained approval by telling the
correctors that they each and collectively were
addressed personally by the author when he spoke
about " the gentle reader." I had a fine time of
it, and thoroughly enjoyed myself.

And here I may conveniently mention a
gentleman with whom I had for years a correspondence, but only twice met in the flesh. On
one occasion I saw him at the wayzgoose of
Messrs. Bradbury and Agnew's employés, and a
second time at this very dinner of the Correctors
of the Press. I refer to the late Mr. Pincott, who
for a very long time was the principal reader of
Punch. He served under all the editors. He
knew my father and his celebrated colleagues. I
am sorry to say I never had the pleasure of
speaking to him, although we were on the friend-
liest terms through our correspondence. When
I got the *Punch* pages for final revision in the
absence of the editor, Mr. Pincott was kind
enough to send me a letter calling attention to
any little slip that he had noticed on going through
them. But he was always careful to give his
suggestions for the amendments of the mistakes
in such a manner that no wound was inflicted on
my *amour propre*. He always assumed that my
knowledge was equal, nay, probably superior, to
his own. " As I knew the Chinese language consisted of " whatever it did consist. " I had not
forgotten the disposition of the Austrian soldiers
at the battle of so and so." " I was aware of the
chief provisions of the treaty of such a place which

authorized such a thing" and so on. Mr. Pincott
never allowed for a moment that my knowledge
was not equal to anything contained in that pleasing work the *Encyclopaedia Britannica*. And as he
had read the copy of my father—he said my writing
resembled his—he used now and again to give
me anecdotes about him. This was after business
had received strict attention and the time had
been reached for recreation. I often regret that
I never was absolutely introduced to Mr. Pincott.
As I have said, I saw him twice—he was pointed
out to me—and I heard him make a very capital
speech, but I never had the pleasure of a conversation with him. I wish I had kept his letters
but, truth to tell, that final revision of the *Punch*
pages, especially when it took place during my
editorship of the *Sunday Times,* was a very
laborious duty. I was glad to get it over and have
done with it ; and I fear consequently that the
extremely interesting letters of my friend, the
erudite Mr. Pincott, found their way into the
waste-paper basket.

And now, having disposed of the Lectures to
Editors in our proposed Press University, I
come to the staff. I admit it would be difficult
to teach a recognized " newspaper man " (the
name bestowed upon gentlemen of the Press by
their American cousins) anything that he does not
know already. But I am afraid that the thirst
for news sometimes leads to over-zeal. Not very
long ago, when Mr. Rudyard Kipling had published his celebrated poem about " flannelled

fools," a correspondent to the *Times*, signing himself " A. A.," protested that he had a poem just as good upon the same subject, but he had kept it locked in his desk, prompted by patriotic motives. There was some curiosity to identify the author of the letter. The general opinion was that there was only one poet of commanding importance with those initials. To my surprise, I got a telegram from the editor of a well known low priced daily paper, asking me to either deny or confirm the report that I had written the letter to which I have referred. As the telegram was reply paid, I sent off an answer in the negative. As a matter of fact, I have never in my wildest dreams thought of receiving the post of Poet Laureate. I have now and again knocked off lines for a song, but those lines have never been of conspicuous merit. I never wrote a line of poetry for *Punch* in my life. Neither of my editors would suffer verses from my pen to appear in the *London Charivari*, and when I was in command I followed what I considered a very proper precedent ; so it will be seen that I lay no claim to be the heir of Tennyson, or Swinburne, or Austin, or even Shakespeare. Judge of my surprise when I read in the low priced paper (a most excellent periodical) to which I have referred an announcement that I had requested them to state that I had not written the letter signed " A. A." that had attracted so much attention. I heard subsequently that the same telegram had been sent to the literary men mentioned in *Who's Who* with the double vowel initials. I was Arthur à Beckett, and perchance I might have been " A. A."— hence the wire. But after all it was only a good joke. But sometimes over-zeal takes another and not so pleasant a shape. A short while ago there was a discussion about the nature of the " news investigator," a gentleman who, I fancy, has been confused with the " newspaper man," from the western coast of the Atlantic Ocean. It was then said that in the race for news the " news investigator " took steps that should have been avoided by gentlemen of the Press. And this assertion came from the Lord Chief Justice him-self. I am inclined to agree with the chief, because I have seen in my day a good deal of this over-zeal—nay, on one occasion had to preside over an inquiry into a case of alleged misbehaviour on the part of the Press during the transmission of the news of the late Queen's death from Osborne to Cowes. I called together the editors of all the London daily papers, and was pleased to be able to subsequently report that the mem-bers of the Institute of Journalists had been proved innocent of any misconduct. The over-zeal to which I have called attention on that occasion proved to be of foreign extraction. I am afraid that the cause of this over-zeal is the keen com-petition for " the latest intelligence." One of these " news investigators " told me that it was not his fault.

" You see," he said, " a lot of us fellows are sent off to get the best stuff we can. If any of us has the start of the others, it does him a little good and us a lot of harm. If we would all agree to put such a piece of news, so to speak, out of bounds, it would be right enough. But while we can get direct intelligence from Old Nick himself there will be somebody ready to interview him wherever he's to be found."

" Do you refer to the printer's devil ? "

" No; to an individual very much senior to that young gentleman, and, when we really want him, not nearly so accessible."

But I fancy things are on the mend in this direction. Since the Lord Chief Justice and other distinguished members of the Bench expressed a strong opinion upon the subject of the methods of news investigation, the nuisance seems to have disappeared. So much the better. From what I have heard, this kind of journalism is better managed in the United States—the land of its birth. There the news investigator—I am told— if he cannot get at the object of his search, writes what he thinks should have been said at the proposed interview, and takes care not to give his supposed interviewer too much away. If he did, his last chance of getting at him would be gone. In England the " news investigator " does not invent ; he gets his news and it is genuine. It is only the method of its collection that is in fault. Beyond this " over-zeal " I can see no blemish in the rank and file of the British Press. " Log rolling " is now a thing of the past. I am not at all sure if it were ever a thing of the present. It used to be said that one author acting as reviewer praised another in satisfaction of an expected return compliment when the author praised became himself an author reviewer. I do not think the expectation entered into the transaction. They both are authors of repute. A knows B, and Mrs. A knows Mrs. B, and the two writers are friends. A produces a book which gets into the hands of B. " Must say something nice about poor old A's book," says B, and forthwith writes a good notice, not because he wants A to return the compliment, but because he and his wife, Mrs. B, know what a struggle Mrs. A has to send the children to school on the allowance, and to stretch the fortnight's annual visit to the seaside to three weeks. Then when B does write a book, and it does get into the hands of A, he thinks something of the same thing.

" Hallo ! here's old B's book that he was boring us about. Not half bad, I dare say ; probably a new departure," and he chuckles at his little joke. " And a very effective cover. Ought to do well. No row with the firm of publishers. No, they advertise in our columns."

And then with an easy conscience A writes a column of praise about B's book, which enables B (before the returns come home) to get another order from the same publishers for another book. Well, if the British public object to this sort of thing, I believe if I were either A or B I should exclaim, " Hang the British public !" or even something just a trifle stronger.

But here again I think the salaried staff require a little advice. It is rather dangerous to trust too much to such an unbusinesslike thing as gratitude—you had better get an agreement. I happen to know that there is an earnest movement on foot to establish a custom of the trade. The chief representatives of "newspaper law" are doing their best to come to some agreement that will be valuable in the courts as a guide to their lordships. There are cases in which the newspaper man has given his entire life to his employers and then received a few months' notice. I have heard of three months' notice being increased to six months, with, perhaps, a further arrangement — not worth the paper it was written on — thrown in as an inducement for quiet and peaceful and pleasant acquiescence. Of course, if a journalist finds himself in such a position he must make the best of the case. His position will be greatly strengthened if he be a member of the Newspaper Press Fund —an admirable institution ; I have been on its council for years — and if he has health and strength he may light on his own feet. And, after all, if worst comes to the worst, is there not the hope of Mr. Chamberlain's Old Age Pensions ?

In conclusion, as I have said much about my father, and a great deal too much about myself, I should like to pay a last tribute to my brother, Gilbert Arthur à Beckett, the second "à Beckett of *Punch*." My friend Mr. Spielmann in his *History* has made a very kindly reference to him, which it

ADVICE GRATIS

has given me great pleasure to reproduce. But nothing more touching was ever published in *Punch* than the verses I now quote. They were written by E. J. Milliken, and appeared a fortnight after my brother's death—

GILBERT à BECKETT.

<small>BORN APRIL 7, 1837, DIED OCTOBER 15, 1891:</small>
"Wearing the white flower of a blameless life."—*Tennyson.*

GILBERT THE GOOD ! title, though high, well earned
By him through whose rare nature brightly burned
    The fire of purity.
Undimmed, unflickering, like some altar flame
Sky-pointing ever. Friend, what thought of blame
    Hath coldest heart for thee ?

A knightly-priest or priestly-knight wert thou,
Man of the radiant eye and reverent brow ;
    Chivalry closely knit
With fervent faith in thee indeed were blent ;
Though upon high ideals still intent,
    And a most lambent wit.

Serene, though with a power of scathing scorn
For all things mean or base. Sorrow long borne
    Though bowing soured not thee.
Bereaved, health broken, still that patient smile
Wreathed the pale lips which never greed or guile
    Shaped to hypocrisy.

A saintly hearted wit, a satirist pure
Mover of mirth spontaneous as sure,
    And innocent as mad.
Incongruous freak and frolic phantasy
Were thy familiar spirits, quickening glee,
    And wakening laughter glad.

Dainty as Ariel yet as Puck profuse
Of the " preposterous " was that wit whose use
    Was ever held " within
The limits of becoming mirth." His whim
Never shy delicacy's glance could dim,
    Or move the cynic grin.

THE à BECKETTS OF "PUNCH"

But that Fate's hampering hand lay on him long,
He might have won in drama and in song
    A more endearing name.
But he is gone—the gentle, loyal, just,
Whence all these things fall earthward with the dust
Of fleeting earthly fame.

Gone from our board, gone from the home he loved!
With what compassion are his comrades moved
    For those who sit alone
With memories of him! Gracious memories all
A thought to lighten, like that flower his pall,
    And hush love's troubled moan.

Farewell, fine spirit. To be owned thy friend
Was something to illume the unwelcome end
    Of comradeship below.
A loving memory long our board will grace,
In fancy, with that sweet ascetic face
    That brows benignant glow.

INDEX

311

INDEX

INDEX

313

INDEX

314

INDEX

INDEX

INDEX

INDEX

INDEX

INDEX

323

INDEX

INDEX

INDEX

INDEX

INDEX

INDEX

INDEX

INDEX

INDEX

INDEX

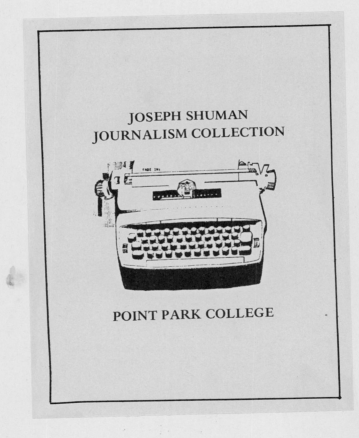

JOSEPH SHUMAN
JOURNALISM COLLECTION

POINT PARK COLLEGE